SOUTHERN
JUSTICE

SOUTHERN JUSTICE

A chilling cold case examination that uncovers how an
innocent Australian woman was found guilty of murder.
And why she must be freed . . . now!

COLIN McLAREN

hachette
AUSTRALIA

Author's note: In a number of instances, pseudonyms have been used in this book. At other times, names have been withheld and identifying features have been altered. I have transcripts, recordings and affidavits to back up all interviews and court documents that support the facts outlined in this book.

 hachette
AUSTRALIA

Published in Australia and New Zealand in 2019
by Hachette Australia
(an imprint of Hachette Australia Pty Limited)
Level 17, 207 Kent Street, Sydney NSW 2000
www.hachette.com.au

10 9 8 7 6 5 4 3 2 1

 A catalogue record for this
book is available from the
National Library of Australia

978 0 7336 4175 6 (pbk.)

Cover design by Christabella Designs
Cover images courtesy Shutterstock and the family of Sue Neill-Fraser. Internal photos courtesy of Sue Neill-Fraser's family and author's collection
Map by Wing Sum Siu
Typeset in Adobe Garamond Pro by Kirby Jones
Printed and bound in Australia by McPherson's Printing Group

For Rush

My four-year-old grandson. You are my light, my innocence, our future. Go lightly, little fella.

The truth is like the sun; you can shut it out for a time, but it ain't going away.

Elvis Presley

Author's note

NINETEEN-SIXTIES MELBOURNE, THE INNER-CITY SUBURB of Richmond. Home to a network of narrow bluestone laneways, painters and dockers, hard men with broken noses, my three siblings, my ma, and me. Our family life consisted of schlepping our wares from house to hovel, trying to stay clear, as best we could, of a violent, drunken father and his no-hoper mates. I learned early that grog and violence fuel each other and that safety usually comes with the men and women in blue uniforms. How I welcomed the familiar wail of a police siren piercing the night. The louder it called, the closer it came, the safer I felt. But Struggletown was good to me in many ways. It taught me right from wrong, good from rotten.

A decade on, with a crisp passport attesting to my nineteen years and adult status, I jumped on an early model Jumbo Jet and smoked my way to Europe, anxious for my life to unfold. The Northern Hemisphere has drawn me back many times in the forty years since that maiden voyage. Travel became my lifelong passion, my university, and I now know parts of the globe better than my hometown, Melbourne. I returned home at the age of twenty with a thud for the birth of my only child, Chelsea. Being her father has taught me about pride, and the softer things in life. We've sort of schooled each other; she's my best mate, my greatest supporter and kindest critic.

Parenthood meant it was time for a career. Due to my early life experiences I've always understood the downhearted, had empathy for the needy and knew not to be intimidated by crooks. The blue sirens beckoned and I applied for a career as a cop. I marched out of the police academy at the same time Lindy Chamberlain was marched into prison. Her wrongful incarceration would trouble me in years to come, a huge reminder of shoddy police work. The 1980s and 90s was a great time to be in the job, a time when dodgy detectives were being challenged and smashed by innovative forensic processes. I embraced it all and climbed the ladder, relishing the hunt for some of the country's worst, facing off with rabble, villains and killers on a daily basis. Not all of them were missing teeth or had dark blue tattoos – in fact, some of the worst wore suits.

I rose to the top of my game in the Victoria Police, holding the rank of detective sergeant and task force team leader, serving in crime squads and travelling the country. I approached every crime – small or large, complicated or not – as a puzzle: one that must be solved for the sake of the victim who needed answers. This became my working raison d'être.

After a decade of cutting my teeth in crime, I was chosen to serve on four nationally significant task forces, one after the other, each with an emphasis on murder. Unpicking the atrocities and sheer cunning of organised criminals, pederasts and Mafia big-shots became more fascinating with each task force assignment. Cold case murders, major narcotics deals, kidnappings and rapes featured on my job sheets. There was no room for white-collar scams in my life. By the close of the 1990s I had worked on more task forces than any other detective in the nation. I had also gained work experience with the New York Police Department, the Metro-Dade Police, the Los Angeles Police Department and the Italian Anti-Mafia unit. And hunted crooks in most Australian states and as far afield as Malta, Greece, USA, France and New Guinea.

At the peak of my investigative career I was coaxed into the elite Detective Training School to share my knowledge, to show the wannabes how to do it right. As a permanent lecturer at this finest of academies I taught detectives and sergeants as well as countless quasi-law enforcement staff the correct methodology to solve crime. I went on to create a specialist investigators course, *Field Investigations*, on how to manage crime scenes, decide which avenues of inquiry to explore and how not to stuff up an investigation. I am proud to say that entire course is still on the curriculum, taught four times a year.

Arguably the proudest moment of my career – over and above infiltrating the Mafia or stopping the run of a gang that blew up an interstate law enforcement building – occurred as I sat in parliament listening to new legislation being passed. A law to prohibit the possession of child pornography. Legislation that would arm cops with the power to destroy paedophilia rings. For a year I had doggedly lobbied politicians and ministers across Australia to create this simple yet powerful tool and, as a reward, was invited to watch as it became law. I resigned from the force soon after. I had seen it all, possibly way too much, and had an urge to tick other boxes. Along my journey I had received my fair share of commendations, which I tossed into a bottom drawer. The memories of working alongside the very best detectives and forensic scientists of my era were far more important to me – and still are.

Fresh out of the cops, I leaped into a new challenge as a hotelier and restaurateur with my chef-qualified daughter. Together, we gained six 'chef hat' awards. Food was my passion and wine is still my treat, but after washing way too many dishes, my past niggled at me. I missed the thrill of the chase. I needed to put myself back in the game, but not in the front stalls this time, more in the bleachers.

I began to work globally as an investigative journalist and documentary filmmaker, producing TV programs, including a probe into the death of the thirty-fifth President of the United States. In 2014, *JFK: The Smoking Gun* was awarded Best International Documentary – History at the Atom awards, voted by film makers and professionals. My JFK documentary caught the attention of the American Academy of Television Arts and Sciences' Emmy Awards. I was invited on to their judging panel due to the level of research and persistence I put into my investigative documentaries. For four years I have had the honour of being the only Australian on the panel. My categories (as judge) are 'Best Documentary' and 'Best Major Investigative News Story'. I also produced a two-hour exposé of the real cause of death of Princess Diana – *Princess Diana's Death: Mystery Solved* – and a six-part TV series on the demise of the New York City Mafia, *Mafia Killers with Colin McLaren*. There were many others. I sometimes write newspaper and magazine articles and am often called upon to review criminal cases for law firms in Melbourne. In 2018 the terrorist-style bombing of the aforementioned law enforcement headquarters came back into my life again. With fresh DNA identification techniques my suspect was ultimately charged with murder and attempted murders, giving me another career highlight. I have also penned five books on topics ranging from the Mafia and crime gangs' multiple murders, to the heroics of World War I.

This, my sixth book, seems to me the most disturbing. By a long shot. The story may shock you. It has certainly had a profound effect on me, and I don't say that lightly.

Enjoy the read and get involved. Perhaps get angry. It's a story we've heard once too often in our past. However, this one might not go away for a while.

Colin McLaren

Contents

Prologue

IF YOU ARE READING THIS, THEN I HAVE PROBABLY BEEN KILLED. That's an arresting, if clichéd, way to start a book. And, as outlandish as it sounds, I genuinely had those thoughts. As robust an involvement as I have had in criminal investigations, over four decades, even staring down the Mafia, I have never been so worried for my liberty and wellbeing than during the past three years. In that time, I've shifted from caution through to mild paranoia and on to wild anxiety as I've discovered my emails have been hacked, as well as my bank accounts. I recently discovered prying eyes have analysed every transaction page of each bank account I held for the past three years, in search of any blemish, any irregularity. Every text and voice message I received was apparently logged and read. I've been forced to jump from my usual mobile phone and email accounts to a series of encrypted text and email services to allay some of my concerns.

I'm not going mad. I never indulge in theatrics, nor do I waste time talking up conspiracy theories. I am a man of facts, someone who searches for truth rather than listening to longwinded theories or giving credence to conjecture. I can't stand bullshit and I detest those who grab a slice of gossip, spit on it and polish it, only to pass it on with their own spin.

I had a long career in Victoria Police as a detective, over two decades of chasing down some of the worst villains in recent history. And I was fairly good at it. I hold the distinction of being Australia's most experienced task force detective. Task force detectives take on the most challenging of investigations – the worst criminals, the toughest cases – and are afforded the best resources to get the job done. This allows a detective to blossom, to open his or her mind and to consider an infinite range of avenues of inquiry and ensure no stone is left unturned in the search for the truth.

I might add that, during my career, I was always supported by the very best team of investigators, criminal analysts and surveillance hounds.

By the time I strolled into early retirement I had amassed enough tall stories to keep me busy at a dinner table for the rest of my days. Or so I thought. So I embarked on a new career as an investigative journalist and documentary filmmaker, continuing my work of searching for the truth. My expertise is researching cold cases.

Yet, here I am, a man of serious experience, and I fear I am being watched, listened to and followed.

As I write this, I'm sitting under a banana tree by the pool of a sleazy hotel in Colombo, Sri Lanka. This is where I have run to, to escape the watching eyes of people who would rather I was not so focused on finding the truth. I arrived here on a hastily booked flight from Melbourne four weeks earlier. I took the first destination on offer and Colombo was it. Despite being a seasoned traveller, I had never given Sri Lanka a thought until the attendant at the Qantas frequent flyer call centre suggested it as an option. I can still hear her rattling off destinations; she had obviously tuned in to the fact that I was keen to get out of my own country. Fast.

I commenced my run because everyone I was working with was being arrested. My first reaction was to head to the tranquil beachside resort of Noosa Heads and tuck myself inside the spare bedroom of a swanky unit owned by a couple of mates. And think. They're the sort of friends who don't ask questions. At least not for the first week. Their curiosity eventually got the better of them; they started looking at me sideways and their questions came in a deluge.

I guess it was warranted given my anxiety and constant phone calls to lawyers and newspaper journalists. I'd switch from one throwaway phone to another. At one point I had three of them on the go, a maddening management task. As my predicament escalated, I received sound advice from my lawyer: 'Disappear, get on a plane. And write that bloody book!'

That advice exacerbated my case of the heebie-jeebies. I caught a flight back to Melbourne, grabbed my car and hit the road for central Australia, via Adelaide, via Port Augusta, via bull dust.

In central Australia, I pulled up to a payphone in a near-dead bush town and called my little sister Bev and her husband. He drives long-haul road trains insane distances through the outback. She works in welfare, helping Indigenous folk in need. I figured she may as well help me too. They're surrounded by red dirt, saltbush, hard men and harder women. Living in that sort of environment soon schools a person not to get too inquisitive, and that suited me fine.

For a fortnight I sat on a rickety bar stool and drank icy cold beer at the local tin-shed pub and ate Bev's cooking as I tried to work out where to run to next. For all my hard-won detective smarts, I soon appreciated how difficult it is to hide. To change your personal infrastructure. For all the benefits of the internet, it sure has made disappearing difficult. I actually started to think about how hard it must be for drug dealers. Or pimps. Or scammers, operating a criminal empire under the radar. Damn, those guys must be smart. And how on earth do they remember all their numbers, passwords and codes?

Eventually, I had my flight details sorted and I made the hard decision to head back to Melbourne, a two-day drive. While still at Bev's I'd started to develop chest pains. Since 2011 I have had a heart condition. Funny expression, that. I had a heart attack back then that resulted in a quadruple bypass. Things have been touch-and-go ever since. I've had my fair share of false alarms, in and out of ICU. Hidden in my sister's house, I felt the pain returning. I needed to get to my family doctor and my clever, winemaking cardiologist. I hit the road, laden with aspirin and bottled water, a bag of throwaway phones and an entanglement of chargers and cables, always fearful of being pulled over. It was a rotter of a journey, shared by dozens of long-haul transporters. When I arrived home, I tossed out about twenty CDs of music I never wanted to listen to again.

I checked myself into the safe hands of my cardiologist. He knew the reason for my pains and hastened my test results. Diagnosis: my diaphragm was badly knotted up due to my extraordinary stress levels. This was what was causing the pain that felt like a heart attack across my chest. Now my cardiologist was also telling me to 'Get out of the country — before you really have a cardiac arrest.' I jumped on the flight to Colombo, home of the string hopper and fragrant curries. As well as the most obsessive cricket fans on the planet. Colombo also boasts wide boulevards lined with an impressive array of colonial buildings surrounded by techno-green lawns that look like they've been clipped by hairdresser scissors. Within a week I was on the mend and writing the manuscript for this book. It's amazing how the body adjusts, how it can change to a lower gear once you leave troubles far, far away.

The reason for my flight and the madness that pursues me is simple. I went in search of the truth. And I believe I found it. I researched a controversial 2010 murder conviction in Tasmania. I exposed a system that I consider defective. The wrong person was locked up, the partner of the deceased, a cleanskin. Sue Neill-Fraser, someone who had never been in trouble with the law, not even a traffic violation, suffered the worst miscarriage of justice I have ever seen. She's now rotting in prison, nine years into a 23-year stretch.

My three-year probe as an author and documentary filmmaker would uncover a dangerous blend of what I judge to be abysmal police crime scene skills, shoddy investigative principles and procedures and an alarming case of tunnel vision. I also found a trove of evidence that was totally ignored by Tasmania's finest. Naively, I compiled a dossier of over fifty pages, highlighting the flaws in the investigation and the mountain of missed evidence. I thought Tasmania's head lawmakers might welcome having this debacle brought to their attention, and perhaps undertake a fresh and independent investigation.

The case had already attracted *60 Minutes* and *Sunday Night* television specials. Authors and journalists had written about it and numerous articles had appeared in the national press. Everyone in Tasmania had an opinion on the case. Politicians and journalists debated the finer details of the murder. There was even a feature-length cinema release of a documentary about the saga, *Shadow of Doubt*, and a play about it, *An Inconvenient Woman*, performed by the Tasmanian Theatre Company in October 2017.

I was far from being a lone voice in declaring the wrongness of Sue Neill-Fraser's conviction. A large number of Tasmanians, mostly based in Hobart, were stirred up enough to start a 'Free Sue' campaign. They had observed a number of legal and law enforcement issues in the state in recent years that worried them and recognised Sue Neill-Fraser's case as a perfect storm of what they believed was the decline in law enforcement and the judicial process in Tasmania. Intriguingly, a number of politicians backed the campaigners, offering to speak out publicly and lobby within their circles of influence.

But once my dossier was handed to those in power, they did not accept it. Those high up in the police and political hierarchy ignored what I had found. They did not act on the new evidence that might exonerate a woman who had suffered the loss of her companion and of her liberty. Instead of embracing the work done for them (by myself) and investigating my suspects further, the Tasmanian cops turned their attention on investigating anyone who dared to have an independent opinion about the death of Bob Chappell, one that differed from their own. That meant me, and those I was working with to right what I, and others, believe is a terrible injustice.

Part I

A harsh reality

What I wouldn't give, some days, to be out on the 'back run' with a good horse, dog, and a mob of sheep. You can't beat communing with nature in the bush.

Having spent my childhood travelling the UK and Australia, I now feel I would like to investigate Asia – maybe hire a boat and travel the islands. I love meeting new people. I loved travelling on a shoestring – copy of *Lonely Planet* tucked firmly under one arm – and I am also interested in hearing about others' perambulations, which ensures others flitting off to remote parts of the globe will write, keeping me entertained with their adventures. I need to accept the fact (finally) that any travelling I do from now on will be solo, rather than with Bob. We did everything together...

Excerpt from a letter from Sue Neill-Fraser to a friend, sent from prison, 2013

The lady in orange eyewear

In May 2016, I found myself squeezed out the end of a twelve-month gig pulling together a documentary into the real reasons behind the death of Princess Diana. The doco revealed previously uncovered facts, and exposed a cover-up by police, aimed at hiding the identity of the man driving a car that collided with the limousine Diana was travelling in.

With forensic professor Dave Barclay from the United Kingdom, I had begun work on another documentary project. This one was a reinvestigation of the horrific murder of Nicole Brown Simpson, OJ Simpson's wife. The project had stalled, however, and I was waiting for television executives to greenlight the documentary when my telephone rang.

It was my agent, Cathy. She is my filter, listening to the offers that come in and picking the ones I should consider. She threw a quickie job to me. Eve Ash, a television producer who had just read two of my books, wanted to pay me for a day's discussion of a case I knew nothing about: the murder of Hobart radiation physicist Bob Chappell. At the time of his death, Bob was sixty-five. His yacht, *Four Winds*, was moored on Sandy

Bay, a tiny cove famous as the end of the annual Sydney to Hobart yacht race, near to Hobart city. These waters are part of the Royal Yacht Club of Tasmania. Bob had spent the night of 26 January 2009 aboard, undertaking fiddly repairs on his boat. His 54-year-old de facto wife, Sue Neill-Fraser, spent the night at home after having lunch with Bob's sister, Ann Sanchez. Home was a modest weatherboard house about three kilometres from the Sandy Bay foreshore. Bob and Sue had bought the yacht a month earlier, in December 2008, and Sue had sailed it down from its Queensland mooring to Hobart. Bob was too frail and unwell to travel the full distance. He had developed a nose bleed in Brisbane and flew home, annoyed at missing out on his maiden voyage on his new yacht.

Just after daybreak on Tuesday, 27 January 2009, the day after Australia Day, *Four Winds* was seen taking water. It was sinking. The Monday had been the holiday addition to the long weekend. Water police boarded the 53-foot vessel and after establishing who its owners were, they rang Sue to tell her that her yacht was in trouble. It was then that they realised Bob was unaccounted for.

The police found traces of what appeared to be blood on the four steps leading out of the wheelhouse and onto the upper deck. There were no obvious signs of a struggle, insofar as nothing looked as if it was broken. However, there were serious hints of violence. Worryingly, blood spatter was found on the walls each side of the steps leading down to the saloon, which is the sitting, socialising, eating and lounging area of the craft, located in the centre of the yacht, with bedrooms and the toilet branching off the saloon. Even at first glance the blood spatter indicated violence at the steps. And someone had opened a water inlet valve and cut a 75mm pipe to the toilet. Police thought this would have been enough to eventually sink the big yacht had it not been for a passing local out for a morning stroll, who raised the alarm.

Four Winds was certainly in strife: it had taken on enough water to soak the lower legs of the first policeman who climbed on board. The police decided to salvage the yacht, a task that was undertaken with haste. Inexplicably, the thought that the yacht may be a potential crime scene didn't take full priority against salvage. In my mind, there should have been equal attention to both considerations. Instead, the yacht was towed to nearby Constitution Dock so Sue could look over the craft and offer insight as to where Bob might be. Sue knew as much about his whereabouts as the police did. Nothing. It had been noted that the Emergency Position Indicating Radio Beacon (EPIRB) was missing. When activated, the device, which is waterproof and acts as a GPS tracker, emits an alarm and a flashing light.

To be fair, the police had an extremely difficult crime scene before them. Such a scene would test the skills of the most experienced detective. The yacht should have been taken instantly to dry dock. It never was, and never has been. Instead, for nine years it has sat bobbing on the water. Once they knew Bob was missing police should have also cast a massive net around all and sundry associated with Bob Chappell, the Sandy Bay foreshore and Hobart's yachting fraternity. Detectives in Tasmania rarely deal with murders; there are few homicides in the island state. It stands to reason their skill set would be tested. Investigative skills are learned over time. Perhaps it is not surprising that, although there was no forensic evidence or eyewitnesses to link Sue to a murder, within 32 hours of the yacht being salvaged, Sue was the one and only police suspect. A motive offered by police was that Sue wanted out of the relationship, a proposition that Sue's adult children scoffed at. Bob was never seen again; he simply vanished. As did the murder weapon, if one in fact existed.

After being arrested on 20 August 2009, Sue Neill-Fraser was placed on remand for murder, a guest of Risdon Prison, a maximum-security facility with a maze of razor wire, concrete walls and 15-mm-thick glass windows. Her murder charge gripped Tasmania and news spread to the mainland. She became something of a celebrity with many in Hobart rapidly forming their views on her guilt or innocence. A fair slab of the community, persuaded by a media whose depiction of the crime was informed by the police view, thought she was a murdering, calculating bitch. This is to be expected. Police and the media invariably have a close working relationship; they need each other.

Any detective worth their salt knows the importance of getting the media onside. It's common practice for cops and journos to hold up the bar at their favoured watering hole on a Friday night. A few beers from a journalist will invariably loosen the lips of the staunchest of cops. In reverse, any half-decent detective knows that if he wants to sway public opinion, taking a journalist out for a few beers and a greasy chicken parmigiana is usually worth its weight in carbohydrates. In contrast, Sue Neill-Fraser was locked out of making any comment. She was incapable of countering the wild stories that appeared about her in the media. She faced trial in September 2010, was convicted on purely circumstantial, and highly speculative, evidence and sentenced to 26 years imprisonment.

* * *

Despite the case's many intriguing elements, I told Cathy to inform Eve that I was busy. I was reluctant to take up another cold case study within a police force's territory. At least not a case that was still so ripe in police terms. But Cathy kept calling me, suggesting I get involved. After all there was a woman – of advancing years – who may have been wrongfully incarcerated. Eventually, at Cathy's insistence, I agreed to a meeting at Eve's home in the upmarket suburb of South Melbourne.

Eve had been following the case for over six years and had amassed a swag of material from a group of lawyers who had banded together to establish 'fresh and compelling' grounds for a leave-to-appeal process. It was Sue's last-ditch effort to prove her innocence and change the mindset of the judicial system in Tasmania. Everyone involved in the pro bono effort was working feverishly, studying the evidence and pulling together documents to be used in the leave-to-appeal hearing (which I will refer to simply as her 'appeal').

A few days before my meeting with Eve Ash I received a box of files and papers, enough to show me that the case to find who killed Bob Chappell was, at the very least, complex. By the day of our meeting, I was prepped and ready to go, although still reluctant to be involved. I walked up to the front door of Eve's house, the biggest in the street, to find the entrance covered in CCTV cameras and doorbells. I chose one and heard a ding-dong inside. The door was opened by a tiny woman in her sixties wearing a bright orange knitted jacket, orange beads and a matching pair of orange spectacles. Even her hair was a mess of brownish-orange locks. I walked in and shook her hand. I had no sooner released it when a man thrust a camera in my face, which I immediately demanded he remove. Eve was very quick with her comeback line. Cathy had agreed that our meeting would be filmed and the camera would be a constant during our briefing. Eve smiled. I looked at the artwork.

I was guided down the hallway into the open-plan living area of the straight-out-of-*Vogue*-magazine home. Everything about the place was spacious and luxurious. The height of the ceilings, the size of the rooms and the acreage of floor space. Even Eve's partner, Paul, was large, standing six-feet-four in the old scale. For a moment I stood self-consciously in the centre of the room, and then it hit me. I was surrounded by wall-to-wall pictures, maps, drawings, quotes, post-it notes and scraps of paper. There was a massive bird's-eye photograph of Sandy Bay and the mooring which once held the yacht *Four Winds*. I completely forgot about the camera as I became engrossed in the material. Slowly I turned 360 degrees, taking in every clipping, picture and item stuck to the walls. It was as if I was standing inside a detectives' muster room. The attention to detail, the effort, astounded me. My mind opened. My thoughts started to spin, slowly initially, then faster the more I read and studied. I had never seen such an effort by a civilian. I didn't say a word. In clichéd Sherlock Holmes fashion, I applied inductive reasoning to it. And followed the links. I viewed the sketches and Google map cut-outs. I ticked off the associations and double-checked the theories. I followed the picture painted by Eve, nodding occasionally and shaking my head once or twice at things that, in the absence of further details, seemed unlikely. Finally, I stood back in mild awe, and smiled. I had been there an hour, and it felt like minutes.

I was trying to understand what Eve's role was in this intriguing case. Principally she was a filmmaker and, I discovered, a very talented one. She had spent twenty years making educational workplace training films, mostly in Los Angeles. She had created a lucrative business using talented actors from the LA scene. I ended up watching a few and as a fellow documentary filmmaker I was hugely impressed. There was a comedic slant to each film similar to that in Ricky Gervais's television series, *The Office* and *Extras*, but funnier. The Bob Chappell murder was no laughing matter, so what brought her to this story?

Eve told me that she'd had a young man, Mark Bowles, working for her, whom she held in high esteem. He left to take up a job offer in Hobart and ended up marrying Sue Neill-Fraser's daughter Sarah. They planned to live happily ever after in Hobart, near Bob and Sue. Then came the murder and Eve, seeing anomalies in the police investigation, volunteered to help. And out came her cinematographer's camera.

Eve had amassed hundreds of hours of footage. She had filmed dozens of interviews with people close to Sue and her family and those who had been close to Bob; with others who were part of the police investigation; with neighbours near and around Sandy Bay. She had even interviewed people who had nothing to do with the case, ordinary men and women in the streets of Hobart. Eve passionately believed in Sue's innocence. That was what motivated her.

I ended up spending six hours in Eve's muster room, discussing every aspect of the case. I also met one of Australia's great cinematographers, Tim Smart, the man who had shoved his camera in my face. Eve had made a documentary about Sue's case (*Shadow of Doubt*, released in 2013) and Tim had been her co-producer on that project. Now they were making a six-part TV series. Tim has an impressive background, having worked on countless Australian films as far back as George Miller's *Mad Max* and most of the Paul Hogan films, to name but a few. Despite his impressive CV, Tim had the appearance of a homeless bum. For all his worldly experience, he looked like a crumpled-up dishcloth in his unironed clothes. He was also a bit of an enigma. He would prove to be great company in the months ahead as we searched for what happened on board *Four Winds*, and an asset as we prowled the streets of Hobart among the homeless, junkies, thieves and vagabonds.

By contrast, Eve appeared to be every bit the Miss Marple type. Like Jane Marple she was very skilled and tireless to boot. She was doggedly determined to find the truth of what happened to Bob Chappell – which was wonderful, as long as Sue was blameless. I wondered if Eve had ever doubted Sue's innocence or given it any objective thought. I knew I would. I would approach this job like any other, with an open mind. I wasn't interested in taking up Eve's offer to meet Mark and Sarah Bowles or jumping straight into a 'Sue is innocent' mindset. It was crucial that I remain objective. Not to jump on anyone's bandwagon. I also didn't want to meet Sue as, with all my experience, every accused or convicted person has the same mantra to offer; 'I was framed, I am innocent'. So common was this cry for help that my only real value was to research the case without any influence upon me. Besides, should I find out anything that went in favour of Sue's innocence, it would be of more value if I had no association of any kind with the convicted Sue Neill-Fraser or her family.

Instead, I chose to go it alone, as an author does, researching his material. I kept reading, kept asking questions. I soon learned that everyone working on the case was doing so pro bono. It was arduous work because the lawyers involved had to fight for every piece of information, no matter how small or insignificant. The state of Tasmania seemed to have pulled the shutters down, resisting any move by Sue's legal team to advance her case. It had become a shit fight.

By dusk I had overdosed on Bob Chappell and his sad demise. Just before I left Eve's place, I grabbed a red marker pen and walked around the walls of the living area laden with pictures of possible suspects. I drew a circle around three of the faces. 'These three have serious questions to answer around the death of Bob Chappell,' I said, voicing my Holmesian deduction after hours of consideration.

I had been sucked into the world of Eve Ash. I wanted to know who killed radiation physicist Bob Chappell.

The Crown's case against Sue Neill-Fraser

IN ANY MURDER TRIAL IT IS INCUMBENT ON THE CROWN – the Tasmanian Director of Public Prosecutions, in this instance – to present a case against the accused person, drawing on evidence the police have gathered during their search of the crime scene, on the background of the accused, and on witness statements and relevant facts. For police, from the time they step into the crime scene until they present their evidence, it is usually a long and arduous process.

Solving a murder relies on carefully assessing the circumstances and details surrounding the homicide. These include the position and location of the body, its condition and the site of any wounds, and the forensics and facts within the crime scene. Some bodies throw up clues that can lead a detective to answers. Witnesses may point police in the direction of a suspect. Often a murder weapon can be linked to someone associated with the deceased or will be in the possession of a person of interest. Fingerprints can make short work of the detecting process, offering undeniable identification. As can DNA, the most important recent breakthrough in forensics, which can clinch the deal for detectives via tell-tale hairs, skin tissue or bodily fluids, irrefutably linking a person to a crime. In helping police build their case, a myriad of experts in a myriad of subjects can underpin an investigative theory. In this age of ubiquitous CCTV cameras, detectives can often access footage that will sink a suspect. Just as damning can be paperwork like receipts, banking records, threatening letters or cards, and emails, text messages, tweets and Facebook posts. The possibilities for types of potential evidence are never-ending. In the case of who killed Bob Chappell, the police had none of the above.

In fact, the Crown case lacked any real evidence. There was no body. That is a big worry for any detective in a murder case. Not only was there no body, there were no witnesses nor any forensics linking Sue to the killing. No known cause of death and no known time of death. Any theory of how Bob was killed is pure speculation. No one on this planet knows how Bob Chappell died. Except, if he was murdered, his killer or killers. He just disappeared off his yacht moored 300 metres from shore in the rapid tidal waters off Sandy Bay. Anything beyond this is conjecture. Bob Chappell could have faked his own death, for instance. Maybe he planned to escape the life he was living and, with a cup full of his own blood and the cutting of one rubber toilet pipe and the opening of one valve, slipped away into the night. Never to be seen again. I don't want to sound flippant, but it's not impossible that he is lying on a beach in the Caribbean. I write this to make a point. If there is no body, the most compelling evidence is usually required to convict someone of murder.

The trouble with crime scenes is they can play an investigator for a fool. They can trick a slow-thinking, tired or inexperienced sleuth into seeing what's not there. It happened to me in my early days as a detective. I looked but sometimes didn't see, or I saw what I wanted to see. The more crime scenes you investigate, the more you hone your skills and the better you become. With training and dedication to the art and science of crime scene management, you become proficient.

I believe Bob Chappell was murdered. But I would listen to any theory to explain his disappearance, as I should if I wish to remain open-minded. He may have simply over-extended his skills while carrying out repairs on his yacht and injured himself cutting the toilet water pipe. That could explain the blood on the steps leading out of the wheelhouse. He may have tried to summon help, grabbed the EPRIB to raise an alarm and then fallen overboard in the dark and drowned. He was a frail 65-year-old. The EPIRB was found washed up a kilometre or so away on the water's edge near Wrest Point Casino. It hadn't been activated.

All these theories are feasible in a case where there is no body and no supportive evidence or motive. Did I say no motive? The Crown did put forward a flimsy incentive for Sue to kill her de facto husband. They claimed she wanted to quit her relationship with Bob. This dovetailed with their next theory, that Sue stood to gain financially from Bob's death, from his assets, plus his half share in a yacht – that, according to their story, she inexplicably tried to sink. This theory didn't wash with me. Why sink your motive?

Like the Lindy Chamberlain conviction in 1982 for the murder of her infant daughter, Azaria, Sue's guilty verdict has generated enormous scepticism and much concern about our system of justice. And so it should. The system needs to be questioned. It is an adversarial system that pits two sides against each other in a courtroom battle and occasionally creates an outcome that shocks and dumbfounds. A robust democracy ensures that we can discuss these cases openly and without fear. Or, at least, it should. In the case of Bob Chappell's disappearance and likely murder, the attempted discussion has brought down ridicule and intimidation upon those questioning the quality of evidence used to convict Sue Neill-Fraser. I scrutinised the case for over two years and I've suffered threats against my liberty from police. That's not in line with my idea of what Australia stands for. The notion that any one of us can be arrested and incarcerated for offering a considered opinion that questions the quality of our justice system is abhorrent.

The jury in Sue's trial were persuaded to convict her on the sum of three falsehoods attributed to her; one trump card, by way of a Crown witness who told a devastating story; and one theory put forward by the (then) Director of Public Prosecutions, Tim Ellis.

According to the prosecution, Sue told police three 'cunning lies' to hide her culpability. Each 'lie' was repeated over and over to the jury during her trial. The first 'lie' centred around where Sue was on Australia Day. She claimed that she had a quick lunch with Bob's sister at the Royal Yacht Club before taking her dinghy out to the yacht to visit Bob. She stayed a while and learned that Bob intended to remain on the yacht overnight to undertake some minor repairs. She returned to shore and then visited Bunnings hardware store before going home.

The police set out to firm up Sue's alibi. They were able to confirm that she had a quick pie-and-sauce lunch with her sister-in-law and then went out to the yacht. They hit a hurdle when they checked the CCTV videotape from the Bunnings store, which closed at 6 pm that day. Sue didn't appear on any footage from 26 January. That discrepancy, they claimed, was her first 'lie'. But perhaps it was simply an error on her part, or maybe none of the cameras within the store happened to capture her image. Whatever the explanation, I fail to see what turns on whether or not she was at the hardware store. The Crown wasn't alleging she went to Bunnings to purchase a murder weapon or anything to conceal the crime or to use in disposing of Bob's body. And at her trial, the Crown neglected to tell the jury that Sue's telephone records proved she had telephoned Bunnings at 1.04 pm on Australia Day. They also didn't call evidence from Sue's daughter Sarah, who recalled her mother telling her on that day that she was intending to go to Bunnings to buy anti-slip mats for the yacht.

During their investigation, police had an IT expert examine Sue's home computer. Among the data was evidence of two searches on the Bunnings website, undertaken on 24 January 2009, two days before Bob Chappell's disappearance. Perhaps Sue had simply confused the date of her Bunnings visit. The telephone call and internet searches may have been preparations she undertook before heading off to the hardware store. Whatever the explanation, I fail to grasp the relevance of whether she visited Bunnings with regard to Bob's disappearance. Perhaps the police simply took the view that in the absence of anything to corroborate it, a story is a lie.

Bear in mind too that Sue was asked her whereabouts on Australia Day a short time after she was given the news that Bob was missing, and that there was blood in the yacht. Both she and her family later claimed that she was in shock. The shock of losing a loved one must impact on the inductive thinking of a detective when assessing the person/suspect they are trying to understand. It appears not, in this case.

The next 'lie' was that Sue claimed she was at home alone the entire night Bob disappeared. As part of their investigations, police installed a listening device in Sue's kitchen. Weeks after the murder they heard her talking about going down to the Sandy Bay foreshore on the night of Australia Day. She had never disclosed this late-night walk to police. Why not?

After an intense investigation it was discovered that Sue received a bizarre phone call late that night from Richard King, a man she had never met before. Richard was a friend of Bob's adult daughter, Clare. After introducing himself on the phone, he told Sue that he had been talking to Clare, and that she had a bad feeling about the yacht. Specifically, that her father, Bob, would be in danger on the yacht, he might die and the boat might sink. Clare had mental health issues. She wasn't close to Sue or to Sue's adult daughters. The police verified the odd late-night call from Richard King and spoke to Clare. It was evident that Sue's only involvement in this part of the story was that she had answered Richard's phone call, but why didn't she mention it to the police?

Sue explained that she didn't divulge the strangely clairvoyant call predicting Bob was in harm's way because of Clare's mental state. She simply didn't want to get Clare into any trouble. Nor did she want to further fracture her already fragile relationship with Clare by throwing her into a police investigation. Sue had no reason to suspect Clare would harm Bob, nor could she explain why Clare came up with her uncanny prediction.

Telephone records confirmed that Richard called Sue at 10.05 pm and that he and Sue spoke until 10.35 pm. Records also show other calls that night after dinner between Sue and one of her daughters and her mother. Sue claimed that she was rattled by what Richard had said. She tried sleeping, but well after 11pm she went down to the foreshore to check on Bob. It was dark. She looked out towards where *Four Winds* was moored and saw nothing unusual. She did see what she took to be a group of homeless people gathered around a lit gas cooker near a yellow Ford sedan on the foreshore. She felt uneasy about the homeless people and would later tell police about them, over and over, but the police showed no interest in the network of homeless misfits living in the area.

The police were interested, however, in a *10# call made from Sue's home phone early the following morning at 3.08. (Dialling *10# reveals missed calls to the phone from which the call is made.) This service would let Sue know if Bob or Richard had tried to phone her while she was down at the foreshore. A logical explanation. There had been no further calls to her home phone.

There is nothing in the police log to indicate that Richard or Clare were ever treated as suspects or persons of interest. That they both predicted harm to Bob Chappell on the night he disappeared demands they be – at least – persons of interest. Neither was surveillance or any other investigative tool directed at them. This lack of inquiry into Richard and Clare given the odd phone call is, in my view, a sign of incomplete investigative work by police. Especially with Richard relaying Clare's thoughts that her father might die and the boat might sink. I find it disturbing that on the very night Bob Chappell was apparently murdered, speculation that he was in danger was bandied around by members of his family. It's just as troubling that the source of this information was not a target of the investigation; at the very least the lead should have been followed up for completeness. Again, nothing about the bizarre call from Richard King has anything to do with Sue Neill-Fraser being Bob's murderer. Clare wasn't formally interviewed until May 2009, four months later. Once more, perhaps the police took the approach that, in the absence of anything to corroborate it, Sue's story was a lie.

The third 'lie' concerned what was to become a key piece of evidence in the prosecution's case. On the morning of Tuesday, 27 January, when *Four Winds* was discovered apparently sinking, a male occupant of 26 Margaret Street, Sandy Bay walked outside into the chaos of emergency vehicles and media and found a red jacket lying on the fence of his front yard. It was the sort of jacket a yachtie would wear, or a snow skier. Sue owned five or six such jackets. She was not only a sailor, she was also a keen walker, horse trainer and bush camper. There was always a jacket of one type or another strewn about in the life of Sue Neill-Fraser.

Police showed the red jacket to Sue that same morning it was found and told her where it had been discovered. Was it hers? they asked. Sue glanced at it and told them no, she didn't think so. She had no recollection of having lost a jacket nearby. Again, she was asked this crucial question only a couple of hours after learning Bob was missing, when, according to her daughters, she was in shock. Certainly, images of Sue, taken on that morning show a woman who, on the face of it, appears to be either racked with fear or distress, or is acting. Later, according to the Crown, forensic tests on the jacket would show that it did belong to Sue; her DNA was found on the collar and cuffs. So, was this a lie? Or an honest answer from a

woman in distress who had other things on her mind? Or was
there more to the story of the red jacket?

The Crown's trump card in its case against Sue was certainly
the testimony of Phillip Triffett, whose name appears in the
police investigation log. Each homicide has a log, the record of
what detectives did during their inquiries: whom they spoke
to, how many suspects they had, what inquiries they made and
so on. It is used to justify the police's actions and rationale in
charging an accused person. Phillip Triffett's name was first
recorded in the investigation log into Bob's disappearance and
probable murder at 4 pm on 28 January 2009. It was next
logged at 8.30 am the following day, 49 hours after Sue was
told her yacht was sinking and her partner of two decades was
missing. Triffett and his then girlfriend, Maria Hanson, were
interviewed by a detective.

On the day Bob went missing, Sandy Bay locals told police
about their boats being broken into and their dinghies stolen
in the days and weeks preceding Bob's disappearance. During
my research I discovered that break-ins were as common as
prawns. Trinket stealing, mostly, with imbecilic vandalism
an added irritation. Every now and then a boat was sprayed
with graffiti, vitriolic gutter-speak splashed across a bow or
stern. I kept digging, asking yachties and boaties to recall their
hard luck stories. There were many to be heard as I stepped
aboard the boats and shook the calloused hands of the fishing
community.

The yachties and fishermen suspected the homeless street
kids who sometimes frequented the foreshore, chasing cash to
fund a night of boozing or drugs. Some of the boaties named
names. Others told police, never to hear back. But among the
young punk thieves was an older bloke, a bum whom I'll call

'Pablo' who owned the worst yacht on the bay. Both he and it drifted round like a bad smell. One night a cray fisherman gave him a knuckle sandwich to the chin, trying to scare him away from the moorings. Another day the cray fisherman awoke to the news that he had suffered another break-in. Along with nine other boats across the water. The break-ins were a pandemic. One fisherman had his million-dollar craft vandalised. He caught the young thieves in the process, and doled out a hiding, only to have his boat burned to the water line and his small business ruined.

It wasn't so much the stolen goods – fridges emptied of beer, GPS equipment, wet-weather gear and lifejackets trashed or taken – more the mindlessness of it, that irritated the boaties. It had become so common that they had given up calling triple zero. When the cops were called, the response was dismal. They rarely turned out, reluctant to step away from their warm squad cars.

The night of 26 January, Australia Day, was typical. Oddly, for mid-summer, it was officially the darkest night of the year and ripe for pilfering. A jet-black sky canopied over the festive cheer and beer of one of the nation's rowdiest public holidays. A short distance away at Blackmans Bay, the sun had retired over a landscape of well-to-do homes and lush forest. The foreshore looked deserted. On the knoll, just up beyond the tea-trees was a construction site. An attractive prospect for thieves, especially the locked shed filled with tools, booze and food. In a wink, the lock was snapped and the shed looted. The thieves bolted, most likely by dinghy, into the dead of night, and onto their next target. This was the undeniable backdrop of life for the owners of pleasure craft and professional fishing boats circa January 2009.

But the focus of the police investigation was firmly locked on to Sue. Boat break-ins got short shrift. Triffett's evidence against Sue was the main game.

Triffett's first of two statements painted a damning portrait of Sue. According to Triffett, he and Maria Hanson met Sue and Bob in the 1990s. They became friends, socialising from time to time. From the statement's second paragraph, the flavour of the insight Triffett was offering into Sue became evident. Triffett claimed that Sue told him that Bob was mean. He told police that he believed the relationship between the two of them 'was not what I would describe as a loving or passionate relationship. It was not like a normal relationship; it was more business-like.'

It's intriguing that Triffett was able to offer this opinion as there had been a falling-out between the two couples in 1997 and they had not seen or spoken to each other in twelve years. Triffett went on to mention Sue's business ventures with a gentleman of senior years named Bob Martyn (incorrectly spelt Martin in Triffett's statement). In the 1990s, Triffett recalled, Martyn and Sue had some dealings in real estate. 'I don't recall the details but I recall that there may have been some issues with Sue making all the money from the land and Bob Martin was only receiving remaining blocks of land from the subdivision as payment for his part in the business deal. I don't know any further details but I believe that Bob lost a lot of money. She was cunning and manipulative and had a knack of getting things to work out for her without really upsetting [sic] or making it obvious.'

Triffett told police that he and Maria were at Sue and Bob's house shortly before their friendship fractured. Sue allegedly told Triffett that she was having problems with her brother Patrick over an expected inheritance. Sue's mother was poorly and likely soon to die. Triffett claimed, 'Sue said that she wanted to put Patrick overboard to get him out of the inheritance picture. Maria and I passed it off as a joke and Sue didn't go into any details.' Later in his statement, Triffett claimed that Sue tried to wrangle him into helping her murder Patrick. 'Sue then started talking about Patrick again and how she wanted to get rid of him. I realised then that she was actually serious about it. Sue told me that she wanted me to go out on the yacht with her and Patrick to deep water, as she called it. I was to push Patrick overboard after weighing him down with a tool box and things off the yacht and then sink the yacht closer to shore, near the marina, whilst Sue rowed back to shore.'

The oddity in this comment by Triffett is that Sue's mother wasn't in poor health. Her family can attest to this. She lived into her mid eighties, dying in 2015. How does this square with the pending death and inheritance caper back in the 1990s claimed by Triffett? But, police failed to check this vital corroborative fact.

Triffett said Sue showed him a white hosepipe that needed to be rigged up and explained how the bilge pump had to be rewired backwards in order to sink the yacht. Apparently, Sue never brought up her murderous plan with him again. Triffett's statement is ambiguous, timing-wise, but he seemed to suggest this happened in the 1990s. Certainly the falling-out between the couples occurred in 1997 when Triffett and Maria visited Bob and Sue at their Alison Street house in Sandy Bay. Triffett claimed that before dinner, and out of Bob's hearing, Sue said, 'Bob was waking up in the night and running around the house with knives looking for intruders ... Sue said, "Bob's got to go". She said, "What we talked about with Patrick has to happen with Bob."' Triffett claimed that he challenged Sue about her proposition in front of Bob and she denied it. The two couples were never to speak again. Phillip Triffett's statements, if somewhat Hollywood in tone, were certainly damning.

At Sue's trial in the Supreme Court of Tasmania, Triffett admitted that he had criminal charges pending (for which he was not convicted) for possession of 'over 1000 rounds of ammunition' at the time he gave his statements. Just prior to Sue's trial, he had also pleaded guilty to unlawful possession of a power tool and a set of timber stairs. He was discharged without conviction. Sue's defence counsel told the court that Triffett was charged with these offences after being raided by police on 7 January 2009, less than three weeks before Bob Chappell went missing from his yacht. The question was put to Triffett: 'Did you seek cooperation with police in this matter as a means, perhaps, of getting you out of other problems which had developed as early as 7 January 2009 when police ... searched your house?' Triffett denied the suggestion. However, he did agree with the proposition that he was hopeful of assistance from police if he provided information about Sue's past.

At the same Supreme Court hearing, Triffett mentioned helping Sue install new fuel injectors in the engine of the yacht she'd previously owned and sailed in the 1990s. When questioned by Sue's barrister, Triffett was unsure how many injectors were in the yacht's engine.

Maria Hanson also gave a statement to police describing Sue and Bob's relationship as 'anything but passionate or openly loving'. Similar to Triffett's characterisation of it as 'not what I would describe as a loving or passionate relationship'.

Maria also mentioned that she fell out with Sue after a long friendship and thought that 'Sue is quite capable of killing Bob. Bob was a frail person and Sue has always been a strong person. I don't think that Bob has been part of Sue's long-term future plans ever since they commenced a relationship … now that the girls [Sue's daughters] are older and have left home Sue has no use for Bob.'

The question is, having not seen Bob and Sue for twelve years, how would either Triffett or Maria know how their relationship was travelling? How on earth was Maria qualified to give an opinion on Sue's capability with regard to murder? Surely such an assessment should be left to someone like a psychiatrist, but only after extensive contact with Sue over many professionally structured consultations.

Maria recalled the visit she and Phillip Triffett made to Bob and Sue's home. However, Maria said that it was Sue's brother Patrick, not Bob, that Sue talked about. '… she found him wandering around in the early hours of the morning with a knife, thinking that there were intruders in the house'. Again the language was similar, except for the obvious contradiction. Was it Bob or Patrick who was wielding the knife, running around the house looking for intruders? Discrepancies like this are worrying.

So is the fact that when I read both sets of statements they appear laced with police-speak, the words police fall back on or use subconsciously. Every witness statement or affidavit should be in the words of the witness. Or, if the witness's language is rough or their vocabulary is poor, it might be altered slightly to assist the court. But using a witness's actual words is important so that police cannot be accused of leading the witness or authoring the statements. The near exactly similar phrasing of

Maria and Triffett's statements raises questions for me about how they were recorded. Maria Hanson never gave evidence at the murder trial of Sue Neill-Fraser, although her statement was tendered to the court. She produced a medical certificate and was excused. Strange place, Tasmania.

Further, there were no corroborative witnesses to support Triffett's and Hanson's accusations. This strikes me as decidedly odd, particularly as the evidence helped to convict Sue Neill-Fraser of murder. I must say at this point that I see Phillip Triffett as nothing more than a witness in the investigation into the death of Bob Chappell. A very fascinating witness. One who clearly has many layers to his character. It is clear from Triffett's and Hanson's statements that their friendship with Bob and Sue ended acrimoniously – which would suggest even more reason to meticulously verify their testimonies. Maria's daughter would have been worth talking to, surely? She was a young adult back then and knew much about Triffett and his relationship with Sue. Her insight, as I would discover, was nothing short of disturbing and something for independent authorities to probe.

It also transpired that Bob Martyn, who, according to Triffett and Hanson, had suffered at the hands of Sue, wanted to give evidence to police about his business dealings with Sue Neill-Fraser, and what he knew of her relationship with Bob Chappell. Martyn was a man of some stature in the Hobart community. He was, and still is, proficient in the mechanics of boats and yachts, and worked in a professional capacity for the Hydro-Electric Commission in the 1990s. In those days he knew Phillip Triffett well, having watched him mature into manhood. He also knew Maria Hanson, Sue Neill-Fraser and Bob Chappell. A good deal older than the four of them, he enjoyed their company, and helped them when he could. Martyn's corroboration would have been useful in underpinning Phillip and Maria's evidence, one would think. But he was ignored by the police, who, he felt, dismissed him as a seventy-year-old pensioner and, initially, by Sue's own lawyers.

Despite Martyn's frustrations at not being heard back when the allegations against Sue Neill-Fraser were ripe and the police were building their case, he would not be silenced. He had attended much of Sue's trial and heard way too much evidence that troubled him. His persistence eventually paid off. Barbara Etter, the lawyer who represented Sue in the years following her trial, finally sat him down and let him tell his story. The result was a nine-page affidavit dated 24 September 2014. Martyn knew that his evidence may be too late to save Sue from serving out her sentence, but he needed to set the record straight. After swearing the accuracy of his affidavit, he stepped back and waited. All that happened was that Bob Martyn got older. Then, in December 2017, he met with investigative journalists Patrick Carlyon and Anthony Dowsley from the *Herald Sun* newspaper and reaffirmed the story he'd first told Barbara. He was just as adamant.

Martyn recalled working on Sue's first yacht (the one Triffett recalled had injectors and an electric bilge pump and which he also said he worked on) in 1992: '... there were no fittings to allow for the discharge of water through the hull. This vessel was not fitted with an electric bilge pump.' Furthermore, the vessel only had one injector, rather than multiple ones.

In his affidavit, Martyn swore that he never told anyone that Sue had been financially dishonest with him, and that Sue was not either cunning or manipulative. He further stated he had had no falling-out with either Sue or Bob Chappell. Rather, he said both Sue and Bob became afraid of Phillip Triffett when he and Hanson began spending a lot of time at their house after a fire on Hanson's property. 'Sue subsequently told me that she had to sever their relationship' as she told Martyn of her concerns about that fire and that she feared for her safety.

Much of what Martyn said was verified by the listening device that was placed in Sue's home. She was also recorded years earlier in an interview with a private investigator, Dennis O'Day Snr, talking about the breakdown of the friendship between Triffett and Hanson and her and Bob. The recording and its subsequent transcript came about after Sue became fearful of her relationship with Triffett. Sue went to talk to two detectives about her concerns and also Dennis O'Day Snr, the private investigator. Unbeknownst to Sue, Mr O'Day taped the conversation, which fell into police hands.

Both Martyn and Triffett were interviewed for the two-page *Herald Sun* exposé about Sue Neill-Fraser's conviction for Bob Chappell's murder that was published on 10 December 2017. Martyn firmly stated his belief that Sue was innocent and was shocked at Triffett's claims. Triffett also gave his opinion: 'She's as guilty as hell.'

* * *

Martyn arrived in Hobart a few days after *Four Winds* was found sinking and came to the aid of Sue and her family, searching the bayside foreshores in the vain hope of finding something, anything, that might help shed light on Bob Chappell's fate. He had the opportunity to observe Sue closely, noting that she had years earlier suffered an injury to her coccyx and had a dodgy hip. He was aware that Sue had had a bad fall from a horse. He did not notice any injury to Sue's hand; specifically, he did not observe a cut to her thumb, something the police claimed she had at the time of Bob's disappearance, and which they submitted as evidence at her trial.

One has to wonder why Bob Martyn's evidence was never sought or offered to the court. I would have thought if the Crown relied on naming Martyn in the damning testimony from both Phillip and Maria, then surely someone in the detective muster room in Hobart might have rung up the old guy and asked him to verify their explosive statements. Certainly, they had Martyn's telephone number. He had left it with them often enough.

* * *

For over two years Barbara Etter, Sue's lawyer, stayed on a dogged quest to uncover Phillip Triffett's background, demanding to know if a police file existed on him and, if so, what was in it. I would end up studying her files, all 2600 pages she had amassed over many years. Most of the correspondence dates from 2012 onwards, when Sue's appeal processes were well underway. (Barbara was not involved in Sue's original trial.) I sorted each document in chronological order, trying to follow Barbara's work, the contacts and letters she wrote and received. The task took months. The trove of documents demonstrated how Barbara used Tasmania's Right to Information (RTI) process and how she battled Tasmania Police to get information. She wrote to the Ombudsman frequently, as well as to senior government officials, the Minister for Police and the Commissioner of Police. Each time the police refused to give her information on Triffett, it only spurred her on to write even more letters and make more appeals for information.

I came to admire Barbara for her tenacity and hold her in high esteem. Her doggedness was impressive. I have never seen a more dedicated effort from a lawyer to gain facts to help a client in need. The cops hated her, and the court administrative system wasn't endeared to her either. I would hear time and again in Hobart that the wheels of justice were gaining speed to get rid of Barbara, who came under an extraordinary amount of pressure in her role as Sue's defence lawyer. However, Barbara was reluctant to assist anyone other than her client. I could never understand that, and still don't. Barbara could be best described as a lone wolf, one who, due to her quirks, could only work alone.

After meeting Eve, I telephoned Barbara, who worked closely with Eve, in an attempt to break the ice and begin to build a working relationship. It wasn't a long phone call, just a set of pleasantries. She greeted me cordially but declined to supply me with any details whatsoever. She followed up our chat with a text message, *Great to be in touch! Look forward to working with you.* It was possibly the shortest letter of engagement I have ever received. So, here I was, an author on research, and an aid to the defence of Sue Neill-Fraser. It was then that I realised I had fallen into the frypan. But, what else could I do, something about the case smelled very wrong and, in my view, no investigative journalist could just sit on their hands and do nothing.

After that it was all one-way traffic with Barbara. I would find stuff out as I researched the case and feed it to her, but I could expect nothing in return. As a compromise, she told me that to access court documents or copies of the police files I should approach Eve, who had a complete set of everything.

I started to get a complex and wondered if I had body odour, but it was just the way of Barbara.

I find most lawyers to be very inward people, whereas detectives are the opposite. The former usually sit twenty-four hours a day, seven days a week at a desk, constructing or deconstructing legal argument. They play everything to the letter of the law. They hang off definitions and meanings as they craft their arguments. Privilege seems to drive them, and underpins their thinking and relationships with others. This can lead to an aura of secretiveness. Lawyers are also schooled to argue a position, regardless of the validity of that position. A bare-faced lie can be argued in favour of their client before the court. Or against another person. This manipulation has always seemed contrary to justice to me. I saw this in my police career and I would see this throughout the Sue Neill-Fraser case. I will never agree with it.

Detectives, on the other hand, are mostly in the back streets of society chasing filth or hitting doors with sledgehammers. They require information, lots of it. They need cooperation from every side of society, every government department, every business and every individual. A detective is only as good as the information they gather. I have always thought that lawyers work in tunnels and corridors, and their thinking can be restricted. While detectives work in vast landscapes, wherever the investigation takes them. They are forced to take on everything, to be open-minded. To embrace everyone, regardless of social standing, ethnicity or creed.

I am a great believer in sharing information. I've been on four nationally significant task forces and we shared all our material. But here I was, studying the circumstances into the incarceration of Sue Neill-Fraser and I was faced with one-way traffic in the information stakes. It was different. But, as I've said, Barbara was nothing if not tenacious. Eventually, in February 2014, after Barbara had sent off yet another complaint to the Police Commissioner, an RTI letter arrived on her desk confirming there was a file on Triffett. It contained 'statutory declarations and documents related to other persons' previously unknown to Sue's defence team. A paper gold mine. But some of the file was heavily redacted. All the police would offer was a range of documents that showed Triffett had been raided on 7 January 2009, nineteen days before Bob Chappell went missing. He was charged with unlawful possession of property and an ammunition offence. Triffett was not convicted of either of these charges. There was also a list of more than forty items of power tools seized by police that same day. Everything in the file suggested the tools were seized from Triffett's home. There were also police reports related to break-ins, including thefts of power tools, and the victims' names. Tools similar to the forty power tools seized from Triffett's house, and with serial numbers. One report stated: 'This MO is consistent with reputed MO of Triffetts of Half Moon Marsh.'

Another notation dated 13 February 2009, nineteen days after Bob Chappell went missing, and over a month after the raid on Triffett, indicated that almost all the power tools were returned to Triffett and signed for on police receipt #209781. The thirteenth of February 2009 was also sixteen days after Triffett contacted police and offered assistance with their investigations into Sue Neill-Fraser. This was also a couple of days after Triffett's offer to assist was placed before the office of the Director of Public Prosecutions (DPP) and discussed. Triffett and Hanson would go on to make their statements to police. Friday, 13 February was a very lucky day for some.

Whilst Barbara's letter openly discusses the Dennis O'Day Snr tape recording – circa 2001 – where Sue outlines her fears of 'reprisals down the track' the police (not the Commissioner) would go on to deny the existence of the tape and transcript and an acrimonious relationship between Sue, Bob and Triffett. However, on 20 February 2012 Sarah Bowles, Sue's daughter, received a copy of the transcript from a simple RTI application. I also have a copy. The detective sergeant who interviewed Sue on 4 March 2009 for murder even mentions, at length, the Dennis O'Day Snr taped conversation. The sergeant's Q&A wanders over ten pages about the history of acrimony between Triffett and Sue and Bob.

Worryingly, police reports on Triffett and the transcript and tape recording had not been mentioned at Sue Neill-Fraser's trial.

* * *

The prosecution's final blow against Sue Neill-Fraser smelled like a carcass in the late afternoon sun. When she inspected the yacht after Bob disappeared, Sue thought a small set of wrenches was missing. She qualified this in court by saying, '… you know, they come in a plastic wrapped-up thing and they're for working on the small nuts on a motor'. Not hard to imagine what she meant: every kitchen has a small wrench in a drawer, along with a screwdriver or two – the sort of tools that might come in handy in any household.

Yet at her trial (where Sue had chosen to give evidence), DPP Tim Ellis completely distorted Sue's claim. In his cross-examination of her, Ellis changed the 'small set of wrenches' to a 'big wrench' and suggested she'd hit Bob over the head with such a wrench. This description was repeated a number of times, as evidenced on page 1297 of the court transcript: 'Big Wrench'.

There is not one skerrick of evidence to show that a big wrench had ever been on *Four Winds*, yet Mr Ellis focused on just such a tool.

In my view, DPP Ellis's closing address to the jury was alarming. 'She's [Sue] walking backwards and forwards and delivers a blow — a blow or blows, or maybe stabs him with a screwdriver, I don't know. He doesn't look round, and so the body doesn't have any marks of what you'd expect if someone had come down there, a stranger, intent on doing him harm. The body, I suggest, would have marks consistent only with [blows] being delivered by someone who he knew to be there, who he knew and expected to be behind him.'

Mr Ellis also told the jury, 'Now I've suggested that wrenches have been on her [Sue's] mind as a sort of implement that was used to kill Mr Chappell.'

It must be the idiot in me, but I can't see anything in the material from the police investigation that I read that details a big wrench, or any injuries sustained by screwdrivers. In fact, without knowing what happened to Bob's body, I can't allow myself to have an opinion about how he was killed. Or what injuries he sustained. It's pure speculation. How could such statements be delivered at a trial? And why weren't they tossed out?

Towards the end of the trial, the judge, attempting to explain to the jury the difference between voluntary and intentional acts and involuntary acts, reached for an explanation and 'a terribly heavy wrench' to make his point. 'So, for example, if she was walking through the boat and tripped and fell and happened to be carrying a terribly heavy wrench which hit him on the back of the head causing death, that wouldn't be a voluntary or intentional act.'

Eventually the jury retired to consider their verdict. They returned from their deliberation and asked a simple question about the difference between murder and manslaughter. The judge again offered examples. 'So let's take the example of hitting a man on the head with a wrench. If an assailant who has no wish to kill the victim hits the victim on the head with a wrench, very hard, you might think that that's intended … So if an assailant hits someone on the head with a wrench, for example, and if that bodily harm that's intended, a head injury caused with a wrench … For example, if the assailant thinks, "I don't care whether he dies or not, I'm so angry with him, I'm going to hit him on the head with this wrench."'

The jury retired again and ultimately came back with a verdict of guilty. In his sentencing remarks the judge stated, 'It's quite likely that's what happened.' (That is, it was 'quite likely' Sue hit Bob over the head with a heavy wrench.) 'But I don't consider that the evidence is sufficient for me to make detailed findings as to the manner of attack.' However, the wrench examples had already been given to the jury before they made their minds up.

In all, there were twenty-four references ('a wrench', 'a big wrench' 'a terribly heavy wrench') made to a wrench being either a weapon of attack or a possible murder weapon. This despite Sue only ever saying that the wrenches on the yacht were 'little ones, for working on small nuts'.

In the end, Sue Neill-Fraser braced herself, white-knuckled in the dock as the judge delivered his sentence. 'Ms Neill-Fraser is now 56 years old. She has no prior convictions. She apparently led a blameless life until she murdered Mr Chappell. Otherwise, there is almost nothing that counts in her favour for sentencing purposes. She did not plead guilty. She has shown no remorse. She has not said or done anything that would assist in the finding of the body. There is no suggestion that Mr Chappell said or did anything to provoke this crime, or even to warrant hostility on the part of Ms Neill-Fraser. It was a deliberate killing for the purpose of some sort of personal gain. It warrants a heavier sentence than most murders.'

Sue was sentenced to 26 years, later reduced on appeal to 23.

* * *

This misplaced focus on the wrenches or wrench on *Four Winds* is similar to a misrepresentation in the Crown case against Andrew Mallard, who was wrongfully convicted of murder in Perth, West Australia, in 1995. Mallard was accused of killing a woman with a 'large wrench' and went on to serve twelve years of his life sentence before his name was cleared and the real killer was identified. The corrupt case centred around the invention of a 'large wrench' that police claimed Mallard used to bash his victim to death. They even had Mallard draw a picture of the non-existent wrench. The Western Australian police department along with the Director of Public Prosecutions and the judiciary spent years fighting a team of brave Mallard supporters, lawyers and disillusioned witnesses.

It would take the intervention of my friend, Professor Dave Barclay, a Scottish forensic scientist – considered amongst the world's finest – brought in to review the mess with an open mind, to blow the corrupt case open. Dave wrote a scathing report and his team exposed the 'large wrench' theory as hogwash. An invention.

Dave's review would also identify the real killer through a palm print left at the crime scene, as well as link the killer to the real weapon. It was a masterly example of forensic and investigative work and a stain on the Perth cops. An independent inquiry ultimately revealed the truth and justice prevailed, but not before the lives of many good people had been ruined. The similarities with the Sue Neill-Fraser case are remarkable.

Into the cesspool

ONE COULD BE FORGIVEN FOR THINKING THAT SANDY BAY and the idyllic waters off the Royal Yacht Club of Tasmania are the natural habitat of Hobart's wealthy and beautiful, people at ease with the likes of Mary, Crown Princess of Denmark, arguably the area's most famous export. It is indeed a sailing mecca that often hosts the crème de la crème of Tasmanian and Australian society. Prestige and fashion meet the very finest in nautical engineering. But it's also the gathering place for many of Hobart's homeless people, junkies and thieves, who, tucked away in the shadows, look over the display of luxury with envious eyes.

Two of the faces on Eve Ash's muster room wall were tough guys, both about 50 years of age, living rough in the area. They affected me like a thistle up my arse. I'd focused on the men for several reasons: they were known to each other; indeed, they were best of friends. Both men were sailors, so they knew about the workings of yachts. Both men lived at Sandy Bay. One of them, Stephen Gleeson, had lived in the immediate area, sleeping rough inside his car – a yellow Ford sedan – which was parked on the spit of land known locally as Rowing Shed Point that looked over Sandy Bay and the *Four Winds'* mooring, only 250 to 300 metres offshore. His car also afforded a good view of another yacht moored close to *Four Winds* that was owned by the other man whom I was intensely interested in, 'Pablo', the guy who'd been punched by the cray fisherman in an attempt to scare him away from the area. *Four Winds* and Pablo's yacht were moored close together, and close enough to shore for Gleeson to see anyone who was on board or to hear them if they were calling out. This was Gleeson's small world.

Both Gleeson and Pablo had a history of violence, had been charged with criminal offences and had served time in prison. They lived a hand-to-mouth existence and were considered undesirables by the yachting fraternity. Police had spoken to Gleeson very briefly on the morning Bob was discovered missing. Gleeson was asleep in his yellow Ford sedan when police tapped on his window and woke him up. Sue Neill-Fraser and Bob Chappell owned an almost new dinghy. Locally, it became known as Sue's dinghy, used for getting to and from the shoreline to the *Four Winds* yacht. Sue and Bob would place their dinghy into the water at the shore area immediate to the spit of land known as Rowing Shed Point, metres from Gleeson's car. When they were finished with the yacht and dinghy for the day Sue often tied 'her' dinghy to a land mooring at the yacht club, only 200 metres away, before going home. Out of sight of Gleeson and others. Hidden by the rowing sheds.

At trial, police claimed the dinghy, which they maintained she used to access *Four Winds* to murder Bob, was found bobbing in the shallows only metres from Gleeson's car. Yet, remarkably, they would ask him nothing about this anomaly. Indeed, nothing seemed to interest the police about this man. Yet he and his best mate on the yacht fascinated me.

I could only shake my head at why police weren't more interested. To me, their presence that morning, so close to the action, demanded close examination.

During my research phase, I read police reports, obtained through Barbara's Right to Information applications, that indicated Stephen Gleeson occasionally passed on information to police. In reports dating back to 2007, it was stated that he told police about drug dealers and illegal gun sales and later even mentioned that he had been nearby when Bob Chappell was murdered. On one occasion he told police that a man who had lived with him had, at one time, killed another man. Such is the life of the homeless and the vagabonds of society. They see and hear much within their underworld. What I took from this was that Gleeson might one day talk to me. I tucked that into my back pocket of thoughts.

Pablo and Gleeson had both been formally interviewed by police about Bob Chappell's disappearance. When Eve supplied me with a copy of their Records of Interview (ROI), I almost snatched them from her hand. I was eager to learn what they had said. Then I made a discovery that would puzzle me greatly. Gleeson was only formally interviewed due to Barbara's insistence, and not until 2012. Three years after Bob's murder. His interview led police to interview Pablo a month later. Barbara, like me, thought that both men should have been interviewed by police in 2009.

I was dumbfounded as to why it had taken the head of the investigation, Inspector Peter Powell, three years to interview them. In any investigation I was involved in, persons in such close proximity to the crime should have been hauled in on day one and interviewed thoroughly. With the knowledge of their criminal backgrounds, surveillance should have also been thrown at both men, along with mobile phone taps and listening devices. Criminals talk. The rougher and tougher the criminal, usually the more they chat, comparing notes. And on it goes. The potential evidence that could have been snared by covert measures is endless. But Gleeson and Pablo never made it to the hit parade of the investigation until 2012, two years after Sue's incarceration. Surely there must be something in the ROIs (records of interview), I thought, that would explain why any potential evidence they may have wasn't thoroughly investigated. Let's not forget, they might have been crucial witnesses too. I polished up my eyewear and started reading.

An ROI is a verbatim account of an interview between an individual and two police together in the one room. Usually there is a detective leading the interview; in this case it was Inspector Powell. However, both police will often pose questions to the suspect or person of interest. That's where the saying 'good cop, bad cop' comes from.

I read Gleeson's ROI first. I was amazed that he had offered an unsolicited comment at the beginning of the interview that suggested he thought police wanted to talk about a 'double murder'. Gleeson was not exercising his right to silence; he was keen to assist. But Inspector Powell didn't seem interested; he never probed.

Throughout the interview, Gleeson continued to voluntarily offer up Pablo as a suspect in the murder of Bob Chappell. It is common for crooks to dob on each other, especially if the case under question is serious, so I was not surprised to read the allegations made by Gleeson. The trouble was, each time

Gleeson suggested his friend Pablo might be involved in Bob Chappell's murder, the two police interviewing him changed the subject or shifted the focus. On three occasions Gleeson attempted to steer the interview back to Pablo.

Reading the verbatim record of the interview was a shock. Not for its content, but more for its lack of content. Gleeson nonetheless went off on his own tangent a few times, offering up relevant information about Bob's murder, especially about three key issues. First, he suggested that there was a girl on board *Four Winds* the night Bob went missing: a 'sixteen-year-old homeless girl'. Next, he hinted that the girl's boyfriend might be involved in Bob's disappearance. Thirdly, and equally intriguingly, he said he had gone to the Hobart Police Station a couple of weeks after the murder and given information to a policewoman, who advised him to 'stay in fit with him [Pablo]', meaning that Gleeson should stay friends with him, to keep getting information. To me, this was smart thinking by the policewoman.

Gleeson had expected to hear from the police, following up on his information. When he told the inspector that he wanted to talk about another murder – a double murder – Powell brushed him off. The police wanted to deal with other issues first, Gleeson was told, 'then we can have a talk to you about that and get some more detail. Just so that we don't confuse the issue.'

Powell never did get around to having that talk or getting that detail.

Gleeson had no trouble recalling Australia Day, 2009. He had been sleeping in his car at the Rowing Club jetty for about ten months. He also recalled emergency workers approaching him the following morning and police having a brief chat with him. The police asked if he knew Bob Chappell. 'No,' Gleeson said, 'but I knew his missus, all right.' He had helped Sue lift her dinghy in and out of the water. Did he know Bob Chappell personally? he was asked again. 'Yeah, [from seeing him] lifting the dinghy out of the water. And I come, "Can I give you a hand, mate?" Well, that's not knowing him,' Gleeson answered.

Gleeson was asked a few more times about how well he knew Sue, but he didn't offer any new information, until suddenly, he dropped a bombshell about Bob. '… word has it that he had [a] sixteen-year-old homeless girl on board, right?' The police showed no interest, telling Gleeson, '… I'm not sure that we need to go there but if you're saying that, I don't know where you would have heard that rumour from …'

Powell ignored the comment. He moved on.

The conversation shifted to Sue Neill-Fraser's demeanour. Gleeson was shown a single photograph of Sue and asked if the image was of the woman whom he helped with the dinghy from time to time. The single photo identification is peculiar because police and courts have clear rules about identifying suspects or persons of interest. Single photograph identification is taboo, because it can be suggestive. It can make a witness feel obligated to positively identify a person based on that single image. A folder of eight photos featuring similar looking and similarly aged persons is the ideal way to ask a witness to identify someone. It's neither suggestive nor unfair. Yet Gleeson was shown a single photograph, which he agreed was of Sue Neill-Fraser, but immediately he tried to shift the direction of the conversation back to the girl. 'So the point I'm making is with the sixteen-year-old girl …'

It's clear that Gleeson was eager to tell police about the possibility of a sixteen-year-old girl being on the boat with Bob

Chappell on the night he was murdered, but Powell continued to deflect his comments, even when Gleeson suggested that Bob's wife might have turned on him because she found out he was a 'rock spider' (a paedophile who preys on teenagers or children for sex). Perhaps Gleeson really did know something. Perhaps he was privy to a secret facet of Bob Chappell that may (or may not) explain his murder.

Gleeson might have had it a bit jumbled, a little mixed up, as witnesses often do, but the fact that he kept telling the police about a sixteen-year-old girl was important. I'd expect the police to then ask questions along the lines of who, what, where. The simplest would be, 'Okay, Stephen, tell us everything you know about this girl.' Instead, the response to this gem of an insight into what may have been happening aboard *Four Winds* that night is dismissal. 'I don't know what value there is in speculating about all those sorts of things because I'm just trying to clear up some other issues with you,' Powell said.

It's important to reflect on Gleeson's words here. Based on his belief that a young girl was on the boat, or perhaps because he'd heard someone else say it, he may well have been of the opinion that Bob Chappell was up to no good. It's easy to see the link. Witnesses often join too many dots at times. People are like that. They jump to conclusions. It's for the detective to unravel the truth. But Powell's response was to shift away from this crucial information. In fact, the police were already well aware that a teenage girl called Meaghan Vass may have been on the yacht that night. At the very least, they knew that her DNA was discovered on the yacht. Furthermore, they knew that on the night of the murder, Meaghan was missing from the halfway house where she was living. They knew, too, that she was suspected of being involved in break-and-enters. So, any revelation about a '... sixteen-year-old homeless girl on board' the yacht should have been 99.9% pure gold to a detective.

Every detective with any level of experience knows that the key thing you are searching for to help you solve a crime is often discovered in a word, a comment that jumps out at you. Something that is 'intimate' to the crime you're trying to solve. Something that smacks you in the face as information only the perpetrator or a witness close to the action could know. Yet, Gleeson's information about a girl on board the yacht was ignored. By the time Gleeson gave this interview, Sue Neill-Fraser was a convicted murderer serving 26 years in Risdon Prison. Perhaps it's no wonder police weren't interested in probing his information further. They already had someone in the bin for the murder. Someone found guilty by the court – there was no need to probe further if you believed you had the guilty party in prison.

To be clear, I found no evidence whatsoever that Bob Chappell was involved in anything untoward, as Gleeson suggested. However, I did find overwhelming evidence that supports Gleeson's assertion that a girl was on board the yacht.

Gleeson went on to tell the police interviewing him of his experience with boats, yachts and army sea-going vessels. He had been around boats since he was a child. He also spent twelve years in the army, five years of which were in the Army Eights, a boating unit. Clearly, with that sort of background, he would know his way around a yacht. Again, police didn't probe him on this. They moved on.

They did ask Gleeson one question that related to the girl on the yacht. Did the name Meaghan Vass mean anything to him? Gleeson said he didn't know 'the name' Meaghan Vass. The police didn't, however, ask him to look at any photographs of Meaghan or any young girls who may have been in the vicinity of *Four Winds* or the area of Sandy Bay around the time Bob disappeared.

Gleeson did say that he knew many teenage boys who frequented the area in which he lived in his car. He went on to discuss the young people who hung around Rowing Shed Point. They would approach him when he was sitting in his car 'drinking plonk' and ask if he would buy alcohol for them. They were generally under-age, and Gleeson knew them 'pretty well'. Again, the police mentioned the name Meaghan Vass, to which Gleeson offered nothing. With the number of young people coming and going from the area immediately around where Gleeson's car was parked, it would be standard practice for police to try and identify them, see if they turned up in police records and possibly track them down and interview them. Perhaps they might have had something to offer about the events of that night. But they didn't. Let's not forget Sue's supposed second 'lie', about being down on the water's edge late that night and seeing homeless people milling around a gas burner. This could only have been Stephen Gleeson's gas burner and his young 'plonk' drinking friends. So, was Sue really telling the truth?

The police did establish one important point: Gleeson never saw Sue or Bob with any young people. But when Gleeson attempted to again raise that he had heard that a young girl was involved in the events on the yacht, he was shut down.

At this point of the interview the line of questioning shifted to a friend of Gleeson's, someone inconsequential to the investigation, leaving the issue of the homeless girl to flounder.

Yet Gleeson persevered. Clearly, he wanted to tell police about what he knew or suspected about Bob's disappearance, and, remarkably, he persisted. 'I don't know if this has got any substance to it, but I have come and seen a policewoman here, about [he mentions Pablo]; he's become a good mate, but the police told me to stay in fit with him.'

Powell asked who he was talking about. Gleeson told them he was talking about his mate, Pablo. Gleeson seemed almost desperate to tell them what he knew. Pablo was moored close to *Four Winds* at the time. In fact, the closest yacht to the *Four Winds*. He said. 'This bloke is an expert conman ... the best I've come across, right? And he's not only that, but he's a hit man. Right?'

Powell showed interest. 'How do you know that?'

'Because he's told me. We're mates.'

Instead of asking for more details about Pablo, Powell shut Gleeson down. 'I don't want to bog us down, you know, going over all that stuff.' He shifted away from the issue of Pablo to an administrative matter. This killed the momentum. Pages in the record of interview were wasted on non-issues. Then, the police homed in on Gleeson's history of drunkenness and family violence. 'We are not here to judge you about any of that,' he was told before police launched into more than fifty questions dealing with his record of fights, drinking, carrying a knife and rough sleeping. The result was a very negative picture of Gleeson's past. Powell then asked Gleeson directly if he had any involvement in the killing of Bob Chappell. I got the impression he was then being treated like a suspect, peppered with a volley of questions. Finally, Gleeson was asked if there was anything he wanted to tell police. He simply laughed, bitterly. A short time later, almost heroically, he again suggested police should check out his mate Pablo, but it was a waste of time. Powell wound the interview up. 'Because we want to keep this neat as far as ... this side of things go ... And look, we'll ... conclude the interview.'

And neat it was. The interview ended in double-quick time.

I've done countless interviews with witnesses and suspects and it seems to me that Inspector Powell had no interest in what Gleeson was trying to tell him. I would like to know why.

The next ROI that I read also involved Inspector Powell and the first of my persons of interest – Pablo. The interview was conducted in April 2012, a month after Gleeson's. The first thing that jumped out at me was that police waited four weeks to interview Pablo despite Gleeson nominating him as a suspect for the murder of Bob Chappell. Any number of resources could and should have been thrown at him. At the very least a phone tap on his mobile phone and surveillance may have been warranted. Yet I can find nothing to suggest an investigative effort was put into Pablo. During his interview, he spoke freely to police and admitted owning a yacht that was on the water at Sandy Bay when Bob disappeared. He said that he and Stephen Gleeson were close friends and that Gleeson had, at one time, lived aboard his yacht. He told Powell he was moored close to *Four Winds*. He was 'slightly off to the starboard side' of *Four Winds* and had been watching it the day before.

Pablo's description of where he was moored on that day – 'slightly off to the starboard side' of *Four Winds* – is crucial.

Pablo settled in Hobart in 2007, he said, having come from New South Wales. He had purchased his yacht after gaining funds from an inheritance. He never worked in Tasmania; instead he moored his yacht opposite the Royal Yacht Club. He claimed he'd known Gleeson since Anzac Day, 2008. They were 'very good friends'. Gleeson stayed on the yacht for two months, leaving in July or August of 2008. Pablo admitted to once being a drinker at the yacht club. On Australia Day, 2009, he recalled drinking with Gleeson, who was living in his car, a yellow Ford sedan that was always parked at the Rowing Club (Rowing Shed Point).

Pablo also admitted to having numerous criminal convictions, including for discharging a firearm in public, malicious injury, drunkenness and 'robbing tools'. He had done prison time for malicious wounding after stabbing another man. When asked to describe himself he said he was 'excitable probably … I was shorter tempered than what I am now.' He said his temper and tendency for violence increased when he drank.

Usually when police plan an interview they begin with questions about a low-level issue. These are used to warm up the suspect by asking about something not too contentious or incriminating. Once the suspect starts responding and answering, the detective will up the ante, moving on to more critical subject matter, issues closer to the matter under investigation. This didn't seem to be the case with Pablo. The police appeared to be having an easy-going chat, framing their questions in a very leading way, with the expected answer already inserted. This is unusual as it carries the risk of the suspect's answers later being thrown out in court, should the matter get that far. I always had one rule when interviewing suspects. To try to make my question shorter than the expected answer. Each time. It tends to get the suspect talking. Occasionally the police did ask a relevant question, albeit very directly. 'Did you ever know a girl, a young girl, called Meaghan Vass?' 'No,' Pablo answered.

Police then made it very clear that they were discussing the incident involving Bob Chappell on Australia Day, 2009. Pablo denied knowing Bob, but admitted he was familiar with his yacht, *Four Winds*. He'd heard about Bob's disappearance from police at the time, he said. (There is no evidence whatsoever to support this. Later, Stephen Gleeson would describe in great detail talking to Pablo about Bob Chappell the morning he was discovered missing.)

When Pablo was shown a single photograph of Bob Chappell and then one of Sue Neill-Fraser, he said that he didn't know either of them. In fact, he said he hadn't even heard Sue's name, despite her conviction for Bob's murder being arguably the biggest news story in Tasmania for many years. Despite being moored 'just off the starboard side' of *Four Winds*, Pablo denied knowing Bob or Sue at all.

After a discussion, the police and Pablo agreed he'd first moored his yacht opposite the Royal Yacht Club in January 2009. Pablo said he was moored 'about 300 yards offshore'. He was pretty familiar with Bob and Sue's yacht, recalling *Four Winds* was a little further from shore, and 'slightly off to the starboard side' of his yacht. As a 53-footer, it was much larger than his, Pablo said, and made a joke about the arrogance of people with big yachts. The police began sketching a diagram to illustrate how close the two yachts were to each other.

Pablo mentioned that on the day before Australia Day, he saw *Four Winds* sailing towards the Derwent Sailing Squadron (the next yacht club south of the Royal Yacht Club) and then on to Bruny Island, a distance of some ten nautical miles. Bingo! He did know them. Perhaps he'd spoken to Bob Chappell or Sue Neill-Fraser, something he had denied. Yet he must at least have seen Bob Chappell at the helm of *Four Winds* or working around the yacht, if he had also seen the yacht sail to Bruny Island. Yet he kept saying he didn't know him, and hadn't seen him or spoken to him. Powell probed him a little about his claim of not knowing Bob or Sue. 'So you never spoke to them?'

'No, no,' Pablo said.

Perhaps Pablo had helped them with their dinghy, the detective suggested, but Pablo stuck to his guns, 'Nope.' Interestingly, Pablo went on to say that Gleeson 'helped them a couple of times'. And again said his yacht was close to the *Four Winds*.

The next topic of conversation was intriguing. Pablo stated that he was on the water, moored opposite the Royal Yacht Club until November 2010. Neither Powell or the other officer queried this. They hadn't done their homework. Pablo, in fact, moved his yacht on the same day Bob Chappell went missing. Not to return. This should have been evident from many avenues of inquiry, not least from photographs taken that day and afterwards. Pablo had moved his yacht to Constitution Dock, the main docking area of Hobart. In time he would sell his yacht and leave Tasmania altogether.

Curiously, Pablo claimed to have seen virtually nothing relating to the investigation into Bob's disappearance, witnessing none of the commotion on the morning of 27 January 2009: no police or emergency staff, no vehicles, water police or salvage yachts or boats. He never noticed the journalists, cameramen or the crowd of stickybeaks milling around. Bear in mind there was a major salvage operation in progress to keep the *Four Winds* afloat and a police search of the vessel, tasks that involved dozens of people. Pablo, apparently, was oblivious to the commotion and the biggest news story for years, all happening metres away from him, unable to recall any of it. Why? Because he had already gone. He claimed that he went ashore suffering from a hangover. He spoke to his close friend Stephen, who told him about the salvage operation – the cops, the fire brigade – but Pablo saw nothing.

The police cut to the chase. 'Did you have anything to do with Mr Chappell's disappearance?'

'No,' Pablo said. 'Not at all. I didn't even know the person.'

'Did you assist Susan Fraser or anyone else in either, you know, killing him or getting rid of his body, or hiding his body?'

'No.'

'Did you yourself kill Bob Chappell?'

'No.'

'If I said to you that someone suggested to us that you were a hit man, what would your reaction to that be?'

'I reckon that'd be laughable,' Pablo answered.

'So, I take it you're not a hit man?'

This last question in particular made me wonder. Who would frame a question like this? There was no stealth, no cunning, in the police approach. No criminal in his right mind would answer anything other than 'no'. I couldn't help but wonder what Inspector Powell might have done if Pablo had answered in the affirmative. Perhaps all the clocks in Tasmania might have stopped!

A police interview is many things. Most of all it's an inquisition, a skilful probe into the behaviour of the person under scrutiny. The detective should know his or her subject matter extremely well and have spent hours preparing questions and planning the best approach. Each question should be a step towards where the detective is leading the interviewee. Slowly,

slowly is the age-old adage that detectives use when preparing an interview. It's like a set of building blocks: use one at a time. It's inappropriate in such a process to ask a question with an answer suggested in its wording. The questions need to be short. The answers, ideally, need to be long. Or at least telling. Once an answer is received, the next question is presented. And on it goes, building up to a set of questions where – hopefully – the suspect has nowhere else to go but to divulge an incriminating fact or a revealing truth. Trouble is the police, in the case of Pablo, didn't seem to have such a structure. And to ask a man who has been around the streets and prisons for a good deal of his adult life if he was a hit man got the answer the question deserved.

Pablo was asked again if he'd ever been on *Four Winds*. His answer was no. Remarkably, when the police asked the next question, they provided Pablo with the answer. 'And you certainly didn't go on there on Australia Day, 2009?'

'Definitely not, no.'

Pablo was asked 486 questions – the high point being, 'So I take it you're not a hit man?' – and answered them all, and Inspector Powell finished up with nothing.

Pablo had the background and history to fit neatly into the mould of gold-star person-of-interest category. So why the fluffy interrogation? Was it because the information, given two years after Sue's conviction, was seen by the cops as unwanted or unnecessary?

Oddly, Pablo never told his best friend Stephen Gleeson that he was setting sail the day after Australia Day. He just upped and went. Yet he told the police that he was around, didn't leave until November 2010. Such an oversight by police indicates they were never serious about the interview with

Pablo. It was a casual chat. One that could have been done on a pair of bar stools over a couple of beers. Tasmania Police missed Pablo altogether.

Barbara would complain for two years about this extraordinary situation where two obvious persons of interest were not interviewed until three years after Sue was convicted. In the end, due to her dogged persistence, police relented and instructed detectives to interview them both. To appease the lady lawyer. With Sue already convicted and in prison for 26 years, reduced to 23 years, the case was closed. Were they simply going through the motions? Certainly, the interview methods were lukewarm at best. To me, the red tick on the job sheet next to Bob Chappell's murder and Sue in prison explains why it seemed that there was no need for further digging.

It was around then that I started to feel sick in the stomach.

Part II

A search for the truth

It quickly became obvious I was the subject of close scrutiny ... if investigators' efforts were largely focused on me, the likelihood of finding out what happened to Bob would be diminished.

I thought it was to be a search for the truth. Not for one moment did it occur to me that it would be the gatekeepers of our legal system who would refuse to follow up leads or investigate even blindingly obvious suspects.

It has been a pretty horrific few years for us ... no one in our family had ever been involved in the criminal justice system, and we were therefore naive when it came to interacting with police. We had faith that if mistakes were made, there were checks and balances (appeals) to address them. Now, in hindsight, our world view has changed, and of necessity we find ourselves tumbling about in the 'eye' of a turbulent fight for justice.

As more time goes by since Bob disappeared, the more clearly I see what has happened and just how outrageous the claims made by police and prosecution actually were ...

Excerpt from a letter from Sue Neill-Fraser to a friend, sent from prison, 2012

Assessing the crime scene

IN LATE 2016 I WENT TO HOBART FOR THE PURPOSE OF researching the crime scene. As a foodie and traveller, I had always enjoyed Tasmania; still do. I fell in love with its cool climate vignerons and amazing artisan cheesemakers and farmers who offer up some of the best produce in the world. My only disappointment is with its capital, Hobart, with arguably the worst array of hotels of any of Australia's big cities, and with the most exorbitant room rates. I would stay in many of these tired dumps, while eating and drinking exceptionally well, over the two years I researched my book into the death of Bob Chappell.

Any crime scene analysis is a methodical chore, one that must be carefully deliberated over. Anything other than the forensic and physical evidence within the scene itself must be excluded. There is no room for wild conjecture or what-ifs. A detective must be guided by facts. A case can be won or lost on the accuracy of the crime scene assessment. Should a detective base his or her crime scene analysis on something that doesn't exist, the court could, rightfully, toss the case out.

I was lucky on that first visit; *Four Winds* was still in town. The day it was discovered taking on water at Sandy Bay it was taken to a police-controlled mooring at Constitution Dock, two nautical miles away. After one more day it was towed to Clean Lift salvage at Goodwood. The salvage yard is a sealed area, guarded by impressive steel gates and fences, and it is where the police finished their forensic examination. Nine years later, *Four Winds* is still there, still on the water. Chris Smith, the salvage agent who helped recover the yacht, ended up buying it at public auction. Chris is a keen yachtsman and he saw a bargain in the 53-footer. He didn't seem to care that the yacht was the most famous nautical crime scene in Tasmanian history.

Chris plans to retire soon and sail off to Japan. He likes the design of *Four Winds* and has never thought of altering anything except the aesthetics. When he bought it, the yacht was still in the same condition as the day he emptied the water from it, the day Bob was found missing. Chris was kind enough to allow me access to the yacht for as long as I wanted and for many repeat visits.

As an ex-detective, with a speciality in crime scene assessment and cold case studies, I am able to bring something unique to my career as an author and documentary filmmaker. I can embrace my research with a skill set unparalleled to others in the game.

The first thing I did was check the weather records for the night of Bob's disappearance. It was, officially, the blackest night of the year, registering 0.1 per cent on illumination charts. To put that in perspective, a full moon will register up to 99 per cent. In practical terms, on the night of the murder, you would have been struggling to see more than 10 metres in front of you, especially on the water. *Four Winds* was one of the biggest yachts on the water, standing out like a beacon on a very dark night.

On my first visit aboard *Four Winds* I walked the massive yacht with slow steps, over and over. Inside and out. To a novice, it's an impressive craft. Big, sturdy and with a surprising amount of room. The above deck area would be similar in size to a small apartment's floor space, with roughly 50 square metres of walking area. Only one gate on the starboard (right-hand) side allows access onto the yacht. Only one door opens into the yacht's wheelhouse, four steps down from the deck, where there is a large steering wheel, a chart table, shelving and comfortable furnishings for a long-haul trip. Another three steps down from the wheelhouse is the saloon, large enough for a gathering of up to eight people, seated and standing. Two lounge suites covered in blue fabric sit opposite each other, each with a large skylight hatch above. The hatches open to allow fresh air and light into the vessel. Off the saloon are the sleeping areas, as well as the bathrooms. A galley runs along each side of the saloon: one is a full kitchen, albeit smallish; the other is a laundry and storage area. Below the saloon is the engine room, where the V8 motor is bolted to the hull.

I would spend countless hours over many months on the twin-mast yacht, walking, looking, thinking and referring to the police images, the many witness statements, my own interviews with Chris Smith and the affidavit of Chris Dobbyn, the marine surveyor looking after the interest of the insurance broker, who held a policy on the yacht. Over the deck I would walk, back downstairs, around the wheelhouse, then down further, into the saloon. Looking up and down and sideways. In and out of every crevice. On my knees, lifting panels, following water pipes, finding valves, opening cupboards, pulling out drawers, looking for insight into what happened on Australia Day, 2009.

One of the police photographs I studied showed a 200mm-long bladed knife. It was out of place, on the floor of the wheelhouse. It belonged downstairs, in the kitchen galley. The blade was wet, probably due to the water that entered the vessel when it was flooded or perhaps it was splashed during the salvage operation. It held no secrets to the crime, but it screamed of a police blunder. There was a shoe impression on the blade, matched to a policeman's boot. A policeman had stood on it! The knife was highly likely to have been the murder weapon. If it had once been stained with blood, it was now washed clean, most likely during the salvage operation, as it lay above the flood line.

Near to where the knife lay is a set of steps going down to the saloon. Blood spatter stained the walls on either side of the steps. The pattern of the blood spots went outwards, away from where the blood first came into contact with the walls. The individual blood spots were in the shape of a light bulb, but very tiny, a classic sign that someone – probably Bob – had suffered trauma at that point. My assessment was correct. The blood matched Bob's DNA. The knife and the blood spatter, and the relationship of the two, told me that Bob was initially struck on the steps and probably pushed into the saloon where he was finished off.

No detective can possibly place an interpretation on how the crime had unfolded without studying a copy of the forensic officer's report on the *Four Winds*. The scientist who worked the crime scene sprayed Luminol on the interior and exterior of the yacht. Luminol, a soluble substance which is lightly sprayed to surfaces, reacts to haemoglobin, thereby indicating blood. If blood is present it gives off a bluish glow. Luminol acts like a road map, charting the violence suffered by a victim, as well as the offender's actions. It's a bit like following the dots, really, when trying to understand a crime scene. To read the scientist's notes in Bob Chappell's case is to see certain areas of the yacht lit up like a Christmas tree, such were the positive indicators.

The forensic scientist located eight blood spots from the blue-cloth lounge suite underneath the skylight hatch on the starboard side of the saloon. Five of these samples were blood positive, a one in 100 million positive identification as belonging to Bob Chappell. Each of these samples was elongated in shape, in a vertical manner. Vertical in shape says much to the detective. It means the blood drops on the cushions started their journey well above their final destination. It's all to do with gravity. As the blood dropped and hit the cushion, it trickled downwards: hence the vertical elongation. An astute detective would be asking the question: what's above the blood drops? Answer: a skylight hatch. Big enough to pass a body through.

This is just one example of how detectives could have pulled together the salient points to unravel Bob Chappell's cause of death and understand how the killing took place.

The forensic scientist's handwritten notes had been obtained by Barbara Etter via a Right to Information application. The scientist had tested the walls beneath the same skylight hatch with Luminol and got a positive reading around the area of the wall clock and barometer, as well as on the bulkhead cupboard immediately beneath the skylight hatch and behind the cloth-covered sofa. This told me the lounge suite played a major role in the death of Bob Chappell. Or, more likely, the disposal of his body via the skylight hatch. A classic example of inductive reasoning and sound deduction.

The Luminol testing went on. The scientist gained strong indications of blood on the outside roof of the saloon as well: 'numerous Luminol positive areas on both walkways ... drops and stains, forward area ... not repeated elsewhere on deck ... on the cabin roof'. That tells me all the action was around the skylight hatch and the forward section of the yacht. Not the rear of the yacht!

I moved on in my assessment and made more observations inside the saloon. The low ceiling height in the saloon made it clear that it would be difficult for any killer or killers to make overhead blows, as a fist carrying a weapon would most likely hit the ceiling on its upward stroke before it hit the target. Wielding a weapon in a fit of rage often causes marking. There were no marks on the ceiling. Another observation stood out like the proverbial dog's balls. The yacht was never scuttled. It was merely flooded.

Scuttling a yacht – inundating it with water so that it sinks – requires many small actions. Each water pipe must be cut and all the water valves opened, including the engine water pipe. On *Four Winds*, this large pipe, once severed, would allow a devastating amount of water to gush into the engine room. Equally catastrophic would be the cutting of the kitchen galley pipe. In short, there are many pipes and valves on the *Four Winds* that, for a villain wanting to truly scuttle the yacht, could all be accessed in minutes. Then cut or opened. Scuttling the yacht could be done and dusted in less than fifteen minutes, yachting experts told me. And down to the sea bed it would go. But, the murderer or murderers never did all this.

Four Winds had only one valve opened. And only the toilet waste pipe was cut. The six automatic bilge pumps had also been disabled. That's all. Nothing else. Why? Easy. Bob Chappell was killed on the floor of the saloon. The floor would have been covered in blood, skin tissue and hair. Not to forget the many fibres from clothes belonging to Bob and to whoever killed him as they wrestled around, throwing punches and fighting. The killer(s) may have been injured, should Bob have got in a punch or two. Plus tell-tale fingerprints would have been present. DNA would have been everywhere. You couldn't expect to fight and then kill a man and tie him up without creating a smorgasbord of evidence on the floor of the yacht for prying forensic scientists.

It's that floor area that needed to be flooded. To wash away and destroy evidence. The fastest way to flood the area was to open the closest valve and cut the toilet pipe. Bingo! Instant water, a metre or so near to the area that held all the forensic secrets. It would have rushed in and done its job within minutes. Then the killer or killers would have been off the yacht to dispose of the body.

In my opinon, the police had it wrong within the first hour of their arrival. *Four Winds* wasn't scuttled. It was flooded to wash away evidence from the saloon floor. Nothing more. Nothing less.

This raises questions about the offender(s). It's highly likely it was someone with knowledge of DNA and forensic science. Someone who might have been convicted in the past by such evidence and therefore knew the importance of washing a crime scene. Someone with a criminal record. And someone with yachting knowledge.

Nevertheless, for all the offender(s)' attempts to wash away evidence on the floor, DNA was found on *Four Winds*:

including in the form of a large puddle of fluid on the upper deck, close to the saloon skylight hatch (identified in March 2010 as belonging to Meaghan Vass); and in a mixed batch of matter from at least three contributors, found near Meaghan Vass's DNA; and on the levers of various skylight hatches. What this tells me is that the offender(s) never thought of any telling evidence above floor level.

Meanwhile, the issue of the removal of Bob Chappell's body was central to my crime scene analysis. In my opinion, Bob was beaten to death in the saloon by two or more persons, probably males. The murderer(s) tied rope around his body and pulled him out of the saloon area via the open skylight hatch on the starboard side, which is more than wide enough to execute the task. The rope was part of the rigging of the yacht. A length of rope was found dangling through the skylight hatch from the outside roof of the saloon into the saloon itself. The rope is visible in police photographs; its presence teases the astute investigator. This clue is vital to understanding the crime scene and cannot be ignored. But it was.

In my scenario, the killer or killers rested Bob's body momentarily on the saloon's roof. Bob's blood dripped down onto the cloth-covered lounge suite immediately under the skylight hatch. Elongated vertical blood drops are evident on the lounge, their shape indicating that at some point his body was above where the drops fell. This is Detective 101 stuff. Logically, I can see no other explanation.

Another fact that supports my theory is that about $6-worth of coins was seen scattered over the roof of the saloon by the first responders and photographed by police. They most likely fell from Bob's pockets while his body was being pulled through the skylight hatch. The same coins were noticed by the salvage agent's teenage son, who was on board and kept a keen eye on the currency, as kids do. I spoke to the kid, now a young man.

On the saloon roof, the outside surface of the yacht, there were as many as twelve black scuff marks made by shoes or boots. This indicates that one or more persons were standing on the white surface and were performing a strenuous task in the area of the skylight hatch. Some of the markings were jet black in colour, indicating real force from boot to white surface. Sailors never wear black-soled shoes or boots; they wear white or neutral-soled footwear or go barefoot. I was able to discount the first responding police as the source of the marks and the coins, as the main salvage operation was focused at the rear of the yacht, outside the wheelhouse door, near the rear mast, where the pump and hoses are set up.

Interestingly, a Detective Milazzo wrote in her notes that there were marks on the main deck area. She wouldn't have done that if fellow police caused these markings. She also stated that the rope to the main mast (forward of the skylight hatch) had been disturbed. This was where the rope dangled into the skylight hatch. The same detective noted that a torch and a juice or water bottle, found in the yacht, were foreign to the vessel. This detective, at least, seemed to be approaching the crime scene with an open mind; however, she would play a minor role from then on. That disappointed me.

Inside the saloon, above the blue lounge suite and about a metre or so above floor level, there were unexplained scuff marks on the wall, way too high above floor level for any normal behaviour. This was near to the barometer and wall clock, where the rope dangled into the saloon. There were fingerprints, too, at the same height. Yet there is no analysis report on these prints. The fingerprints and scuff marks were photographed by police; however, they withheld this information – more than fifty images – from Sue Neill-Fraser's defence team until 2017 when I got to view all the police images. This is a typical example of the way the prosecutors – these supposed gatekeepers of the truth – had vital information that may have exonerated an innocent woman. I would dig deeper and find a report by the fingerprint expert who wrote to detectives that there were many latent fingerprints still unidentified from *Four Winds*. I could believe that. (A latent print is one that can be identified to a person or suspect due to its clarity.)

How did scuff marks and fingerprints get up so high, near to the wall-mounted barometer and clock? To me, this indicates that two or more persons were doing something that required real physical effort, immediately beneath the skylight hatch. My theory is that the marks were left as they tried to lever themselves off the wall, while pushing Bob's body through the hatch. From there, it is anyone's guess as to what happened to the radiation physicist.

Chris Dobbyn, the marine surveyor looking after the insurance broker's interests, has overseen the response to hundreds of yacht disasters. He also went on board the crippled *Four Winds*. He recalled seeing a fresh rope burn on the inside surface (the lining wall) of the skylight hatch above the blood-stained lounge suite. It was so fresh that the rope mark appeared white against the tan-stained surface of the lining wall. This is another observation that supports my theory that Bob's body was hauled through the hatch using a rope. This rope burn was photographed, but didn't feature in police analysis of the crime scene.

Chris Smith, the salvage agent, told me some fascinating facts. He, one of the first responders to the flooded yacht, saw a piece of skin, with short grey hairs attached, stuck to the inside surface of the skylight hatch. He thought it was fresh skin. This vital information is also consistent with a body being dragged or pulled through the skylight hatch. Bob Chappell had short grey hair. Chris believed the policewoman photographer working the scene would photograph the piece of skin. She never did. It seems police missed this clue. This is beyond explanation. The photographer did, however, find a very long 'colourless' hair, and photographed it, but the hair can't be seen in the photograph. The supporting notations by police concerning the long hair state that it was found on the 'rear' skylight hatch. Another note states it was on the 'near' hatch. Yet another states it was on the 'forward' hatch. Last I heard, in 2018, police had another go at defining where it was found: on the skylight hatch on the 'starboard side' of the vessel. Who knows where it was actually located?

Chris Smith also studied the fuse box in the saloon area and ascertained that whoever disarmed the bilge pumps did so with some degree of knowledge of yachts and their workings. The person knew which wire to unscrew to cause the bilge pumps to be decommissioned. (Switching off the pumps allows a build-up of water in the yacht's hull, as well as deactivating the automatic siren and mast light, which would have had rescuers come running.) The culprit used a thin, long-handled, flat-head screwdriver to unscrew the housing that held the one and only wire that controlled the bilge pumps. All other housings and over one hundred other wires were untouched.

I noticed in the police photographs a kit of screwdrivers in a moulded case. It was in the laundry, and it was open. Some of the screwdrivers were missing. There were screwdrivers strewn about the floor of the saloon. Not hard to work out who tossed them aside in their search for a thin, flat-headed screwdriver. The forensic notes show that a leading detective noticed the screwdrivers in the laundry, but nothing came of this vital clue. The policewoman photographer was told about the wire being unscrewed, told to take a photograph; however, there are no photographs available. So, this salient point was lost. Instead, police took the position that Sue had turned off the bilge pumps at the manual control switch. A 'fact' that wasn't a fact. In 2016, Chris went over it again with me. He and I just shook our heads in amazement.

I would later learn from a police report that on the night of 26 January 2009, the night Bob Chappell was murdered, unknown offenders had forced entry into and ransacked a vessel that was moored in the Lutana area, north of Sandy Bay. According to the report, the 'power had been turned off at the switchboard'. The modus operandi of the thieves was very similar to that which Chris Smith discovered when he boarded *Four Winds*, where the alarm system was disengaged at the wiring. This is what police call similar facts, or the same MO. It's gold to a detective when hunting a suspect. Yet, along with so much, it was ignored. To brush this crime report aside in a major crime investigation was unforgivable to me.

To illustrate my crime scene analysis, I undertook a video re-enactment, using three male actors to represent Bob and two attackers. Actors are ideal for these sorts of experiments as they are always highly professional and take instructions well. The actors performing the role of the attackers were of average build (not Arnie Schwarzenegger types), and I took some time to find an actor with Bob's identical build and weight. The actor I finally found had an uncanny resemblance to the wiry Hobart radiation physicist. None of the three actors had any involvement with anyone associated with the case.

I had never met my chosen actors before and I briefed them with only a small amount of information. To ensure impartiality, I didn't tell them that the re-enactment was to do with the Sue Neill-Fraser case.

The three actors went to work and we filmed the entire briefing and experiment, including footage of the now-grown son of Chris Smith, who showed us where he had seen the coins. Jeff Thompson, a local Hobart lawyer and yachtsman, was there, to ensure that the re-enactment was legitimate and consistent with the known facts and my crime scene analysis. Jeff had just joined the team with Barbara and was of great assistance due to his extraordinary level of experience in sailing around the world, over two years, with his wife and two kids. It was valuable input.

To my amazement, the two actors playing the offenders tied 'Bob' up and hoisted him through the skylight hatch in double-quick time. The experiment was so successful that I had the actors try a few different versions, just to cover all bases. I made sure they never added anything into the experiment that wasn't part of the original crime scene. No matter the restrictions I threw at them, they easily lifted the body of 'Bob' through the skylight hatch using the rope and the blue lounge suite and walls as props. In fact, the actor playing 'Bob' bumped his head on the side of the skylight hatch, supporting Chris Smith's recollection of finding short grey hairs and skin there when he first boarded *Four Winds*.

Just as riveting was what happened to the coins that were placed in 'Bob's' pocket. They fell out, as scripted, as I had believed they would. (The real Bob Chappell was known to always carry coins, and the children in his life often ferreted through his pockets for loose change.) The footage was damning for the Tasmania Police. It revealed their crime scene analysis was, in my view, an embarrassment to sound detective work.

The police analysis had Sue Neill-Fraser killing Bob Chappell in the saloon area. In fact, the prosecution went a step further. They told the jury at Sue's trial that she clobbered Bob over the head with a wrench and stabbed him with screwdrivers. She then used a fire extinguisher to weigh the body down once she got it into the water. The craziness of this scenario is that there wasn't an iota of evidence that a wrench, heavy enough to be used as a murder weapon, was ever on the yacht, let alone that screwdrivers were used to kill Bob. It was pure speculation.

As for the fire extinguisher, it fell into the same category. There were two small extinguishers on board, both accounted for, neither used in the commission of the homicide. But no large old-style fire extinguisher, and no photos of one either. There was a mounting that had once held an old-style fire extinguisher, probably installed when the yacht was first built decades ago. However, no one could positively prove that a heavy old-style fire extinguisher was on the yacht on 26 January 2009. Indeed, Bob's own sister, Ann Sanchez, who worked at Wormald (which makes and supplies extinguishers) stated that she recalled noticing there was no old-style extinguisher there. Bear in mind, Bob and Sue had only had possession of the yacht for about a month. Mechanic Nathan Krakowiak, who was on board *Four Winds* in mid-January to carry out repairs, only weeks before Bob disappeared, recalled he'd looked for an extinguisher and couldn't find one. Norton Makepeace, a marine electrician, had also been on the yacht to assess some work. He didn't recall an old-style fire extinguisher either; neither did Alan Goodfellow, a works foreman who had spent time on the yacht.

However, the forensic officer made an astute observation regarding the bracket (still screwed to the wall) that had once housed the old extinguisher. She swabbed the bracket and found no evidence of blood or DNA. What this tells me is that if whoever killed Bob then grabbed the old extinguisher to weigh the body down, they did so without leaving any blood or DNA on the fastening clip that held the fire extinguisher. It was a seriously violent crime so it is not unlikely that the offender's hands would be bloodied. As it turns out, the fastening clip was tested and came up negative for blood.

The forensic officer made one further important observation. She noted that sitting on the top fastening bracket of the old fire extinguisher housing was 'a sparkling wine bottle cork'. How could that cork have got there, and stayed there, if a murderer grabbed the extinguisher – in haste – to use as a weight to sink a body? Surely the cork would have fallen to the floor. This may seem the stuff of an Agatha Christie novel or a Sherlock Holmes film, but it is also the stuff that solves crimes. This one tiny fact renders as nonsensical the proposition of Sue Neill-Fraser using the fire extinguisher to dispose of Bob Chappell's body.

The police asserted that Sue tied up Bob and then rigged an elaborate winch pulley from the rear mast to haul Bob's body out of the saloon, up onto the wheelhouse floor and then up again, out the wheelhouse door and onto the deck. This is impossible to achieve, as experts stated at the trial. It would require the winching to be done almost sideways, up two flights of steps and onto the rear deck. What Sue was to have done once the body was on the deck is anyone's guess. But somehow, to comply with the imaginings of the police, Sue was required to dispose of the body alone. In a dinghy. Given Sue's age, physique (somewhat overweight), limited strength, damaged coccyx and injured hip, this seems more than a little unlikely. Additionally, the sailing crew that delivered the yacht from Brisbane to Hobart said Sue was not strong enough to operate the winch alone. Let's not forget that Sue had suffered a bad fall from a horse some years previously and had had back problems ever since.

To reinforce the Crown version of Bob's body being extracted from the wheelhouse, a detective draped a rope from the rear deck to inside the wheelhouse and down into the saloon. He tied it around himself, all '98 kilograms', in an attempt to show the feasibility of lifting someone in the manner the police asserted. This experiment was not filmed. Nor was it photographed. Verbal evidence of the success of the experiment was given at the trial, despite the lack of forensic methodology, independent observation or impartiality. Such an experiment should have been carried out by qualified forensic scientists or a winching expert to ensure correct process, and the entire experiment should have been recorded.

Another issue with this experiment is that no rope was found by the first responders draped in the manner detailed by police. On the contrary, in the police photographs the ropes on the rear mast are all neatly bundled up in their correct positions. Were the police proposing that Sue used these ropes to haul Bob Chappell out of the yacht and then neatly re-bundled them? Surely she wouldn't have so fastidiously played housewife after killing Bob, tidying the crime scene to a pristine condition, while out in the open for all to see. Besides, the ropes and the area surrounding the winch were found to be free of blood or any other forensic matter. Plus there were no scuff marks or tell-tale signs that this area was connected to the disposal of a body.

Fascinatingly, the same forensic officer who found indications of blood inside the saloon, on the blue lounge suite, discovered no such positive results outside the wheelhouse door or near the rear winch. If the prosecution's theory was correct, surely blood would have saturated this location. But none was found.

So how on earth can the police version of the crime scene suggest that Sue Neill-Fraser murdered Bob Chappell? Where is the forensic support for a theory that seems to be just a hunch?

I am reminded of the maxim taught at detective training schools around the world: Failure to search is failure to find. I am also reminded of another maxim useful when working a crime scene: A detective's mind must be like a parachute, always open.

The only rope draped inside *Four Winds* from the outside was photographed dangling into the saloon skylight hatch – the skylight above the vertical blood stains on the blue lounge suite, on the starboard side. Trouble is, these clues needed to be found and investigated. By detectives with open minds.

Me and the boss

AFTER SIX MONTHS IN A LEAKY BOAT, WHICH IS WHAT I called my research into the death of Bob Chappell, I badly wanted to question the key detective in this fascinating case, the now-retired Detective Inspector Peter Powell. Having conducted countless interviews with suspects, accomplices and witnesses to crimes including murder, attempted murder, public bombing, paedophiliac acts, safe breaking, robbery, major drug importation and trafficking, I was itching to ask what made him focus on Sue when the murder occurred on a landscape that was riddled with misfits and villains? What was his thinking in those early days? How did he pick his way through the forest of suspects so quickly to get to Sue?

Up to 70 per cent of homicides can be classified as domestic. What that means is that in a vast amount of murders the killer is either the partner of the deceased or within their immediate family or group of friends. It's a worrying statistic. Consequently, for police, the default position is to focus on the family of the perpetrator in cases of murder. Unless, of course, other evidence, like DNA, fingerprints or eyewitness reports, points to other potential suspects. Usually, this sort of evidence is found after a thorough crime scene assessment, and after all the usual avenues of inquiry have been worked hard and exhausted. It could take weeks. There is much to do before all other suspects can be eliminated. In the case of Sue Neill-Fraser, I was perplexed by the lack of exhaustive avenues of inquiry. There were some door-to-door inquiries done, but they were by no means exhaustive. Many of the occupants were not home at the time of the first door-knocking, and the police reports indicate that there were no return visits by police. And as far as yacht-to-yacht inquiries were concerned, there didn't seem to be any undertaken. Why this key line of inquiry was ignored is a worry. There should have been a log put together of all boats and yachts on the water that night, with occupant details and alibis. Indeed, the log should have focused on those boats and yachts moored or anchored close to *Four Winds*. In fact, the detective sergeant who interviewed Sue for murder noted in his own statutory declaration that there were no thefts from or of yachts or boats in the months prior to the death of Bob Chappell. This is incorrect.

As it was, when it came to retired Detective Inspector Peter Powell, I lucked in. I heard that Powell – who had interrogated Pablo and Gleeson in 2012 – had recently sat down with a well-known author and given a fruitful interview. He seemed to be on the talk circuit and open to chatting about the case.

It was a stunning sunny Hobart October morning in 2016, some days after I'd concluded my crime scene assessment, when we both sat down in the conference room at the Royal Yacht Club. I chose this location for a number of reasons, mostly because it offered a view of Sandy Bay, where *Four Winds* came to grief and Bob Chappell was last seen alive. Where

Pablo's boat was also moored. And because I knew the Hobart cops sometimes drank at the club in the members bar. It was important that Powell feel at home and be at ease.

Peter Powell was a very upright looking man, north of sixty, and enjoying retirement. He walked into the room oozing way too much confidence. He had a strong middle-England accent and wore the tiniest of ginger moustaches on an otherwise clean-shaven ruddy face. He could be mistaken for a character from the British television series *The Bill*. After the mandatory firm handshake, he was kind enough to indicate that he was familiar with my past career and my writing of books. He seemed keen to talk. More than keen, he took his seat opposite me and jumped into the interview. I'd brought Tim Smart with me and he silently moved around the room, focusing his cameras and checking the sound as we got started. I made sure Powell had a large glass of water and two jugs of water on the side. I thought that things might warm up, despite the air conditioning.

We chatted a bit about the notoriety of Sue's case and its similarity to the Lindy Chamberlain saga. As with Lindy's case, there was no body, no identifiable cause of death and a conviction based purely on circumstantial evidence and shoddy DNA analysis. 'So really,' I said, 'is it fair to say she [Sue] got convicted on her own lies?'

Powell was in agreement with this. 'Even at trial she changed some versions of events as well and was quite evasive about some issues. She had what we all think is convenient memory...' The different accounts Sue gave of her movements around the time of Bob's disappearance were pretty damning, in his opinion, and something the jury would have been made very aware of by the prosecutor.

Powell then steered our conversation around to the interviews Sue did with police, which, he pointed out, she could have refused to do. 'On the first morning when Bob went missing, she came down and spoke to uniformed police, and then made a statement later that day. But of course, over the next several months, apart from being spoken to a couple of times, she actually participated in two formal interviews.' Sue wasn't cautioned until her second interview. This seemed unusual to me. Why didn't police caution her if she was a suspect? I have never heard of this happening before. In fact, some legal practitioners might say it was unfair to Sue to not know her rights and to not be cautioned, I suggested.

'We were trying to firm up what the real facts were,' Powell said, 'and we were inviting her to give some answers to some of the questions in our mind. We were quite happy we didn't have enough to charge her, so we didn't have to caution her.'

Really? His answer certainly reveals something about the way Tasmania Police operate. I then pointed out that Sue must have been a genuine suspect, though, because police had installed two listening devices in her house, something they would have needed a judge to approve.

'Well, we had to convince the judge, obviously, that there were things in the whole series of events that indicated that she wasn't being truthful,' Powell said. And Sue did have legal advice. 'In fact, she actually said, on the listening device, that her lawyer had told her not to talk to the police. So she had clear legal advice not to talk to the police, but still did.'

The old-time detective in me thinks that seeing the police knew, via the listening device, that Sue's lawyer had counselled her not to talk to police, she should have been cautioned thoroughly and even had her lawyer with her in the interview room. Fairness, at the very least, would demand this.

Powell believed Sue was wily. 'I do think that she was one of those people that's committed a crime that wanted to appear helpful. I'm sure that's how she wanted to project herself. The fascinating thing I find is that she was also warned by her lawyer that we probably had an LED listening device in her house, maybe a phone tapped ...' They heard her say as much via the device they'd planted. He also believed she deliberately said things in the hope that they would be recorded. 'A lot of the stuff she said, or the discussions she had at home to various members of the family and friends was self-serving stuff you might expect people to do if they think the police are listening to their conversations.'

Like what? I asked.

Things to give the impression she was a good person, he reckoned. 'I think that Sue is a very cunning, manipulative person who is very good at telling a story to people, and being believed, and I think that's part of the problem – she has got the best little support group in some of her close friends and family. But what I find fascinating is, during all that listening device material, Sue never once sat down with her family and said, "Why would they think I'm a suspect?" or "I wonder what really happened to Bob?" ... I would have thought that's just a normal conversation you might have among your family and friends.'

It's the Lindy Chamberlain curse. Sue didn't act or speak the way police expected a grief-stricken woman would. Perhaps police also objected to Sue's poor opinion of them.

'She certainly made a lot of derogatory comments about the police, saying they were just a B team and they were just Mr Plods in suits, and all those sorts of comments,' Powell added.

'Did your boys take that hard?' I asked.

'I don't think, being a detective, you worry too much about those sorts of comments. It's probably not the worst thing that's ever been said about them.'

He'd be right there.

According to Powell, Sue didn't become a suspect until late February or early March in 2009. Then, without prompting, he mentioned our friend, Phillip Triffett. 'We had this witness … come forward and speak to the police on 29 January … he was telling us this story about these conversations he had with Sue in the past about wanting to kill her brother via similar sort of means as to maybe how Bob had died.'

Powell was incorrect about the date. Triffett initially contacted police by phone on 28 January with information about Sue (Powell accepted this when I pointed it out to him) and then came into the police station to make a full statement about a fortnight later. The next day (29 January), according to the police log, it was decided to follow up on Sue's claim that she went to Bunnings on Australia Day. From my reading, this indicates that Sue was well and truly a suspect at this point. But Powell wasn't prepared to accept this. 'As far as checking Bunnings, I think it's quite commonly understood that when someone goes missing, family are always looked at as possibly being involved in the disappearance, murder or whatever.' It was a case of, 'Let's make sure we're doing all the right things from an investigation point of view, and actually confirm that what she was telling us was true,' he said.

Were there any other suspects at that time? I asked.

'I don't want to be too strong and say no, because I'd say that we were trying to work out the sequence of events at that stage.' At these early stages, Powell insisted, it wasn't a murder investigation. A yacht had been sabotaged and someone had gone missing in suspicious circumstances, that was all. I had great trouble with his logic; what about all the blood, I thought. He went on, explaining that because of the delay in determining that they were dealing with murder, the police made a crucial error. 'In hindsight, I think we'd all agree that, forensically, the yacht wasn't guarded well enough at Constitution Dock.' Neither was the scene preserved adequately at the salvage yard where *Four Winds* was first taken, he admitted. The marine police had clambered all over it in their efforts to stop the yacht sinking, and the forensic team did only a basic first assessment before it went to the dock. As a crime scene, it was poorly handled and everyone seemed to play catch-up in their assessment.

At the very least, *Four Winds* should have been taken into dry dock immediately and put under cover. It never was. It just bobbed about in the water and weather, all those months. In fact, it's never been out of the water. Never been treated like a crime scene should be treated: with great care.

'Right,' I asked, 'when was it a murder investigation? The moment Triffett mentioned something sinister?'

'I guess you have to say that makes you more suspicious,' Powell said. 'I certainly don't say that Susan Neill-Fraser was a suspect when Phillip Triffett first contacted police.'

But reading the investigation log, from the day after Triffett rang police, it was all about Sue. It was at this point that I brought up one of my persons of interest, Stephen Gleeson, the man living in his yellow Ford sedan at Rowing Shed Point. The man currently serving five and a half years for attempted murder (knocked down to grievous bodily harm) and with a history of real violence. A bad egg. He'd been living in the vicinity for ten months. Why wasn't he a suspect?

Gleeson was spoken to on the morning *Four Winds* was found taking water, Powell said, but no statement was taken from him. 'There was nothing that we felt made him a suspect other than anyone else who might have been in the area. He became a person of interest much later in the investigation. He wasn't ever, in my view, a suspect, but after Susan was convicted, we went back and spoke to him again.'

That's true. Two whole years later.

Next, I brought up my second person of interest: Pablo. 'There's a fellow in a yacht moored next to the *Four Winds* … He is a man of violence, done lots of prison time, and was living on that yacht for quite some time and been thrown out of all the different yacht clubs here, preceding the Bob Chappell incident.' Oh, and he was moored a short distance from Bob Chappell's boat when he disappeared. Did Powell remember him?

Powell dismissed both Pablo and Gleeson as fifty-year-old alcoholics who'd go on the booze together and end up having a bit of push and shove. That's not a bad description, except he forgot to mention that Gleeson was subsequently convicted of grievous bodily harm after he continually bashed his neighbour over the head with an iron, causing terrible brain injuries. Powell acknowledged that it was a very serious assault, but wrote it off as 'another drunken episode between a couple of drunks'. I thought of all the violence I had seen as a cop, always by men, most of them under the influence of alcohol. We moved on.

Even when Barbara, Sue's lawyer, told police that Gleeson had mentioned Pablo's past Powell dismissed it as 'a throwaway line' made because Gleeson had fallen out with his one-time mate. Additionally, Powell did not comment when I explained alcohol and violence normally go hand in hand. Booze and blood, like peaches and cream. I knew this well from a young age, as I'd grown up with an extremely violent, drunken father. Indeed, that exposure to alcoholics and their violence and a desire to protect people from it was one of the main reasons I became a cop.

I reminded Powell that Gleeson had told police that Pablo might have been involved in a couple of murders, but again he dismissed this inconvenient rumour. 'I don't remember all the details of that now. He was certainly trying to make Pablo out to be a bad egg.' A short time later, he said, 'But my attitude was that they're both drunks – I wouldn't rely too much on anything Gleeson told me, to be honest.'

'Well, one of them is capable of almost killing someone recently and he's doing seven years for it,' I replied, but Powell was having none of it. He kept returning to Sue's 'lies' as the real sign of a murderer. 'Why would an innocent person keep changing their story?'

The key to solving a crime is to keep an open mind. With Pablo and Gleeson's history of violence, why didn't he pull them in for an interview, I asked Powell, particularly as they were both so close to the crime scene? Unbelievably, Powell told me that police weren't even aware of Pablo until after Sue was convicted. This is the point in our interview when I began to sound just a little incredulous. 'But he was the closest yacht to *Four Winds*.'

'Not at the time,' Powell said.

'Yes, he was.'

'He certainly wasn't known to us. Let me say that.'

When I expressed disbelief that police didn't check out Pablo's yacht, the closest to the one off which someone had disappeared, Powell said, 'I'm not disputing his yacht being there, what I'm disputing is that he was on his yacht every night. Lots of my detectives did inquiries at the yacht club. There were certainly lots of appeals in the media for people who had information to come forward. We certainly did a check of our police databases to see if yachts had been broken into, in the last three months ...'

Maybe a little defensive?

What about the identical MO of the vessel broken into on the same night? It seemed that the police had no idea what strife was occurring on the water in January 2009.

I suggested that seeing as the police had a situation where a yacht was sinking and a man was missing, they perhaps should have visited the yachts closest to the sinking yacht and asked the occupants, like Pablo: 'Hey, did you see the guy fall off his yacht ... did you see any foul play?' Powell repeated that he didn't dispute Pablo's yacht was there; he was only disputing whether Pablo was 'on his yacht every night'. Nonetheless, Pablo went unnoticed by police for more than three years.

We then discussed Powell's interviews with Pablo and Stephen Gleeson in 2012, two years after Sue was convicted. I brought up the fact that Gleeson had approached police within a fortnight of the disappearance of Bob, to suggest Pablo could be a suspect. 'He had a meeting with a policewoman. Were you aware of that?'

Powell said he didn't recall that. 'I don't know where you got that information from.' I was beginning to think I was better informed than Powell was.

I reminded him that in Gleeson's ROI, Powell himself (in 2012) made mention of Gleeson going into police headquarters with information about Pablo. But, in front of me, he repeatedly said he didn't remember this. Yet, it's there, on the Gleeson ROI transcript!

We then moved on to discuss the sabotaging of *Four Winds*. Given the manner of the flooding – the cut toilet pipe, the alarm mechanisms turned off, the valve opened – we agreed that whoever did it must have had a very good knowledge of yachts. More knowledge than Powell, it seems, who revealed that he assumed the alarm system on *Four Winds* was simply turned off at the power board. It wasn't. It was unscrewed at the wiring. But the saboteur, whoever he or she was, had done more than that, I told him. Chris Smith, the salvage agent, was the first to respond to the sinking yacht, apart from the police. On opening that panel to the power board, it wasn't obvious to him why the bilge pumps wouldn't work when the Clipsal switches controlling them were returned to the 'on' position. He poked about among the maze of wiring and found a feed wire from the battery packs had been disconnected. Once he'd reconnected it, the bilge pumps came back on, the alarm siren began to sound and the mast light started flickering.

'Which shows again someone's got knowledge of that yacht. Not just that yacht, but knowledge about how it all works,' Powell said. On this, we were in complete agreement. But when I tried to suggest that many other people would have the knowledge and skill to scuttle a yacht, Powell returned to Sue. 'Equally, Susan Neill-Fraser's had a yacht before *Four Winds*, and she's been on this one, and she's gone to a bit of trouble to ask people to show how the technical side all works.'

I had another attempt at widening the frame. 'Stephen Gleeson had a career in the army, in the boat unit.' But Powell dismissed this. Gleeson, he said, compared his experience in the army boat unit to *McHale's Navy*, the comedy television series about a misfit crew in the US Navy. This was news to me. I've read the ROI. Gleeson made no such flippant comment. When I insisted to Powell that Gleeson's knowledge went much deeper – his training included how to scuttle boats – Powell turned the discussion back to Sue. 'Equally, Sue knows that yacht …'

Now, I made my real point. 'But could it have been that maybe the detectives only had one suspect, and one suspect alone?'

But Powell denied this, insisting that in all the initial discussions about Bob's disappearance, police kept an open mind on suspects and possible scenarios. It didn't appear that way to me. I put it to him that Sue was always their only real suspect. Because of Triffett. 'Eventually, yes,' he conceded, and once again returned to talking about her 'lies'. His belief that she tried to mislead police was the clincher when it came to her guilt. What about her trip to Bunnings? he asked. As if Bunnings somehow held the key! Still, I was prepared to go there. Wasn't it possible that Sue, faced with questions only hours after her husband had gone missing, simply mixed the days up? I put to him. But Powell remained unconvinced and our discussion moved on to the bizarre late-night phone call from Richard King, in which he told Sue that Bob's daughter, Clare, had told him that her father might be in danger on the yacht. One thing we did agree on – that strangely prophetic call was weird, and Sue couldn't possibly have set it up.

'Clare's obviously got huge mental health issues,' Powell said. 'So I don't know why that call was made.' Detectives spoke to Richard King and Clare about her premonition, but found her 'all over the place, scrambled'. Supposedly, Clare didn't even know that Bob was on the yacht when Richard made the call to Sue.

I put it to Powell that it was a perfectly natural response to that call for Sue to go down to the foreshore to check on Bob and the boat. 'It's a woman rattled by a really crazy phone call about her husband, Bob Chappell, who's possibly going to be in harm's way.'

Powell countered my argument. 'She tells us that it was so dark she couldn't even see the yacht … So she goes home … She's concerned, but not concerned enough to do anything other than to say, "I can't see the yacht, so it must be all right."' Let's not forget, it was officially the blackest night of the year, registering 0.1 per cent on illumination charts. Maybe Sue's comments to police were spot on.

He then brought up Sue's call to the Telstra call return number (*10#) at close to three in the morning. Where he sees suspicious behaviour – Sue checking that no one has called her and knows she wasn't home to answer the call – I see rational action. Sue probably wanted to see if Richard had called again, I said. But Powell made his point: that Sue had initially told police 'I was home all night'.

Powell then brought up what he saw as Sue's attempt to implicate the homeless people living around the foreshore who were having a 'barbie'. 'It was midnight. I wouldn't have thought there'd be Australia Day celebrations still going on.' Why not, I thought?

'But I've made inquiries,' I told him, 'and there were those homeless people and there was that little cooker.' It appeared from our conversation that I was engaged in a discussion with a man who'd made up his mind.

By this stage in our discussion, the Inspector had drunk all his water and more. And I was about to introduce what I saw as a huge misstep in the police investigation. I suggested to

Powell that Sue's conviction was the most striking example of someone being convicted purely on circumstantial evidence in recent Australian history. 'Tell me I'm wrong, but there's only one non-circumstantial aspect to this case that I can find. One scientific fact that's undeniable, if we believe in science. That's a DNA swab that's on the deck of the yacht and that comes up to a young street girl called Meaghan Vass.' This same girl, I said to Powell, was running with a group of young men who were known for doing break-ins.

Powell knew where I was heading. 'There's dispute about whether it's primary DNA or transferred – there was some suggestion it could have been walked on.' The retired inspector had hit on a real nerve for me. At the trial the police, through the DPP, suggested that Meaghan Vass's DNA – a whopping size sample of fluid found on the upper deck of the yacht, the size of a dinner plate, 260mm x 210mm overall – must have been walked on to the yacht under a policeman's boot. Therefore, it must have been secondary transfer.

I wasn't going to let that go through to the keeper without comment. 'Transference of DNA, scientifically, is rare as hen's teeth,' I stated. I firmly believe, that due to the sheer size and amount of fluid, any suggestion it was secondary transfer was pure fantasy. Sure, a tiny speck of DNA might be transferred by the sole of a boot, but the puddle of DNA on the upper deck couldn't, in my view, ever be considered anything other than primary transfer. From the owner of the fluid.

We pushed this point back and forth between us for a bit until Powell admitted he believed that Meaghan Vass was on *Four Winds*, just not on the night Bob disappeared. He was now having an each-way bet. He suggested that she stepped onto the yacht at the Clean Lift salvage yard, days after it was salvaged. Even though there was no evidence of any kind to suggest the secure yard had been broken into or entered. Nor was there any evidence that *Four Winds* was broken into while at the yard or that anything was disturbed or stolen. No images of the girl had been captured on the yard's CCTV either.

'There's another possibility,' Powell said. 'It happened at Constitution Dock. Just because we can't see her go on that yacht doesn't mean she didn't.' He was now fishing. The CCTV had no footage of any intruder on the yacht.

I offered a third possibility: that Meaghan was on *Four Winds* when Bob Chappell was murdered. But Powell was unconvinced. What was her motive for being out there? he asked. How would young street kids have the technical knowledge to sabotage a boat? I put my spin on it. 'Misadventure. She doesn't need a motive. There's an opportunity. She's running with a lot of street kids – petty criminals, breaking into yachts.'

We debated this possibility. Powell noted that *Four Winds* was the furthest yacht from the shore, so not the most obvious target for 'a little thief'. I countered with the fact that the *Four Winds* dinghy wasn't tied to the yacht – a sign that 'no one is aboard'. It was also the biggest yacht in the bay – a prize. Then I mentioned, again, the rash of break-ins. 'I've spoken to so many people who've had break-ins where they were woken in the middle of the night on their yacht, to a thief standing inside the cabin, other thieves standing on the deck, stealing things, and they disturb the thieves.'

'It's interesting,' Powell said, not willing to give an inch, 'given most of these people never report it.' In fact, I had been told boat owners were reluctant to report thefts as the police did little to assist.

Powell had previously stated in a taped interview with Eve Ash that Meaghan Vass had some associations with some young male offenders, 'under-age offenders, that have been in the past guilty of breaking into boat yards and stealing things off boats'. This gelled with what he stated to me, at the yacht club interview, that most of the 'people that she might have been mixing with, most of their DNA is already on the database'. Personally, I found this comment one of the most telling from Powell. I saw it as a neon sign, flashing an obvious message to detectives. What this means in police terms is the vast majority of DNA held on the database belongs to criminals who have been arrested and charged with crimes. During their arrest their DNA is taken for the database to match against other crimes or future crimes. Therefore, indirectly, what Mr Powell was telling me was that Meaghan was in company with criminals. Trouble is, at the time Meaghan had been identified against her own puddle of DNA on the yacht, this flashing neon sign had faded to black.

In the later part of our exchange we had a moment or two where we got a little testy. Powell didn't much like my implication that the Hobart police had been less than thorough in their investigations and were ignorant of the extent of the break-ins on the yachts on Sandy Bay. How could police have known about the break-ins if the victims didn't report them? he asked. Hardly justification for ignorance, in my opinion.

He switched tack a little. *Four Winds* wasn't the obvious choice for thieves looking for easy pickings, being the furthest yacht from the shore. Another reason why it was likely that it was someone who knew Bob was on the boat alone who killed him, he said. He also said it was the *Four Winds* dinghy that was used to get out there. Perhaps suggesting, as the dinghy was Sue's, it must have been Sue involved in the killing.

We then engaged in a conversation about the two records of interview with Sue Neill-Fraser. Powell agreed that it may well have been in Sue's best interests not to give evidence. 'I'm the first to say: if I was running that defence, I might have run it differently … She was in a difficult position because when there's no confessional evidence, no eyewitness evidence – it's circumstantial – how does it look if you don't give evidence? … it probably did her a lot of harm because of her manner and the way she presents herself.'

I suggested that police weren't being entirely fair when they failed to caution Sue in her first interview. The police were then able to use everything she said, cherry-picking any inconsistencies to build their case against her. She might have been more careful in what she said if she knew she was a suspect. We rehashed some ground over this aspect of the case, but Powell insisted the interviews were all above board. 'We were backed by the Director of Public Prosecutions.'

To me, an ex-detective, Sue's ROIs were fascinating. In the first, as I pointed out to Powell, the detectives interviewing her said almost nothing. They just let Sue talk. And she did. On and on. And Sue is a talker. Sometimes, Powell said, he got the impression Sue was trying to convince the police of her story: 'Sometimes she's trying to lead you off the question a bit, I think, or lead you away from the question or explain it a different way. This is where she tended to change her stories.' But usually, he admitted, having someone who talks a lot in an interview is a benefit to police.

It was a clever technique to let someone talk their head off, I agreed. 'She just sits there, just blurting it all out, and you gather it all in – it's like a big hoover machine.'

The second record of interview was entirely different: it was an interrogation. Question after question. This time around the police cautioned Sue three or four times. While my opinion was that Sue's first interview was the one where the damage was done in terms of police building their case, Powell disagreed. 'I think the second interview was what really sunk her ... she was being caught in a situation where she was contradicting herself. I guess that's the difference when people are not skilled witnesses, or experienced witnesses, isn't it?'

'I've never had any doubt that she killed Bob,' he added.

'You still don't?'

'No.'

We had been speaking for almost two hours. Powell looked exhausted, out of sorts, not quite the man who strode into the room with a story to tell. His face was scarlet as he gulped air from his empty glass. The final twenty minutes of our interview were telling. I asked his thoughts about the public campaign to free Sue. He was dismissive of her 'little support group'. 'My view is, I think the general public are happy with the result.'

As we wound up the interview, Powell paid me a compliment. 'You've done your homework.'

* * *

The interview with Powell revealed the thinking of the leader of the investigation into Bob Chappell's disappearance and, in a broader sense, that of his team. It confirmed there was only ever one suspect, Bob's de facto wife, Sue Neill-Fraser. This was odd. In fact, it was wildly out of whack with what might be expected, considering the mix of thieves, violent men and homeless people on or near the water that night. I was flabbergasted that the police had no knowledge of the level of petty theft from pleasure craft and fishing boats in the area. I was equally amazed at Powell's reaction to Pablo and Stephen. What did police need, I wondered, to have an individual fall into the category of a person of interest?

I thought back to the first day I got involved in the case, when I visited Eve Ash's muster room, studying the vast array of material she had amassed. After six hours I'd been able to pick up a red marker pen and place a circle around the faces of three people – Pablo, Stephen Gleeson and Meaghan Vass – and state with a reasonable degree of certainty that these three people potentially could provide crucial information. What troubled me was that the retired inspector couldn't see what I saw. Our thinking was so different. How could he discard every detail that underpinned my thought processes? One of us was right, and one of us was wrong. It was shaping up to be like a cricket test: the Englishman versus the Australian. It was day one and there were many more overs to bowl.

But nothing shocked me more than the police's bouncer: their attitude towards Meaghan Vass, whose DNA was found on *Four Winds*. While Powell conceded that she had most likely been on the yacht (which destroyed the ridiculous secondary transfer theory) he wanted to place her on the yacht at the Clean Lift salvage yard days after Bob Chappell's murder. Despite there not being a skerrick of evidence that the salvage yard suffered a break-in at the time, or any indication from Meaghan herself that she'd been there.

Powell showed himself to have a closed mind on Sue's possible innocence. Nor was he willing to concede that Sue probably didn't tell malicious lies but may have been muddled after hearing the shocking news that her partner was missing, believed murdered. One thing I was deeply worried about was the lack of procedural fairness towards Sue, in particular during her two police interviews. She wasn't cautioned during the first interview and later her words were cherry-picked to weave a circumstantial case against her.

My sense of logic, my train of thought and my conclusions about Sue's actions on the night, and the presence and actions of others, such as Stephen, Pablo and Meaghan, were vastly different to Powell's. Nothing that was said during our two-hour conversation altered my thinking about Sue's role. Indeed, it reinforced my thinking.

One comment worried me above all others. Powell thought it strange that Sue Neill-Fraser never walked around her own home audibly professing her innocence for hidden listening devices to pick up. I still think of this comment often, as I dwell on the case. Must we outwardly profess our non-involvement in a crime to appease prying cops on the hunt? Powell's thinking was dangerous. Sue Neill-Fraser was living alone. Her loved one had been murdered. She was occupying her home and her thoughts in total isolation. So why would she mutter anything into secret police listening devices?

The red jacket

As in any new research, I wore out my boot leather walking the beat, banging on doors. Even though the killing had happened eight years earlier, I, researching this book, could hardly be critical of the original police investigation for failing to undertake intense door-to-door inquiries if I wasn't prepared to do the same myself. Even if it was in the freezing cold that is Hobart in winter.

I had read volumes on the case, but I had never been to Sandy Bay before. For the first hour or so I just strolled around, taking in the landscape, getting my bearings. The first thing that jumped out at me was how tiny the bay was. Although there were two large yachting clubs, side by side, the actual beach area along Marieville Esplanade was barely 150 metres long.

I was anxious to see the finger-like protrusion of land known locally as the Rowing Club shed area, or Rowing Shed Point. This was where Stephen Gleeson had parked his yellow Ford sedan, in which he slept, way back in 2009. I stood in the exact spot that the police photo showed Stephen's car had been parked. Looking out onto the water, I had an uninterrupted view of where *Four Winds* had been moored on Australia Day, 2009. And where Pablo had more than once stated his yacht was moored. There was a toilet block at the street end of the finger of land, then a line of sheds ran all the way to the end of the point. The sheds were about five metres in height, effectively a massive wall that blocked all the view from the south. The yellow Ford sedan would have been sheltered from the elements and also from prying eyes at the Royal Yacht Club or the Derwent Sailing Squadron. I could understand why Gleeson had chosen to camp on this tiny peninsula: he was protected. And it was here too, only three to four metres from his car, that Sue's dinghy was found untethered, bobbing in the water, seemingly abandoned. The location of the dinghy would work its way into my thinking, never letting go. That thistle up the arse again! I stood there for ages, looking, observing.

I looked at the landscape and clues before me. From where I stood I studied the row of houses along Marieville Esplanade, which ran along the foreshore. I took particular note of the house on the corner of the esplanade and Margaret Street, 26 Margaret Street, a red-brick house. A crucial exhibit for the prosecution had been located on its front fence: a red jacket with Sue's DNA allegedly on the inside of the collar and cuffs. Clearly, for her DNA to be identifiable, Sue would have had to have worn the jacket a number of times.

By then I was possibly more intrigued by this item of evidence than the dinghy or any other, save for the DNA of Meaghan Vass found on *Four Winds*. Sue was initially uncertain if the jacket belonged to her. The Crown contended her uncertainty was an incriminating lie. It maintained she

killed Bob Chappell and dumped her jacket on the fence as she
fled the area.

I kept looking at the corner house where the jacket was
dumped, then back to where the yellow sedan was once
parked, then at the spot where Sue's abandoned dinghy was
found, and then out to where *Four Winds* had been moored.
Round and round I turned, looking at one thing after the
other. The untethered dinghy wouldn't let go of me. As I
looked, I kept thinking. Inductive reasoning. Deduction.
More thought. *Four Winds*. Sue's dinghy. Yellow Ford sedan.
Red jacket at 26 Margaret Street. Sue's dinghy. You could rule
a straight line to connect them all. My mind's eye kept seeing
the closeness of the dinghy to the yellow Ford. I was becoming
obsessive about this odd fact. Odd for many reasons, none
more concerning than the fact that the dinghy was motorised.
And untethered. Abandoned.

It was obvious to me that the four points were related.
It was an offender's flight path; there could be no doubt of
it. Evidence of flight – how an offender leaves the scene of
a crime – can be telling when you're attempting to solve a
crime. Did the offender run or drive away from the crime?
Sometimes you can chart the path the criminal took by the
exhibits left behind or the items they discarded as they ran
away. I just didn't know yet what the red jacket was telling
me. I knocked on the door of number 26 and spoke to the
owners, but my inquiries were fruitless. The red-brick house
seemed to be involved only insofar as that was where someone
dumped the jacket.

As most experienced detectives do when confronted with a
handful of facts that don't necessarily add up, I applied logic.
Why on earth would Sue kill Bob then motor her dinghy over

to the rocks, abandon it and run to 26 Margaret Street to dump her jacket? In doing so, she would risk being seen (and heard, because of the outboard motor) by Stephen Gleeson, who was in his car at the time, or by others on the foreshore celebrating Australia Day. It didn't make sense. Logic went against pinning these actions on Sue. The jacket was hers, undeniably, but logically there was no reason for Sue to dump her dinghy so close to Gleeson's car if she had, indeed, killed Bob Chappell. Bear in mind she would have been covered in blood – her hands, her arms and her upper torso, knees and shoes. As well as stressed and battered and bruised, as one might expect, murdering her partner, as well as exhausted from dumping the body.

When it was time for her to skedaddle home, why on earth would she motor her dinghy towards Gleeson's car, then run past him, a man she knew, who could identify her? And why would she then toss her DNA-covered jacket onto the fence of a house within spitting distance of the foreshore for the owner to find? It did not make sense. As detectives say, it didn't fly.

The most worrying aspect of the entire police theory stands out like dog balls. If Sue killed Bob, in the way suggested at her trial – bashed him over the head from behind, causing blood to spatter in all directions; then winched him out of the yacht and carried him into the dinghy; and, finally, dumped his body somewhere – why was there no blood found on Sue's jacket? Neither was there any DNA belonging to Bob. No saliva, hair or skin tissue samples belonging to him. No fibres from his clothing. Not a skerrick to indicate a black widow murderess had worn that jacket that night. The complete lack of any forensics indicating Sue wore the jacket while killing Bob Chappell, or wore it when fleeing the scene, is the single biggest weakness in the Crown's case. Indeed, it damages its case beyond recovery. It serves Sue's innocence, not her guilt.

I didn't care a hoot who killed Bob Chappell, as long as the facts and the circumstances supported the theory of who was responsible. If I could prove Sue was guilty, by way of my own reckoning, I would be just as satisfied as if I proved her innocence. I had no loyalty to anyone involved in the case. All I was seeking was the truth. The lack of DNA evidence on the red jacket undermines any premise that Sue Neill-Fraser was linked to the *Four Winds* crime scene because of the jacket. The whole police case was flawed.

If Sue had killed Bob, it would make much more sense for her to motor her dinghy away from *Four Winds* and leave it tied adjacent to the Royal Yacht Club, where she usually left it. In this position she would have been on the blind side of Stephen Gleeson – shielded by the massive rowing sheds – and out of sight of others on the peninsula and foreshore. Once she tied up her dinghy, she could have easily sneaked away, hidden from prying eyes.

My analysis was borne out some time later by the findings of one of Australia's most respected forensic scientists, Mark Reynolds, who gave evidence concerning the dinghy at Sue's appeal in the Supreme Court of Tasmania. Fourteen swabs were taken from inside the dinghy and, in short, Reynolds stated that none came back positive for blood. No blood! Indeed, there was no forensic evidence whatsoever inside Sue's dinghy to suggest she had been involved in Bob's murder.

Yet someone had left the dinghy untethered near Gleeson's car, as if in a rush. Or perhaps they'd felt safe motoring the dinghy to that point, despite the obvious possibility that Gleeson might look up and see them. And someone had placed Sue's red jacket on the fence of 26 Margaret Street. But who? And why? Most importantly, what was their connection to Bob Chappell's death? And why wasn't the dinghy soiled with blood? I believed the clean dinghy and clean red jacket were the keys to solving who killed Bob Chappell. After many hours staring at that single dot on the harbour I came up with a theory, based on salient points and logic.

Someone, maybe as many as three or four persons, stole the dinghy from where Sue had moored it near the yacht club the afternoon before. They motored out to *Four Winds*, with ill intent, weaving past sung-out, wrung-out Australia Day revellers, towards the biggest yacht on the harbour. The familiar purr of an approaching dinghy would not have disturbed Bob Chappell.

Once on board, there was an almighty act of violence. This caused one person to flee. That person was not part of the violence. They may have been at odds with the violence or just petrified. Perhaps they left their DNA, located on the yacht. The person fled in the dinghy to the rowing shed rocks and abandoned the dinghy. That same person had picked up and worn Sue Neill-Fraser's red jacket while on the yacht. The jacket was dumped at no. 26 Margaret Street as the person ran from the foreshore. Abandoning the dinghy next to Gleeson's car was of no concern to this person.

This theory ticks all the boxes and indicates the jacket thief was innocent in the death of Bob Chappell. Hence the dinghy and jacket were devoid of any forensic evidence. No blood!

The more I rolled it around, the more this seemed to fit the facts. I grabbed my notebook and set about doorknocking many of the houses in the area, as well as the two yacht clubs and the string of marine equipment and repair shops. I was in search of anything to help solve this case. Three days later I was done and chilled to the core. The 4°C days had embedded themselves in my bones. I had spoken to almost one hundred people. Most were helpful, a few were dismissive and others tried their best. Two or three simply told me to 'fuck off' and mind my own business. *C'est la vie.*

The first person I spoke to was Bill, an old sailor at the Royal Yacht Club. He'd dropped in for a beer after a bitterly cold day's sailing. He recalled Australia Day, 2009 very well. He remembered that Pablo, whom he described as a 'ratbag' and a 'pisspot', was moored close to *Four Winds*. He'd also heard that Pablo had a young girl on board his yacht. On the afternoon of Australia Day, he'd noticed a dinghy (I found out later it belonged to Pablo) at the end of the Rowing Shed Point where people were hanging around in cars. He also saw people on Pablo's yacht. He mentioned another 'young girl' that his mate Eddie Hidding said he'd seen on *Four Winds* the day before Australia Day.

I chased up Eddie for a chat. He agreed Pablo was an unpleasant sort who was 'bad' and 'angry'. Pablo was moored 100 metres away from *Four Winds* on the starboard side, he said, just off Rowing Shed Point. Eddie's observation was important as he worked in the Bay Chandlery, (a boat hardware store) behind the rowing sheds. Due to Eddie's office facing away from the water, his view of the bay was narrow, but it just happened to include the area where *Four Winds* was moored with Pablo's yacht nearby. He'd seen Pablo's dinghy on the rocks at the rowing sheds daily, close to where Gleeson was living in his car. Several other people I spoke to also saw Pablo, or knew of him, and had noticed his yacht's position in the bay. Eddie told me about another guy he knew, Grant Maddock, who was moored in the same area as *Four Winds*.

I followed up Grant. He had been a yachtsman in the area for many years, part of the landscape in his timber-hulled yacht. He was slim with cascading shoulder-length hair and delicate features. No disrespect to him, but from a distance he could be mistaken as female. We got on well, sharing a table in a coffee shop for six hours. He also recalled that Pablo's yacht was moored close to *Four Winds*. He'd taken photographs of *Four Winds* around that time; however, police now had the images, which were never provided to Sue's defence team. Grant said a friend of his had been moored in that same area. One night, his friend's yacht was broken into and an intruder climbed into the cockpit and announced he was there to steal the dinghy. Break-ins and thefts from yachts and boats were happening weekly back then, Grant said, but owners stopped reporting them because of police inaction. Grant recalled being on the water on the night of Australia Day, 2009. He was in his own dinghy and it was late, about midnight. This information is vital in understanding a flaw in the case against Sue Neill-Fraser. The Crown proffered the evidence, through a witness, that a woman was seen in a dinghy, late at night, travelling across the water in the general direction of *Four Winds*. The witness wasn't completely certain it was a lone woman; however, the prosecution went to great lengths to argue that the person in the dinghy was Sue Neill-Fraser. However, with Grant declaring that he was on the water late that night, his fine features and long hair make it entirely possible that the witness saw a man, not a woman. One more example of the police case being slanted only one way.

Prior to Sue's trial, four witnesses came forward stating that a grey dinghy was tied to the side of *Four Winds* during the afternoon of Australia Day. This information is highly relevant, yet it was brushed aside by the police. Sue's dinghy was new, brilliant white in colour, with blue stripes. Eve Ash tried to speak to one of the witnesses some time later but was met with a wall of silence. He refused to talk to her unless she gave him $10,000. As I learned long ago, some witnesses do it from the heart, others from the wallet.

Another person who was very obliging was a guy called Stephen Catchpool who lived in a large house overlooking *Four Winds'* mooring. He recalled Pablo going back and forth in his dinghy from the rowing club to his yacht in the same area as *Four Winds*. He told police this snippet of information on day one of their investigation, as well as about his own dinghy, which had been stolen a few days before Bob's disappearance. The police didn't seem interested and he wasn't asked to make a statement. His wife photographed *Four Winds*, but police took the pictures and she never got them back. Nor did they surface at the trial, except one picture that was post-murder, showing the yacht taking water. Nothing pre-murder, which may have been valuable.

John, another witness I spoke with, was a charming old sea dog, almost ninety years old. He was on the water the night of Australia Day and knew where *Four Winds* was moored. John was coming in after a day's sailing, but decided it was too dark to reach his jetty mooring safely and dropped anchor for the night around 11 pm. He recalled a man with a slim build and long hair (Grant) who asked if he could help John with his yacht. John was also aware that break-and-enters were rife at that time.

I found numerous people who were aware of break-and-enters on yachts, and the thefts, bashings and vandalisms that sometimes occurred as a result. One of these was a fisherman, Rod. He'd been broken into twice by 'young punks' around 2009. They stole small items and wet-weather gear. A mate of his owned a 30-foot boat that was broken into by vandals who spray-painted the craft. Rod's friend's boat was later burned to the waterline, destroying it outright. It had been worth more than a million dollars.

Another witness, Steve, had a small business near the rowing sheds. He recalled seeing Sue's dinghy at the rocks on the morning Bob Chappell was declared missing. He thought the location of the dinghy odd, as it was normally tied up in the groyne area near the Royal Yacht Club. He knew of Grant. He also mentioned thefts were always a concern for yachties back in 2009.

My door-to-door inquiries were ringing alarm bells. Seven years after Bob was killed I easily found fifteen people in the area of Sandy Bay who recalled Australia Day, 2009 and the weeks preceding it. Most said that thefts from yachts and commercial boats in the area were occurring regularly, as well as vandalism and arson. I filled up pages in my notebook detailing their reports. The thing that jumped out at me was that much of it seemed to be the work of 'young punks', as some witnesses described them. Street kids, probably, knocking off maritime stuff to either feed their drug habits or just get by. If the police had done their job more thoroughly back then, they might have found another fifty witnesses. But to find them they would have needed to put on their leather boots, turn their collars up and door knock, day and night, until they found a half-decent suspect.

In the end, I was convinced that Sue Neill-Fraser didn't dump her own dinghy near the yellow Ford sedan. Likewise, she didn't toss her red jacket onto the fence at 26 Margaret Street. Sure, her DNA was on the collar and cuffs, but that doesn't mean she carried it with her or wore it that night. Anyone on board the yacht could have. Most of all, I was convinced that the owner of the Ford had the key to solving this murder case. He had become my favourite person of interest.

* * *

Much later, more extraordinary information came to light about the red jacket. At the time it was handed to police, a 260mm-long dark hair from someone unknown was located on it. Sue's lawyer, Barbara, pushed relentlessly for the hair to be analysed and finally, in April 2017, eight years after Bob's murder, the DPP finally relented. The hair was tested, but all the DPP would say is that the hair had nothing to do with Sue Neill-Fraser, her family or friends. The police undertook a massive inquiry and a report was written about this strand of hair. I know this much: the DNA contained in the hair matched a young woman who got into a fist fight on the night of Australia Day and was arrested, along with up to ten other brawling women. They breed them tough in Hobart! The woman was transported to the police station in a squad car after 8 pm on 26 January 2009, in all likelihood hours before Bob Chappell was killed. The following morning Bob Chappell was declared missing. Sue was shown the red jacket found on the fence and, at a glance, stated that it wasn't hers. A police sergeant took possession of the jacket and tossed it into the boot of his sedan. The same police vehicle that some of the brawling women were transported in the night before. The sergeant then drove it back to the police station.

How the hair got onto the jacket is not known. Clearly, it is an issue of contamination. But how, why and when? In March 2017, police interviewed a dozen people in an effort to discover how it got there, but reached no real conclusion. However, the police file on this mess does trace the jacket's journey after it was placed in the boot of the police sedan.

Extraordinarily, for a key piece of evidence in a murder investigation, the red jacket was not labelled or placed in a sealed exhibit bag. This is basic Detective 101 stuff. No care was taken to avoid contamination. The jacket was just tossed into the boot of a squad car. The car was then driven to Hobart Police HQ, where it was parked. The sergeant knocked off work at 3 pm. Four days later, a detective asked the sergeant for the red jacket for the purpose of forensic analysis. The good sergeant had no idea where it was. In police jargon, he found himself fat in the middle of a cluster fuck. A panicked search ensued. A check of many police cars failed to reveal the jacket. A broader search was then mounted as the magnitude of the bungle became apparent.

The jacket was eventually found lying on the ground in the car park, metres from the main door to the police station. It had lain in the dirt in the path of 'employees, contract workers, visitors, civilians and persons in custody' as they came and went from the busiest police station in the state for four days. There had been a run of sunny weather, with temperatures around 28 to 30 degrees Centigrade. It had rained on the day the jacket was finally found and there had been wind gusts of up to 44 kilometres per hour. How many stray dogs had sniffed over the jacket in that time, perhaps cocking their leg? How many hobos had picked it up and discarded it? Who can say?

That same good sergeant solemnly declared under the Oaths Act, in his statutory declaration before the Supreme Court of Tasmania, that after he placed the jacket in the boot of the police sedan, 'I retained the jacket' until the detective came and collected it. The police log says the same. At Sue Neill-Fraser's trial, when the DPP asked him if he'd retained the jacket, the sergeant, again under oath, answered unequivocally 'Yes'.

The truth is the Crown's no. 1 exhibit was without a chain of custody for four days. Yet in March 2017, when the inquiry related to the one long female hair on the jacket was underway, the sergeant admitted losing sight and custody of the jacket for four days. If he had stated the truth at Sue's trial in 2010, the evidence relating to the jacket may well have been tossed out. Who knows what would have been the result? The forensic report exposes the level of contamination: there were 'apparent animal hairs present in most areas' of the jacket.

Worse, the forensic scientist's initial report on the DNA found on the jacket's collar and cuffs stated that it was of 'Mixed DNA profile, female DNA present, at least three contributors'. There was, the report said, a one in thirty chance that Sue Neill-Fraser was one of the contributors. 'Neill-Fraser may have come in contact with this jacket, although this isn't readily supported by the statistics.' In other words, it was doubtful that Sue Neill-Fraser's DNA was on the jacket. This finding begs an answer to the question, how did the red jacket end up being positively identified as belonging to Sue Neill-Fraser? And, if one accepts Sue was a contributor, who could the other two be? And why haven't the police and the forensic scientists done all they can in eight years to find the missing two contributors?

Unbelievably, a final analysis, presented at trial, found there was actually a one in 100 million chance that Sue was a contributor to the DNA on the red jacket. What caused the odds to change so dramatically in twelve months for the forensic scientists? From one in thirty to one in 100 million. The change in numbers is a real worry, without explanation.

But the saga of the red jacket doesn't end there. On 23 March 2009, a woman who lived in the area of Marieville Esplanade told police she saw a 'red sailing jacket' as she was walking to work the day after Australia Day, 2009. Her normal route was to walk along the Esplanade, over a small pedestrian footbridge crossing a rivulet, then on towards Battery Point. At 8.15 am she saw a red jacket hanging on a house fence on the other side of the bridge. This bridge is 300 metres away from 26 Margaret Street. She didn't touch the jacket or see anyone near it. In all likelihood, it was the same red jacket later found at 26 Margaret Street. After all, how many red jackets were lying around, on fences, along Marieville Esplanade that morning? More importantly, how did it get from the fence beyond the rivulet to the fence at 26 Margaret Street, where it was found by the owner of the house one and a half hours later and handed to police? It's all sounding a bit dodgy.

The police report on the woman's sighting of the red jacket beyond the rivulet was marked 'Highly Protected'. Why? Highly protected documents are exempt from Right to Information applications. Yet it was supplied to Barbara, Sue's lawyer, through such a request. Probably by mistake. The report itself simply details the garden-variety piece of information offered by the good-hearted citizen. So why the

'Highly Protected' classification? A classification that suits terrorism or similar sensitive inquiries.

Interestingly, by the date the sighting was reported (23 March 2009), the investigation into Sue Neill-Fraser was in full flight, complete with listening devices in her home and telephone intercepts. Perhaps the sighting of the red jacket down the road from where it was eventually located might have posed problems. Any alternate theories on who dumped it and where would have been an unwanted complication.

The entire saga of the red jacket needs to be the subject of a full and independent inquiry to establish the truth of how it relates to Sue Neill-Fraser's murder conviction (if at all), and where it fits in what I consider an inept investigation. An inquiry by highly qualified interstate investigators, headed by a judge.

* * *

I came across another highly protected police report in my research that bowled me over. As I mentioned earlier, on the night Bob Chappell disappeared, another vessel was broken into. The boat was entered and the power was turned off at the switchboard. The same modus operandi as the intrusion on *Four Winds*. This is what detectives call similar facts. The stuff that gets them all excited. However, nothing seems to have come of it. Perhaps the Hobart detectives believed there were two separate incidents on the water on the exact same night where a person or persons with ill intent turned off the power at the switchboard of a boat! I wonder if the cops have heard of similar facts?

And why would the report into this petty crime be classified at such a high level? Attached to the report was yet another labelled 'Protected'. It described an attempted theft of an inflatable boat from Waimea Jetty at Sandy Bay sometime on 18 or 19 January the same year. (Sue's dinghy was an inflatable boat.) The jetty overlooks the *Four Winds'* mooring point. For some reason, the theft was abandoned. The would-be robbers took off, leaving behind a screwdriver and shifting spanner covered in 'blood'. And for some reason, it took detectives two weeks to attend the crime scene.

At each stage of the investigation into this attempted theft, up until 23 February, police noted the 'blood' found on the tools. Then, suddenly, the swab was reported as showing negative for blood. But no samples were sent for DNA profiling, according to the investigation log. Yet there is a DNA results forensic number which shows a blood sample was analysed. Fascinatingly, the forensic 'nil result' is labelled 23 February. By then, Sue was the one and only suspect for killing Bob Chappell. On the police crime report an offender linked to the crime is named, but those details are redacted. Of course, they are. That's what happens in Tasmania.

The overuse of the highly protected classification may well have been a ruse. Effectively, it prevented the information in these reports, gold in the fight to prove Sue's innocence, from being released to her lawyers.

I couldn't help but wonder: if detectives on the local front had done their work thoroughly when break-and-enters on boats and yachts were rampant, would Bob Chappell still be alive?

The man who knew too much

I CAN'T IMAGINE LIVING ROUGH IN A CAR FOR TEN MONTHS on that Hobart waterfront with the elements beating down on me daily, nightly. Especially not in a clapped-out early model yellow Ford sedan. I'd consider it for a night or two in a late-model Bentley with an inlaid walnut bar and Bose sound system, but that's as far as I would take it. Oh, and with a cashmere wool blanket to boot.

Stephen Gleeson did it out of necessity. He was poor. Loneliness had a bit to do with it too, and the Rowing Shed spit gave him contact with the outside world. Tough, he was. A streetfighter who could handle himself. He stood out, not only because his car was painted canary yellow, but because Hobart's homeless gravitated to the area where his car was parked. They also gravitated to Gleeson. He always had guests dropping over for a drink or a sausage cooked on his tiny one-burner gas cooker. Sandy Bay residents saw him as a bum, a nuisance. They wanted the police to move him on, cleanse the foreshore of the boozing men with their un-showered bodies. But the police ignored the rough sleepers, always busy elsewhere, it seemed. Even when investigating Bob Chappell's disappearance from a yacht moored only a few hundred metres away, they disregarded them outright.

I needed to talk with Gleeson. Trouble was, he was in Risdon Prison near Hobart doing serious jail time. He took to a neighbour with a heavy Victorian clothes iron, an awesome weapon in the wrong hands. His original charge of attempted murder was knocked down to grievous bodily harm and Gleeson pleaded guilty to bashing his neighbour's head in, flattening it, almost killing him. Sadly, the victim is now severely brain-damaged, having been ironed out, so to speak, by a one-time rough sleeper.

The rules around visiting prisoners are strict. You need to write to the prisoner you want to talk to and ask to be put on their visitors list. In winter 2016, I drafted a short letter to Gleeson. I wrote that I was an author seeking a chat. I posted it off and crossed my fingers. A week later I rang Risdon and asked if I had been placed on Stephen's list. My name wasn't there. I wrote again. No luck. I tried one last time.

This time, when I called prison administration I was told my request had been accepted. I was delighted. I got to work and studied everything I could get my hands on about Gleeson then booked an airline ticket. The process of visiting Gleeson was arduous. I would fly from Melbourne to Hobart with all its usual delays, and then drive a hire car out to Risdon Prison to undergo the long security process. Every time I arrived at the prison I was required to strip myself of my belt, phone, pens, coins and wallet then present myself an hour ahead of the scheduled visiting time and prove my identity to the prison staff. Once I'd jumped through a series of administrative hoops, I would sit among the dozen or more other visitors, waiting for the call of a guard whereupon I would stand to attention and have a sniffer dog cast its nose over me. Then I'd be marched towards the maximum-security unit. After some serious key juggling by the guard and the opening and closing of a few steel doors, I would finally arrive in a small room full of cameras and guards, and furnished with tiny tables and chairs. Then I would sit, hands clasped, and wait. Stephen would appear, and I would have 45 minutes to talk with him, without the aid of any pen or paper with which to take notes. Nothing but memory to record what he said.

Our meetings would take place under the watchful glare of the guards and on the stroke of the forty-fifth minute it was time to go. I would sit in my hire car in the prison car park, scribbling my notes, trying to recall our meeting in full, one salient point after another. Once I was done, my sequence went in reverse, as I travelled all the way home to Melbourne.

My first meeting with Gleeson went predictably. We sat at our tiny table and made awkward small talk. I was permitted to buy two tokens from administration and used them to shout him a bag of crisps and a can of Coke from a vending machine. Which he destroyed in double-quick time. Gleeson's first question was understandable; he didn't know me from Moses: 'What the fuck do you want to talk to me about?'

I needed to move fast. This guy could call an end to our meeting at any time, and the guards would toss me out. Establishing rapport was everything at this point. I explained that I had previously written a number of crime books and that I was interested in the Bob Chappell murder. He had guessed as much. He told me the head of prison security had warned him about talking to me, that I might quote him in my book. However, he was willing. From day one, he seemed to be interested in talking to me.

Gleeson is a reforming alcoholic. My father was one. Always reforming, always pissed, always violent. I knew the type. As kids, we were punched around the house as my father drank himself into a stupor. But Gleeson had been holed up in prison a couple of years, with no access to booze, so his reforming was going well. Alcoholics often find their foggy, booze-clouded memory improves after a long time off the grog. Gleeson mentioned this was the case with him and that he wanted to discuss issues that surrounded the murder, but needed to go slowly. I liked hearing that. Things would come back to him if he gave himself time to think it over, he said. But I only had 45 minutes.

I learned when I was a young detective that dealing with jailhouse witnesses is hard work. You not only need to build rapport, but to have the patience of a spider. I ended up visiting Gleeson seven or eight times over nine months. He became a great source of information and was earnest in his attempts to help. The first thing I noticed about him was how slowly he responded to my questions. Each one was considered. His face was a picture of concentration and he often squinted as he thought. He would be no good playing poker; his expressions would give him away. Each time I saw Gleeson he became more talkative, but I had to allow him time to think.

Our first meeting turned out to be fruitful. Without prompting, he mentioned that he was interviewed by police in 2012 and 'they were going through the motions, they didn't seem interested in what I wanted to say, they kept cutting me off'. I would agree with that! He moved on to Pablo, mentioning that he was 'cunning and dangerous'. Over the time of my visits, as his comments grew more useful and his willingness to help was established, I sent my notes off to Barbara, Sue's lawyer, who went about turning notes into affidavits.

My great concern in all this was that the loose lips of the prison guards might leak information about my chats to police. I was, ultimately, correct. In November 2016 when I visited Gleeson, two 'suits', detectives, had recently visited him and demanded to know what he was talking to me about. They threatened to charge him with something, anything, should he keep meeting me. This bothered me greatly, and made me realise I must have hit a nerve with my visits to Stephen. Despite the police standover tactics, Gleeson was keen to continue, recalling and telling me what he knew. He swore the affidavits prepared by Barbara detailing what he knew. A lot of it was to do with his mate Pablo and his yacht.

Gleeson always appeared genuine to me. He told me about being at home (in his car) on the night of Australia Day, 2009. He had just walked back from the city after having a few drinks and went straight to sleep at around 10 pm. At about 11 pm he was woken by a tap on the car window. It was a young man. He was with a girl, about sixteen years old and of medium build, with dark hair and fair skin, and 'not too tall'. She was the same homeless girl that Gleeson had mentioned to police in his interview in 2012. Gleeson had seen her hanging around the area a few times. He thought she might have been staying at a halfway house because he had seen her in the company of a female carer. They would sit around the foreshore, as if on a day out.

Both the young man and the girl sat inside Gleeson's car. He fired up his gas cooker and they cooked sausages, a poor man's feast. Before the two drop-ins left, they 'talked about breaking into yachts, to steal things,' Gleeson said. 'I understood they might be planning to break into yachts that night.' The next morning, he was woken up by the police. They asked him a few questions about the night before, but he told them nothing.

This last comment by Gleeson, that he'd told the police 'nothing', made sense to me. You reap what you sow. Even in the underworld, if you show a bit of civility, as well as compassion, you get the best out of people. Even if a potential witness is a crook or has been on the wrong side of the law, if you treat him or her right, develop a bit of rapport, they'll often talk. That's the key to success. Too many cops expect witnesses and suspects to spill everything in a few minutes. How ridiculously naive.

Over the course of the many meetings I had with him, always accompanied by packets of crisps and cans of Coke, Gleeson's recall of events became stronger and firmer. Eventually, he viewed a number of folders of photos that I was able to bring into the prison in the company of Jeff Thompson, the lawyer who had been recently recruited to Sue's defence team by Barbara. Only lawyers can carry paperwork into prisons and this was the first time I met Jeff, though I came to know him much better in the following months.

One of the folders held eight images of middle-aged men of similar appearance; Gleeson correctly picked out image no. 6 as being of his mate Pablo. (Using eight photographs is the proper way to undertake an identification parade by way of images.) Another folder held eight photos of similar-looking girls, all about the same age, each with dark long hair. Gleeson identified one as being the girl going off to break into yachts on the night of Australia Day, 2009. It was a photo of Meaghan Vass. Bingo!

It's important to keep in touch with prisoner witnesses, so they don't feel they are being used. One of the biggest mistakes detectives make is to stand over witnesses, browbeating statements out of them. Such tactics will only get a portion of what a good witness can offer. The smart detective will spend the time to get the whole shooting match, everything. I felt that I had achieved that, and Sue's defence team was pleased. As was I, for my manuscript.

With the affidavits completed, I tried to stay in touch with Gleeson and 'keep him warm' for court. I actually liked the guy; I thought he was a man trying to steer a better course through life. I visited him often, until the heat in the Tasmanian kitchen got way too hot.

About that time I became worried about the effects my questioning was having. I was stirring things up and by July 2017 I thought it best to keep some distance. I worried Gleeson would feel that I had taken what I needed and then dropped him, taking off back to the mainland. Around that time, Gleeson had a parole hearing coming up; he was hopeful of an early release. I hoped the Tasmanian police wouldn't use this important day to apply pressure for him to alter his evidence. As an old cop and ex-detective, I know exactly how the game is played. I thought that the Tasmanian cops might use my absence to 'poison me' in Gleeson's eyes; that is, to turn him against me. Tough men in jail can be reduced to putty in the hands of officials who can change a life with the stroke of a pen.

I would wonder about Gleeson daily for months to come, recalling what he'd told me the previous year: that two suits had stood over him and threatened to charge him should he continue to speak with me. That threat loomed heavy. Later, I read Stephen's visitor list and confirmed that detectives did visit him in November 2016. He was right. They obviously wanted to turn off the flow of information that was coming my way. In my opinion he was a man who knew much.

A puddle of DNA

Some of the most dramatic breakthroughs in criminal investigations come with the discovery of deoxyribonucleic acid (DNA) at crime scenes. DNA is a molecule that carries the genetic instruction used in the growth, development, functioning and reproduction of all living organisms. Like fingerprints, no two strands of DNA are identical. Unique to an individual, it's usually the final word in establishing a suspect's guilt or innocence. DNA analysis of hair, bodily fluids, blood, semen or skin tissue can prove, beyond an infinitely high standard of proof, whether a particular person was at a crime scene. Or not.

The day *Four Winds* was discovered apparently sinking, a stream of police, forensic personnel and salvage staff came and went as they undertook their various tasks. Ultimately, one of the forensic officers lifted a sample of fluid from the upper deck of the yacht. Its location was logged as 9.45 metres back from the bow of the yacht and just inside the railing on the starboard side, close to the saloon skylight hatch. It was described in the forensic biology report as 'Exhibit no. 20, starboard walkway,

Full DNA profile (female). Does not match any individual currently on the Tasmanian DNA database (Person E) (1 in 100 million).' The officer noted that the DNA material, which was clear with a slight tinge of colour, measured 210 mm by 260 mm (about the size of a dinner plate). It was a significant amount of liquid and ruled out as blood, sperm or other easily identifiable fluids. It might have been saliva or gastric juices. Or, due to the large volume, a mix of both.

With no match found in the Tasmanian DNA database, the source of the fluid would remain unidentified for a little over one year. But in March 2010 it was identified as belonging to Meaghan Vass, a street kid who had been living rough for the past three years. By this time, Sue Neill-Fraser was awaiting trial for murder. At her trial in September that year, prosecutor Tim Ellis stated: 'We've had Meaghan Vass, a sixteen-year-old homeless girl, bullied and chased around … all because some of her DNA was found in the one spot on *Four Winds*, one spot, one spot only, on top of the deck – a sixteen-year-old girl.' Mr Ellis suggested Meaghan Vass was being picked on, treated 'ferociously' because of the DNA deposit. The thing is, it was a pretty large 'spot' of DNA. Indeed, it was a puddle of DNA!

Just as fascinating was another DNA discovery, also found on the upper deck, just near the saloon skylight hatch, close to Meaghan's DNA. Swab no. 19 was described as 'From starboard side of walkway. Mixed DNA. At least 3 contributors present, inconclusive with regards to female DNA. Robert Chappell not excluded as a possible contributor.' While it had a low screening for blood, the fluid was compelling insofar as it comprised material from three different persons. It was also a large deposit, measuring 80 mm by 280 mm. That's about the size of a small loaf of bread. A blue rag – described on the forensic officer's paperwork as a face washer or towel – was also found at the location and labelled 'Item 9, small blue towel/face washer from starboard side walkway, just before the cockpit'.

Let's think about this for a moment. At this one location – the upper deck of the yacht near to the saloon skylight hatch on the starboard side – there must have been a lot going on to create a series of extraordinarily large deposits of DNA. The blue rag is also very telling, when you try to unravel why someone was spitting or dry retching perhaps at that location, and wiping their mouth or face with a rag.

The forensic scientist had gone about her task methodically. She went downstairs to the laundry and noted the presence of two other telling exhibits: 'In Laundry, 2 x rags on top in a clear plastic bag of rags appear to have brownish ?? vomit stains. Agreed – FSST [Forensic Science Service of Tasmania] to dry and ? tox.' (This is a verbatim of what the scientist wrote.)

In layperson's terms, the scientist had found two swatches bearing traces of vomit, which were still wet and sitting on top of a bag of similar rags in the laundry. The scientist collected the swatches for toxicology and other tests. Toxicology can detect if the person who vomited had taken illicit or pharmaceutical drugs or drunk alcohol. DNA would also be present, as would traces of whatever food the person had eaten. All facts that could help solve a crime. The two swatches were given barcodes and exhibit numbers: items 93 and 94. The potential value of these two vomit swatches should not be underestimated. They could be vital, as one of the offenders may have vomited during the murder, or when trying to dispose of Bob's body. It is not unheard of for a killer to vomit at a crime scene, due to the horror involved in killing someone. Additionally, it's highly unlikely that Bob Chappell would have vomited earlier in the day and left stinking rags lying around. Surely, he would have vomited overboard, or in the toilet.

The blue rag found on the upper deck next to Meaghan Vass's pool of DNA could also tell a story. I can imagine Meaghan, the person who left the DNA on the starboard-side walkway, may have sat there for some time. She may have spat and cleared her throat, having recently vomited downstairs. The size of the pool of fluid indicates she cleared her throat a few times, spitting constantly, using the towel to wipe her mouth and face.

These vital exhibits – the blue rag and the two swatches of vomit, given Exhibit Bar Codes 14431-734-9, 14431-733-5 and 14431-669-2 – become even more telling when you consider them alongside swab 19, containing mixed DNA and found in the same location as the blue rag and Meaghan Vass's DNA. It's feasible that swab 19 could contain traces of Bob Chappell's blood. Remember, this murder was very violent, as evidenced by the blood spatters – all identified as belonging to Bob – on the walls of the saloon. His blood sprayed everywhere. Obviously, the murderer would be covered in blood too: on their hands, arms and their face. This may have found its way into their saliva, which they then spat out. That seems logical. The trouble is, this large sample was filed away and is still yet to be thoroughly tested. No detective thought it necessary to request further testing. So, the sample sits in a cupboard in the forensic unit in Hobart, its secrets locked away with it. Odd place, Tasmania.

The two vomit exhibits – Nos. 93 and 94 – were sent to the forensics laboratory. All good up until that point; however, no detective requested an analysis of these vital exhibits either and eventually they simply disappeared. Never to be seen again.

While they'd been clearly logged for analysis by the forensic scientist aboard *Four Winds*, there was no specific reference to them on the subsequent forensic report that was tendered in court. An almost unheard-of anomaly. How could this be?

Item 9, the blue face washer found near Meaghan's DNA, also went to the laboratory. And, like the vomit swatches, it disappeared completely, vanishing not only from storage but from the forensic work sheets and final reports. Why? What secrets could these three vital exhibits have told? What answers have been lost by their disappearance? The handling of these key exhibits defies sound investigative and forensic techniques. There can be no explanation for hiding them from the court process and the defence lawyers.

In my view, all the DNA exhibits found on *Four Winds* which are still in existence should be retested with the latest DNA technology, the Low Copy Number (LCN) method, which is able to detect DNA in its most minute form. In 2016, this method identified a killer in a Mafia murder case that I spent a year working on. Exhibits in that case were so tiny that detectives had thought it unlikely that DNA testing would yield a result. But using the LCN method, a match was found and the Mafia figure – my suspect when I was a detective in the 1990s – was charged in 2018. The DNA samples found on *Four Winds* provided many opportunities for discovering who killed Bob Chappell. Easy work, one would have thought. Additionally, the disappearance of three of the exhibits – the two vomit swatches and the blue rag – must be investigated and an explanation given by the Forensic Science Service of Tasmania.

* * *

Other DNA samples found on the steps leading out of the wheelhouse onto *Four Winds*' upper deck are also hugely relevant in trying to unravel the mystery of who killed Bob Chappell. Yet they remain unidentified.

Like fingerprints, DNA identification is only as good as the number of suspects, criminals or participants listed in databases. Normally, in an investigation such as this, detectives should have begun an elimination process, whereby they reeled in all their suspects and compared their DNA samples with those found on *Four Winds*. However, the Tasmanian detectives failed to do this and so ignored comparative DNA from a string of people. Sampling potential suspects could have confirmed or eliminated persons of interest and helped police gain a deeper understanding of the crime.

Another massive oversight regarding DNA evidence was the mishandling of a '195mm-long colourless human head hair' located near the skylight hatch. At times this 'colourless' description was changed to be 'grey'. Labelled as belonging to 'person D', it yielded a full female DNA profile, which ruled out Sue Neill-Fraser and her daughters as potential sources. All it needed was to be matched to a suspect. Trouble is, as earlier mentioned, the hair was logged as being located on the rear skylight hatch, not 'near' the skylight hatch. Although at one stage the report stated it was located on the 'forward' hatch. The location details were changed again, in 2018, and the police now say it was found on the saloon skylight hatch. A run of simple errors, perhaps; however, the investigation into Bob Chappell's death is riddled with simple errors. Science is meant to be exact, not cut and paste. There has never been an attempt to identify this hair. It was filed away, like the sample of Meaghan Vass's DNA, into a bag, inside a cupboard, in an office of the forensic building, to be forgotten. It still sits there today. That this crucial piece of evidence has not been matched to a suspect or eliminated as irrelevant is inexcusable.

Just as inexcusable is that other DNA samples that were recovered have never been run through the DNA database. Swab 27 was taken from a juice or water bottle and a torch located inside the yacht, neither of which were known to be on the yacht before Bob's disappearance. Remember, Detective Milazzo stated they were foreign to the vessel. Swabs 82 and 83 were taken from the levers on the skylight hatches in the saloon. Swab 81 was taken from levers of the forward skylight hatch, the hatch I believe Bob's body was hauled through. The swab yielded 'Mixed DNA profile, Male DNA present, inconclusive with regard to female DNA.' Lastly, item no. 100, 'an apparent hair', was located near the bottom tread of the steps leading down to the wheelhouse, the same steps that had Bob Chappell's blood upon them. I almost fell off my chair – not from laughing, but from shock – when I found out these swabs and items had either never been examined or run through national databases. Why not? Criminals are known to be transient, and if nothing else, the samples could have been used to eliminate possible suspects, such as the clique of homeless people who slept rough on the Rowing Shed spit.

The mixed DNA swabs – item 9, the blue rag, item 19, the large deposit of fluid with possible blood spots – located on the starboard walkway near the access gate of the yacht were, in investigative terms, the most important forensic evidence located. Why, because they were immediately near to Meaghan Vass's puddle of DNA. Yet they, and other samples of DNA and Person D's hair were left to languish in a dusty archival drawer in the forensic science laboratory of Hobart.

Seven months after Bob Chappell was murdered, the DNA samples remained untested, but Sue Neill-Fraser was hauled into police headquarters and charged with the murder. The DNA samples slipped to the back pages of the police brief of evidence. However, DNA isn't like ink – it can hang around for tens of thousands of years. There was evidence there that just needed to be focused on. My belief is that this DNA is critical to exonerating Sue Neill-Fraser.

The homeless girl

IT WAS IN FEBRUARY 2010 THAT THE SHIT HIT THE FAN. AN extraordinary revelation surfaced that had the potential to smash the police case against Sue Neill-Fraser. It was, of course, the matching of Meaghan Vass's DNA to a sample found on *Four Winds* in early 2009. Until then police had no idea who owned the puddle of fluid found on the upper deck of the yacht.

However, Meaghan Vass had been arrested for theft and her DNA was routinely collected and placed on a database, leading to the positive match. It meant Tasmania's elite major crime squad had a conundrum on their hands, as they'd already charged Sue Neill-Fraser with the murder of Bob Chappell. How they handled it was in my opinion surely one of the most inept responses in Australian police annals.

In March 2010, a detective, whom I will simply call Detective Maverick, who had written up the statements by Crown witnesses Phillip Triffett and Maria Hanson, was given Meaghan Vass's file. Now he had to explain the DNA that placed a street kid and thief on Bob's yacht. He must have been awfully concerned.

Maverick was called to give evidence at Sue Neill-Fraser's trial, and stated under oath that Meaghan Vass, at the time of the murder of Bob Chappell, was staying at Mara House, a women's refuge and halfway house. It was managed by a woman named Shari Collis. In his notes were Shari's written answers to questions he'd asked her. He told the court that Shari confirmed that Meaghan had asked to have a 'sleepover' on 26 January 2009 and that she left Mara House at 3.50 pm. She had agreed to phone Shari later with the phone number of the person she was staying with, but failed to do this. So Meaghan was absent from her care facility the night Bob Chappell was murdered.

When Sue's defence counsel attempted to ask Maverick where Meaghan stayed that night and with whom, prosecutor Tim Ellis tried to shut the line of questioning down. He objected when Sue's counsel asked to see the contents of Maverick's large lever-arch file, labelled 'Vass', from which he was reading. The presiding judge, Justice Blow, then sent the jury out of the courtroom. In their absence, Ellis and Sue's counsel argued over the admissibility of evidence in the Vass file. Ellis argued that it was 'hearsay' and not admissible; it appeared the DPP didn't want details related to Meaghan and her whereabouts on that night revealed. The game was on.

After some discussion, the judge ruled that Sue's counsel could read the 'Vass' file, and ordered a recess to allow him to do so. When the barrister returned he started an argument to recall both Meaghan Vass and the forensic scientist who analysed her DNA. He could see that he needed to uncover new facts that might tell a different story about what happened on the yacht.

After further submissions about the admissibility of the file and its contents, things never went the way of the defence

barrister. Justice Blow announced that he would tell the jury to
ignore the previous evidence of Detective Maverick, as he had
only been told what was in Mara House's records, rather than
seeing them himself. It was hearsay. The jury would be told to
disregard the fact that Meaghan Vass was recorded as being
absent all night from her accommodation and in the company
of another person. The judge followed up with what to me was
a flabbergasting comment: 'I wonder how relevant any of this
is anyway?'

Despite Meaghan's puddle of DNA being found on the
boat where a man had been murdered, the judge couldn't
see the relevance of evidence that pointed to Meaghan Vass's
whereabouts that night.

Sue's counsel continued his fight to recall Meaghan Vass,
arguing that he hadn't had a chance to ask her if she had
visited the area of Marieville Esplanade, Sandy Bay, during
her original court appearance, days earlier. Recalling Meaghan
would help to clear up the anomalies appearing in her story.
Plus, it had come out that Meaghan was in the company
of a young man. He also wanted to recall Carl Grosser, the
forensic scientist who determined that the DNA on *Four
Winds* belonged to Meaghan, and then read an explosive email
Grosser had sent Detective Maverick. 'Given the strong DNA
profile that we obtained from this swab I'd suggest that this is
indicative of the presence of a relatively large amount of DNA
which is more likely to come from bodily fluids, blood, saliva,
than a simple contact touching event...'

This email contradicts the police contention that Meaghan's
DNA found on *Four Winds* was an insignificant amount and
could have been transferred onto the yacht on the boot of a
police officer after the murder was discovered.

I studied the run of emails, word for word. Maverick's reply to this email on 23 March 2010 seems to be asking Grosser whether it was possible to place another interpretation on the presence of Meaghan's DNA. 'I know I'm a pest but this girl is adamant she hasn't been on the yacht, so I'm just trying to work it all out or possibilities, that is. I am reluctant to believe her but I do think that she – was in some involved etcetera … [sic]'

This is, again, explosive content. His notes suffer from poor punctuation, but it appears Maverick is saying that he is reluctant to believe Meaghan's denials and that he believes she was on the yacht the night Bob disappeared.

Tim Ellis, the prosecutor, challenged Sue's counsel's attempt to have Meaghan recalled by continuing to suggest that it was more likely someone else transferred Meaghan's DNA onto *Four Winds*. He offered a convoluted theory: 'Someone may have equally contacted on their footsteps or in some other way her DNA and gone to Marieville Esplanade and got on a dinghy and alighted on the *Four Winds* at any time.' Perhaps he wasn't aware that the DNA deposit was massive: dinner plate sized, remember. He then suggested the DNA 'may have got there a year ago'. A year when the yacht was cleaned for sale in Brisbane, sailed down from Brisbane to Hobart on the open seas and was then moored off Sandy Bay for five weeks in the summer heat? His suggestion was in my view absurd. Was he saying Meaghan Vass was in Brisbane a year earlier?

Ellis also cited concerns for the girl's welfare if she was recalled. 'To get young Meaghan Vass back in for a bit more nasty badgering about where she was on what night would not only be pointless but totally unfair, a girl who's had no fixed address being paraded back in to be badgered about this …'

Justice Blow ultimately ruled that forensic scientist Grosser would not be recalled, neither would Meaghan Vass. 'The question of just where Meaghan Vass was and what she did on the night of 26 January seems to be peripheral ... I think we'd be wasting time and there's no realistic prospect of it making any significant difference if she [Meaghan Vass] were recalled.'

Sue Neill-Fraser's counsel made three submissions to the court: to admit Maverick's comments and notes about Meaghan's absence from Mara House as evidence; to recall forensic scientist Grosser; and to recall Meaghan Vass to answer as to where she was the night Bob Chappell was murdered and in whose company. All three submissions were disallowed. Had the defence counsel got what he wanted, the police case could have been smashed there and then, but instead, in my opinion, an innocent woman went to jail.

Chasing the elusive

I spoke to Meaghan Vass on the phone well before I met her face to face. The call came about because of a woman whom I'll call Gabby. It was a strange connection between these two women: they were both involved romantically with a man I will call Snapper, the head of a motorcycle club. The club's HQ is a rattly old fortified house in the back blocks of Hobart, down a dead-end street of an industrial estate. The type of street any normal person would stay clear of. Snapper was legendary; he had far more women than Meaghan and Gabby vying for his affections, but these two appeared to be his favourites.

Gabby was forty-one and had been involved with Snapper since she was a teenager. She loved Snapper, at least that's what she told me, but motherhood, drugs and life in the bikers' lane had taken its toll. She was a real Aussie battler, the type your heart goes out to, the type who, invariably, can't seem to help themselves. She was worn down with young children and a teenage daughter. But Gabby was no lightweight; you'd know it if you got on the wrong side of her. When I met her, she was serving jail time for driving while disqualified.

Gabby knew Sue Neill-Fraser. They were both jailbirds, sharing the same prison compound. Gabby liked Sue and had become aware of her plight. She also knew Meaghan, who was a regular visitor to the clubhouse. Gabby believed that Meaghan was involved in some way with whatever had happened on *Four Winds*, and thought that she might be prepared to help.

I wrote to Gabby and she agreed to meet me. I visited her for an hour in late November 2016. It went well. The meeting took place in a secure visitors room and CCTV cameras were trained on us, as well as a two-way mirror. I could see the silhouette of someone on the other side, sitting, watching. Obviously a security officer, putting their nose as close to prison reality as they could. Life for a prison guard is a bag of dull tasks: standing watch over has-beens, thugs, wife beaters, paedophiles and society's worst. It's the sort of employment that entices ex-army types or those who failed police recruitment exams. I've always believed they covet the life of a detective; hence their willingness to spy and snitch to those in law and order. Someone like Gabby having an interstate visitor would be fine gossip to pass on. It didn't concern me. I was just getting material for a book, which is what I told Gabby.

Gabby was due for parole at the end of the year. She intended having Christmas with her family and then wanted to re-kindle her friendship with Meaghan. That they were both sexually and romantically involved with Snapper wouldn't interfere with her contacting Meaghan, or arranging for the girl to meet me, Gabby said. She wanted nothing for her assistance, despite a reward being on offer by a group of Hobart people who had taken a strong interest in the case and believed in Sue's innocence.

As I always do, I wrote copious notes the instant I got back to my car in the prison car park. In time, I would become a bit of a fixture, sitting in my car, writing pages of notes. Once or twice I suffered a walk over: a prison guard strolling over to look in my car window, asking what I was doing. I always smiled and told them that I was an author making notes for my new book. It was true, as far as it went. Once my notes were done I would get out of there as quickly as possible.

I agreed to wait for Gabby to contact me once she was out of prison. This was crucial. Gabby had to be the one pursuing me. I couldn't be seen to be chasing her down, demanding her help. Voluntariness is everything in the early days of witness assistance. I bided my time.

Waiting for Gabby wasn't such a bad thing as it meant I could jump on a plane and fly to France and Italy for Christmas for a holiday. I was away the entire month of December, taking in the cold sights of Paris, Bordeaux and northern Italy. I must admit, I never gave Gabby a single thought while I caught up with friends and ate way too much food and sipped far too much Christmas cheer.

It was towards the end of my trip, after having said my goodbyes to friends, that death paid me a visit. After finishing breakfast in a fabulous villa in La Morra, Piedmont, I was planning to pay my bill and head upstairs for a hot shower and then pack my suitcase. I'd had the best few days and was feeling a bit blue about going home. My next stop was Milano, for lunch with two old friends before my flight home. It was a few days into January and Gabby entered my mind for the first time in a while; she was due to contact me. By then she would have been out of prison, on parole.

I walked past reception and took a few paces outside, into the snow. Then, bang! Pain ripped across my upper chest. I knew exactly what was happening. I'd had that exact same pain six years earlier, just before my quadruple bypass. It was unmistakable. I was having a minor heart attack. And I remembered that I hadn't packed my Nitrolingual spray, which relaxes blood vessels, allowing an increased flow of blood to the heart.

Luckily the pain came and went relatively quickly. I hadn't crumbled in a heap, but I had to get to my room and take control of my situation. Immediately after I got through the door, I lay flat on my back on my bed. My mobile phone was nearby. I pulled up my daughter's phone number. I didn't call her, I just waited the pain out, calming myself and breathing slowly. I had done the same thing in Sicily, when the first attack happened six years earlier. I lay there for two hours, letting all the tension fall out of my body. Sipping water. Breathing easy.

I had oodles of time before check-out and I stayed on my bed until nearly 11.00 am. When the pain had gone away and I gently got up, I was in an almost jelly-like state. I texted my daughter, just to leave a message of affection, then tossed my phone into my hire car and drove to Milano airport – via a *farmacia* for a Nitrolingual spray. I made it home, immediately called my cardiologist, who was also overseas, and settled back into a slow routine. While I was awaiting the return of my cardiologist from his holiday, I got the first of what would become many text messages from Gabby. She'd been home for two weeks and had already been in contact with Meaghan. She was optimistic that she would be able to persuade her to meet me later in January. So far, so good. I was grateful for the delay as I needed to sort out my heart issue. In the meantime, I was happy to sit quietly at home, under my family doctor's orders, and take it very easy.

After several more text messages from Gabby, in which she told me she'd re-kindled her relationship with Meaghan, we spoke on the phone. Meaghan was willing to talk, Gabby said, as long as she was not prosecuted. I took this as a hugely positive sign, but I remained cautious. People in this world routinely flip-flop from one position to another at the drop of a hat. Indeed, they can be treacherous as they struggle with the issue of what to do. In my police days I saw dozens of crooks promise the world, offer statements and swear oaths to tell the truth, only to renege at the last minute. Meaghan had to commit to writing a statement or making an affidavit.

Gabby had mentioned that Meaghan kept a diary and confided that she had sneaked a look at it. She saw an entry from 2009 that may have had something to do with the night of Bob Chappell's disappearance. The wording was something like 'It wasn't meant to go like that. [Dodger] did it.' Getting hold of the diaries of Meaghan Vass was now of the utmost importance to me.

One early morning before daybreak in the middle of January 2017, I was woken by a series of text messages from Gabby. She had been up all night with Meaghan and Snapper, talking about the *Four Winds* incident and Meaghan's willingness to assist me. One message just read *Pack your bags*, meaning I should get ready to fly to Hobart to talk with Meaghan. I'd just drifted off again, when the phone rang. It was Gabby and she was with two other people, a male and a younger-sounding female. I was bleary-eyed, standing in my lounge room butt-naked, while Gabby tried to get the young woman to talk to me. She was reluctant, but eventually I was introduced to Meaghan. The man, of course, was Snapper, her boyfriend. We had a four-way chat. Gabby said that Meaghan had been on *Four Winds* the night of Australia Day, 2009. I needed to hear it from Meaghan, I told her. With a heart condition and waiting for my cardiologist to schedule me for surgery, there was no way I was going to Hobart. Not unless Meaghan offered some solid facts. I heard Snapper and Gabby both say, 'Tell him.'

Meaghan spoke to me briefly. Really, I asked a set of questions and Meaghan answered. She was nervous, and I understood why. It was a potentially dangerous subject for her; however, I wasn't going to pack my bags for a wild goose chase, not with my heart in need of attention. 'We were on the yacht partying,' she told me. 'I can't remember but have to think about it. [Pablo] and [my boyfriend] and me. There was a fight. On the yacht.'

When I asked if the yacht was *Four Winds*, she answered: 'The old guy's yacht. Next to [Pablo's].' Meaghan told me that they had used a dinghy and a fight broke out. 'Fuck. I saw it, but I fucked off. Took off.' She escaped the yacht in the dinghy, she said, and Pablo and her boyfriend went back to Pablo's yacht. By what means she didn't say.

All of a sudden, I had a bloody fabulous reason to sneak off to Hobart, instead of waiting on my cardiologist. Naively, I believed I could bowl the Meaghan matter over in a day or two and be back for my surgery. Before I hung up I offered Meaghan the use of a lawyer, and she seemed to be happy with this, but I sensed the matter was an enormous burden for her. She was unsure what lay ahead. As the sun rose outside my window I assured her that I would help where I could. The call ended.

As I went for a shower, the moment was not lost on me. A woman who I was told was Meaghan Vass, the woman with her puddle of DNA on *Four Winds*, had just told me, by telephone, that she had been on the yacht, and that she was in company with others when a fight broke out. It was, for my book, potentially gold.

Over the next few days I traded many text messages with Gabby, all to do with me meeting Meaghan. Eve and Tim gathered their film equipment and we booked our passage to Hobart. I asked Gabby to find the diary belonging to Meaghan with the entry from January 2009. I made it very clear that any conversation I had with Meaghan had to be recorded. I would rent a hotel room in Hobart and all the audio-visual equipment would be out in the open for all to see. There was no other way of doing this. Gabby agreed.

By the end of the week, Eve, Tim and I were in a way-too-expensive hotel room in Hobart opposite Constitution Dock, waiting on Gabby and Meaghan. We waited. And waited. I was used to waiting from my police days, sitting around chewing the fat, sweating on crooks. Crooks, as it turns out, have no sense of punctuality.

Eventually Gabby arrived, along with her kids and a nanny. And did those kids howl! I asked Gabby to lose the kids for a few hours, but she was insistent they stay close by. I don't think Gabby could actually hear the noise, she seemed oblivious to it. She explained that things were in the hands of Snapper, who was driving Meaghan to the hotel. So we sat tight. Meaghan did speak to Gabby by mobile phone on one or two occasions that first day. I heard one of their conversations, which Tim recorded with his equipment and sent to an expert audio technician for enhancement. Meaghan was saying that she was on her way; she was having a shower and working on her make-up. Gabby was direct, stating that we were waiting for her to arrive for a chat; we'd just be sitting around on lounge chairs and talking. Meaghan seemed reluctant to come to the hotel. She said: 'I just want a shower ... I wasn't seeing what was going on ...' There are a number of ways to interpret her comment. In context, I believe Meaghan was referring to being on *Four Winds* and that she didn't see what was going on in relation to the death of Bob Chappell downstairs in the saloon. I come to that opinion due to my understanding of all the evidence as well as the location of Meaghan's DNA on the upstairs walkway. And the size of her DNA, a puddle, a large quantity that suggests she may have sat on the walkway a long time, retching and spitting in fear. Hence, she didn't see what was going on downstairs.

Only Meaghan could clarify this, and she was dragging the chain, keeping us waiting. For about nine hours that first day. Enough time for me to be almost deafened by the screeching of Gabby's kids.

We ended up waiting three long days. There were two or three false alarms as Gabby worked the phones, calling Snapper and – we believed – Meaghan. Meaghan was worried, it seemed. From what I could hear, Snapper seemed to be on our side and was trying his hardest to get Meaghan to the room. Yet for all his efforts, we ended up with little more than sore ears and square eyes from watching television.

During this waiting marathon, Eve, Tim and I had the unpleasant sense of being watched. Strange things happened. Individually, they amounted to nothing, but collectively they made me feel that the Tasmanian police were on to us. When we'd first checked in to the hotel, we'd been issued with three room keys. I asked if the hotel was full. No, was the reply, it was a quiet period. I then asked if we could change our allotted rooms. The reception clerk seemed a tad frazzled by this simple request and we haggled with the manager, insisting on a room change. Over the next couple of days, I'd noticed a lone male sitting in the hotel foyer making an attempt to look inconspicuous. I was convinced he was a surveillance hound. On one occasion I observed Eve as she left the hotel. The lone man got off his chair, walked over to the door and watched her walk down the street. Then he made a call on his mobile phone. Little things, but they happened way too frequently.

My paranoia spiked the day Tim and I were sitting around the wired-up 'meeting' room, waiting for Gabby. We had been up all night and it was now the middle of the day. Both of us were taking a cat-nap, so the suite was in silence and the TV turned off. I was dozing in a chair next to the door connecting to the suite adjacent to our room. Suddenly there was the sound of a key in the door lock. The door slowly opened. I leaped up to find two startled men standing on the other side of the open door. They were in their thirties, with shortish hair and dressed casually in jeans and shirts. I demanded to know who they were, and they stepped back, nervous, looking at each other. I repeated my demand. They apologised and backed away.

I again asked who they were. They were locksmiths checking the locks, one of them said. Bullshit. Neither of them was carrying anything but a key. Certainly not a locksmith kit. It smacked of two covert cops taking a quick 'look-see'. I concluded that Tasmania Police had got wind of our inquiries and had decided to see who we really were, and, more to the point, how professional we were. The two men backed away, refusing to engage in conversation and re-locked the adjoining door. I opened the door onto the corridor and watched them walk briskly towards the lift. We immediately rang reception and asked if locksmiths were on the floor, to which the answer was no.

The three of us suddenly felt very vulnerable. We were a long way from home and without any protection. Tim offered to set a trap. He rigged up a covert camera in the room, a tiny fisheye lens that fitted into the socket of a power point. That night we made a lot of noise talking with the concierge at reception about where we should eat. The hotel management was in no doubt that we were out for the night and we made it easy for surveillance operatives to follow us. Over the next couple of hours, we enjoyed our meal in a seafood restaurant.

When we returned to the hotel, Tim checked the covert camera. He played the footage, which showed someone opening the door from the adjoining room. The door stayed open for just under thirty seconds, then it was closed again, and locked. That was all that was captured. The positioning of the camera didn't allow us to see the faces of whoever had looked or come in. The angle was too acute. However, it confirmed that someone was on to us.

There was still no sign of Meaghan, and I felt for Eve. She was funding the entire operation and was looking haggard. This was the seventh year she had been on the trail, and so far she had nothing much to show for it. We decided to abort the meeting attempt and fly home. We began packing. Checking out, we were met with another unpleasant surprise. The manager had added $250 to Tim's room bill, because, he said, the chambermaid had discovered that Tim had been smoking dope there. The surcharge was for the extra cleaning costs to get rid of the stench of cannabis smoke.

We were standing at reception when this shock was delivered. The allegation was a 'brick'. A blatant lie. We demanded to meet the duty manager in Tim's now vacated room. Within minutes we were with the head man. Eve was ropeable and I had to calm her down, but cleverly, she turned on a recording device.

Once there was quiet, the manager explained that someone must have been smoking dope in the bathroom as the plug hole in the sink showed signs of ash. Now it was my turn, and I called on my previous drug squad knowledge to question his so-called expertise. I demanded that the accusing chambermaid present herself. Of course, there was no such chambermaid. Nor was there any smell of cannabis, cigars or cigarettes. I smashed his ridiculous proposition for six. We left the hotel with a soft-cock apology and Eve followed up with a written complaint, demanding a refund, which they provided. As soon as we were back in Melbourne, as insurance, I had Tim's saliva tested for all forms of illicit drugs. The results were negative, of course.

We were playing in someone else's back yard and we were under the spotlight.

Despite all Gabby's efforts, Meaghan wasn't stepping up. We couldn't keep waiting. Gabby was also showing some troubling behaviour. She was asking for money for her help. Many of her text messages to me were requests for small amounts of money to help her survive and feed her children. Cash for help is a quandary. While it's not unlawful, it's not ideal. It tends to water down the value of evidence. Though every police department in the world offers a range of payments for information, it's not what we wanted to do. Besides, if Gabby pulled a rabbit out of the hat, she might well have been eligible for part of the $40,000 reward offered by the Free Sue campaign, which had nothing to do with me.

In early February, within a week of being home, death came knocking once more. Another heart attack. This time I was only minutes from help. I was rushed to Royal Melbourne Hospital where my cardiologist went to work. I had three stents installed in an artery. I came out of the procedure like a cat that was running out of lives, immensely grateful for another chance. I checked out of hospital on Valentine's Day and very gingerly went home. My cardiologist handed me a spare stent in a tiny jar, in case I needed to do repairs in the future! His idea of a joke. I smiled and took up some serious rest.

During my time in hospital, Gabby had agreed to come to Melbourne. She was willing to sign an affidavit outlining all she knew about Meaghan. Sue Neill-Fraser's lawyers were keen to hear what she would say. I agreed to write up her statement and to hand her over to a lawyer who would do the legal stuff. On 15 February, the day after my discharge, I went against doctor's orders and sat in a hotel room in Melbourne with Gabby for eight hours with a camera and audio equipment. I wrote up twenty pages detailing her involvement with Meaghan. There was only one opportunity to get this done, then I could be free of Gabby and get some rest. I got on with it. Then handed her over to the lawyers and went back to bed. It took me a long while to recover from my heart procedure.

Unbeknown to me Gabby was arrested upon her return to Hobart. She was remanded in custody on charges of possession of handguns, a guest at Risdon Prison again. That's all I heard. Except for one more thing: detectives were mounting an investigation into what she had been up to with me, Eve and Tim. Her mobile phone was undergoing data tests to extract all the communications she'd had with me. That was okay. The police could have simply asked and my lawyer would have posted them a copy of all my texts to and from her. All they would learn was that Gabby had a desire to help a woman in prison and her help amounted to trying to get Meaghan Vass to meet with me. Plus, she'd tried to tickle my till a few times along the way. If they had probed deeply enough they would have seen that on one occasion Gabby and her kids slept in the alcove of a shop door. The woman was practically destitute. Her own mother had kicked her out. Without a home, she and her kids were living a hand-to-mouth existence. But she was still willing to help. Now she was back in the bin, and her children would keep crying. I feared for her future.

I also feared what might happen to Eve, Tim and myself as we decided to push on.

The anchor on the yacht

IN EVERY INVESTIGATION, WHEN THE COINS FALL, NOT ALL of them come up heads. Not all the minutiae relating to a crime is discovered. All you can hope is that you have tried your hardest, covered all the ground, and exposed at least the most important clues. But just as it's easy to miss something in an investigation, sometimes the thing that is missing is blatantly obvious. Staring you in the face. You can see it, you just can't grab it. It's the tease to the puzzle.

I recall the words of Robert Richter QC, one of those working with us to uncover the truth of Bob's disappearance. Robert was the man I would often go to for advice. He is arguably Australia's greatest criminal defence advocate and had joined the pro bono team long ago. The conviction of Sue Neill-Fraser is in his words the worst injustice he has ever seen, and he yells it to the media whenever he can, demanding a royal commission. One day I was sitting in his office, discussing my frustrations. Every now and again Robert comes out with a saying, a few words that make you think harder, deeper. He was referring to Meaghan Vass. 'She is the anchor, Colin. The anchor to what happened. Her DNA is on the yacht. You have to keep researching, keep digging. She holds the key. She is the missing link, and her DNA is your anchor. Don't ever forget that.'

I finally got to meet Meaghan in March 2017. She was then twenty-three years old. I have met hundreds of Meaghan-types before: years living on the streets, issues at home, poorly schooled, angry, smoker, drinker, drug user, long-term recipient of social welfare benefits, and exposed to regular episodes of violence and, almost always, a thief. I know the Meaghan-type well, not only because of my police work, but because I once lived a life like hers. I came from a broken home myself. I was in and out of a boys' home, running amok on the streets as a fourteen-year-old. Eventually, you grow out of it, or at least I did.

Within a day of meeting Meaghan, I got it with her. I could see her hurt and comprehend her eleven-year career on the streets of Hobart. She was a scared 23-year-old and I figured she had been scared since she first ran away from home at the tender age of twelve. And there was another layer to Meaghan's pain that surely made her more withdrawn, more fearful, than her troubled background could account for. A boyfriend she was sometimes living with, Justin Tonner, had been murdered, stabbed to death a year before I met her.

It was due to the decency of a woman whom I'll call Sharyn that my meeting with Meaghan finally came about. Her history was just as traumatic as so many who have lived on the streets; however, Sharyn had great dignity and a real sense of caring. She enjoyed the company of knockabouts and was one of the motorcycle gang hangers-on. She adored bikers. Nothing wrong with that in my view; we humans always gravitate to people or groups that treat us fairly. It was there that she befriended Meaghan. Meaghan, she knew, relied on the generosity of her mates for a bed, often just a couple of cushions on a frayed couch. She had a lot of mates, but few friends. Sharyn saw what I saw in the 23-year-old: someone who wanted to be better, but simply didn't know how.

Sharyn had seen the large 'What happened to Bob Chappell?' billboard erected in the centre of Hobart by the Free Sue crowd. It had been there for many years, offering a $40,000 reward to anyone with credible information that might help Sue. Sharyn rang the phone number on the billboard. She wanted to help and her details ended up being passed on to me. While most callers were just time wasters, Sharyn was clearly different. We met for a quick drink at the Hobart airport. She could see that I was genuine, and offered to broker a meeting with Meaghan, who had been staying in her spare bedroom. I told her I was an author of many books, researching this fascinating case. She was happy to help as long as her name was kept out of it.

While Meaghan was reticent about what had happened on *Four Winds*, Sharyn felt she wanted to talk. And after our drink, Sharyn vouched for me to Meaghan. The vouching system in the underworld is highly valued, and I have used it many times. If someone from that world knows you well enough and thinks you're straight up, they will vouch for you to someone else in that world. The person vouching knows they'd better not stuff up when they speak up for someone. Many a criminal has been bashed or even killed for vouching for someone who ended up being an undercover cop or a 'shitman', a low-life. Sharyn assessed me as I did her, and she vouched for me. And Meaghan agreed to meet me. That's how it works in the concrete jungle.

Initially, Sharyn planned for me to meet Meaghan at her tiny weatherboard home. Then, if we got on, a formal meeting would be held in a hotel, neutral territory. I was told that Meaghan was keen to have support and keen to talk. I offered to organise a solicitor to help Meaghan with any legal issues. The solicitor I contacted, David Gonzalez, arranged his own travel to Hobart. He was Melbourne-based and would remain on standby for the duration. He offered his services pro bono.

Meanwhile, Eve organised a positive psychology counsellor, Kylie, to help Meaghan. Our briefing on Meaghan had hooked her. She had a small window in which she could see Meaghan and, depending on how they got on, Kylie would make herself available for further consultations with her. Next, Eve organised a forensic hypnotherapist, Alfred Podhorodecki, who was happy to act pro bono. Eve had worked with him before and he had a wall covered with qualifications. He also had a strong police background. He had been an inspector with Victoria Police before establishing his practice. His expertise was in relaxing patients who had to remember something difficult or painful. We figured that Meaghan might want to avail herself of both these specialists.

Tim Smart would film the entire meeting to record not only Meaghan's words, but also her demeanour. We needed to be able to show that no one was twisting her arm to force her into saying anything. And Meaghan needed to know we were recording the meeting. We would advise Sue Neill-Fraser's legal team if Meaghan recalled anything useful.

Tim had set up the hotel room with vision and sound before we headed off to speak to Meaghan at Sharyn's house, in a poor part of Hobart about a twenty-minute drive from the centre of town. The neighbourhood was occupied by battlers. Bikers were known to come and go from Sharyn's place and there were eyes and ears everywhere. Any strange car in the street would be quickly detected, especially something like the white Toyota sedan we had hired. We could easily be mistaken for surveillance cops. At least Tim, who would stay in the car, was dressed in his usual never-ironed Western shirt and Levis. His shabby look was an asset when we were dealing with junkies, thieves, vagabonds and riff-raff.

For security, I switched on a small recording device as I approached the front door of Sharyn's house. I had seen two heavy-set bikers, in their leather colours, leaving the house a few minutes earlier. They were half my age and twice my size and I was no match for them should things go wrong. The potential for violence against me was real; however, the meeting was important. At least, should I be set upon, it would be recorded! When I knocked on Sharyn's door her 60-kilogram mastiff-Staffordshire terrier cross came charging towards the front door, barking the house down. He looked at me through the flywire screen and showed me his dentures. Sharyn howled at him to head for the back yard and I gingerly stepped inside.

Meaghan was everything I expected. Underweight by possibly 10 kilograms, she was fidgety and unable to look me in the eye. She doodled in a notebook as we chatted. Sharyn stayed outside with her dog, ensuring a spot of quiet. For the next two hours, Meaghan tried her best to sit still. But failed. She was an emotional wreck. She looked as if she hadn't eaten for a week and she sucked on a bong constantly. Her appearance was stamped with the life she had lived over the past eleven years, and all the hellholes she had been in, through, and out the other side of. I did my best to try to lighten the mood. I made a few jokes and smart-arse comments about life, anything to build a rapport.

Finally, we connected, and Meaghan seemed to want to talk. She made it clear that she wanted to recall what had happened on Australia Day, 2009, but the memories of that night were locked and she hoped to unpick them with me. She was obviously troubled about that night. Something dark had happened and Meaghan was searching for light. She had no faith in anyone except for Snapper. I would have to work to get her to trust me. The good thing was that she said over and over that she wanted to remember, to unblock her mind. I relished the challenge of helping her do that.

As I watched Meaghan doodling I recalled that Tasmania Police hadn't put any time into Meaghan. They had developed no strategy to elicit information from her. In fact, they never actually formally interviewed Meaghan in a record of interview, despite her puddle of DNA found at a murder crime scene. I found that absurd. I remember investigating a double murder in Melbourne and the key to solving the case lay in the hands of one of the murderers' wives. It was incumbent on me to do what was necessary to win the wife over and hopefully get her to give evidence against those involved. It took me eight months. We went from 'Get fucked, I'm not talking' to 'I want to go into witness protection and tell you everything.' I wondered if I had eight months available for Meaghan. I doubted it, but at least I could make a start.

I opened by explaining what DNA is, and that her DNA had been found on *Four Winds*. She made no comment about this, but did tell me that she left Mara House on Australia Day, 2009 and went out with two young men, one a teenage thief, the other her dodgy boyfriend (who I will call Dodger from here on in). She said something happened that night that scared her. 'I mean, it's triggered me not talking about it … I remember knocking around with [Dodger].'

She went out with Dodger for three years. 'It was a thrill. He'd come in a stolen car, you know, we'd drive around.' If Dodger had suggested robbing a bloke on his yacht, 'I probably would have been all for it, you know. It's money for piss, whatever. I was sixteen.' She then made an alarming comment: 'I would have … gone to the ends of the earth for them, you know.'

She remembered the conversation she'd had with me on the phone in January, but she distanced herself from the actual words she said about 'partying' on 'the old guy's yacht' and 'a fight' breaking out. As well as 'I saw it but fucked off. Took off, in a dinghy.' Meaghan said that back in 2009 there were 'homeless young people going around knocking things off yachts. Nine out of ten times it was probably [Dodger].' She thought that 'If it was a scam to get money for piss or something like that, then probably yes, I would have been involved.' She went on to make it clear that Dodger was a thief who stole often. 'We were doing scams to make money so we could get on the piss … shit, we used to do shit like that all the time, and we used to think it was a thrill.'

The conversation drifted back to the violence on *Four Winds*. 'You think something horrible has happened?' I asked her.

'Well, that's what I said. I don't know. Most likely.'

The conversation shifted to her diary. Without prompting, she said, 'Gabby already told you about the diary.' This was significant. It indicated that Meaghan knew I had heard about the entry she'd made in January 2009: *It wasn't meant to go like that. [Dodger] did it.* She thought I was in possession of her diary, and said she thought it would help her memory if she could read through it. But I'd never had her diary, much as I would have loved to look at it and the potential goldmine of evidence it might have contained. And I would never find it. Who knows where it is now?

Meaghan had a mantra. Whenever she wanted to ignore a question or was afraid to answer it, she would say, 'I can't remember.' She was able to recall many things over many years, but as soon as we focused on Australia Day night, 2009, or on the specifics of the thefts – who, when, why, how – she would fall back on her mantra. 'I can't remember.' Meaghan had something locked away in her mind, I was sure, but she couldn't find the key, or didn't want to. At one point she said that she was 'haunted' by the whole Australia Day saga.

Meaghan did recall that her mother had a close friend in the police force, a policewoman detective she named, but I cannot for legal reasons. This was enlightening. I had come across her when I was reading crime reports about the burglaries on Australia Day night, near the water. The policewoman detective's name was on one that had a note about 'Megan', which was written on a report in pen and then obliterated. Trouble was, you could still see the name. Meaghan said the policewoman detective used to babysit her when she was a child. She thought the woman and her mum had spoken back at the time Meaghan was called to give evidence at Sue Neill-Fraser's trial.

She remembered being asked about her DNA by plainclothes police in 2010. 'The last I remember like we'd been to court, or whatever, and I signed some piece of paper, or something, but I'd given all the information that I needed to, and they wouldn't bother, like that'd be it.'

It was those words that troubled me. It was starting to make sense why Meaghan didn't offer a lot of help or evidence at the trial. Perhaps people in authority were assisting her.

Towards the end of our chat I asked Meaghan if she'd been warned off talking about what happened on *Four Winds*. 'If you were with Dodger that night on the yacht, would he have said something to you like "Don't tell ever ...; [don't] ever talk about or discuss [this] or tell anybody"'?

'I don't know, but ...' she mumbled in reply.

'Would that be what he's like?'

'True,' she answered. 'Yeah, I gather. He would have said that. But he probably would have ... he probably would have just expected me to know, you know, if he's doing something dodgy and keep your mouth shut.'

I asked Meaghan if she thought Sue was guilty of killing Bob. Meaghan answered, 'I wouldn't say she was guilty ... It's horrible. I would do anything I could to help her.'

During our meeting, Meaghan whimpered occasionally, and cried once or twice. Any time Dodger was mentioned set her off. On other occasions she doggedly refused to recall anything. Bizarrely, despite her mantra of 'I can't remember', she sat and workshopped her memory for two hours, trying to get closer to telling me what happened after she left Mara House on 26 January 2009.

Meaghan saddened and frustrated me. On the one hand, she implied that she may have been stealing around the time of Bob's disappearance, or at least that she was in the company of those who were. But not once did she admit she had anything to do with the incident aboard *Four Winds*. On a positive note, Meaghan showed a willingness to swear an affidavit about her role that night. 'If you could remember, would you put it on an affidavit?' I asked her.

'Yes, I would … to get her out.' I asked again and she repeated her answer. She even backed up her answer by saying, 'Nothing [about swearing an affidavit] worries me.' This was important to me. By saying this, she opened a door. A door that I might well walk through, in time. I immediately had an idea ticking in my head, one that I would need to think over, and talk to Robert Richter about.

I watched her doodling on a couple of small diaries. I asked her for something to write notes in, and she handed me an old notebook stamped 2016. I flicked through it as we talked and came across an intriguing handwritten comment. Dated July, it read, *I have friends in HIGH places*. What could it mean? It made me wonder.

* * *

Nine months earlier, in June 2016, I had telephoned Meaghan's mother to ask her to broker a meeting between Meaghan and me. There were a lot of very experienced lawyers working on the Sue Neill-Fraser defence campaign, I told her, and perhaps Meaghan could receive an indemnity from prosecution in exchange for telling what she knew about being on *Four Winds* in 2009. She listened. I also mentioned the reward offered by the Free Sue campaign. Perhaps Meaghan would be eligible, if her evidence helped exonerate Sue. Meaghan had a small child whom she had given up. The funds could help Meaghan relaunch her life, I suggested. I was grasping at straws, but Meaghan's mother seemed to be listening.

She agreed to meet me the following day, at Maldini's cafe in Hobart. She mentioned that she had a 'friend who was a police officer'. This worried me. I knew about police culture. I had come from such a culture. If someone is convicted of a crime, police culture demands that from that point forward you reaffirm the conviction. It is extremely rare for police to have an open-minded view on a convicted person. Once found guilty, always guilty.

The next day, as I was heading to the cafe, I received a text message: *Hi Colin. Sorry for last minute notice but I will not be at Maldini's today after all. Too much opposition from my police friend & my family. Cheers.*

Her text was a massive blow. I stood in the street staring at it, hoping I was reading it incorrectly. But it was very clear and very final. Her mention of her 'police friend' would weigh heavily on me for the rest of my research. It still does. Had I hit a nerve? Had the policewoman detective gone into damage control? Had I set off alarm bells by suggesting that Meaghan was a valuable asset in finding out the truth?

I replied, keeping the line of communication open: *This offers the chance to wipe the slate clean on this matter, perhaps. Think it over some more. It would all be done properly and with legal representation. Glad to talk anytime. Colin.*

I never heard from Meaghan's mother again.

* * *

When I left Sharyn's house after my meeting with Meaghan, I asked if I could hold on to the notebook. She nodded. I tucked it into my jacket pocket and then left, setting the mastiff-Staffy cross into a spin again. I could still hear him barking half a kilometre away. When I got back into our hire car I noticed Tim's nervousness. He was wearing a pair of sunglasses as well as a pair of reading glasses on his forehead. He looked as sweaty and fidgety as Meaghan. He confided that after about half an hour he had become so worried he'd crouched down low in the driver's seat, still just able to peer over the steering wheel so he could see the front door of Sharyn's house. A car load of rough-head bikies went past and stirred worry in Tim. What played on him most was my comment, two hours earlier, before I knocked on Sharyn's door. 'If you see bikies arrive be prepared to call the cops. If they start bashing me I'll throw a chair through one of the windows to let you know.' My comment was a mix of correct procedure and humour. The latter was obviously lost on Tim. I made it up to him later that night with three fingers of Sullivans Cove whisky, and a few belly laughs.

During the night I couldn't help but remind myself that getting a witness to give crucial evidence relies on the effort one is prepared to put into that witness. Whether you're a detective or an investigative journalist, the same applies. Show a bit of humility, listen to their heartache stories and you may receive a reward for your patience. You reap what you sow.

The last thing Meaghan and I had spoken about was the hypnotherapist she would meet the following day. She was nervous, but willing. She wanted to unlock her memory. And find out what she was doing on the night of Australia Day, 2009. But she'd added, 'What if it breaks me the fuck out?'

I tried to sleep.

* * *

A bit of a postscript with regard to Meaghan's ex-boyfriend Dodger. Due to my work with Meaghan, and the pressure the police found themselves under, two detectives finally interviewed him in August 2017. Eight years after Bob Chappell's murder. It took all of 38 minutes. Take out the top-and-tail hellos and goodbyes, plus time lost looking for photos, and it might weigh in at half an hour. Their opening question was hardly stealthy: 'Were you involved in the murder?'

Dodger's answer was predictable. Did they expect him to say anything else but no? He also denied knowing Gabby, Stephen Gleeson or Pablo, for that matter, and appeared to have very little knowledge of Sandy Bay. His answers were a series of 'no's and 'nah's. The guy knew nothing, apparently.

When the detectives got around to Meaghan, Dodger claimed to have met her only a few times, 'only eighteen months ago, or something like that'. Putting their first meeting in early 2016. An obvious lie. They were dating back in 2009. This was flushed out at the trial. He mentioned the stabbing death of Meaghan's past boyfriend Justin in that same year as a peg to hang his lie onto. 'She was just fucked in the head. That's the truth to it.'

The two detectives lifted their game, asking a few sleeper questions to catch Dodger out. 'Eight and a half years ago when Bob Chappell went missing, is it fair to say you didn't know Meaghan back then?' When Dodger said this was correct, the detectives feigned surprise. What about the complaints Meaghan's grandmother had made to police that Dodger was hanging around Meaghan in early 2009, they asked. (The grandmother felt Dodger was a bad influence on Meaghan.) Dodger again denied knowing her back then; neither were they ever were boyfriend and girlfriend, he added. Although he readily admitted to being a burglar and car thief, he'd never broken in anywhere with Meaghan and she never stayed overnight with him in 2009, he claimed. Not surprisingly, Dodger also knew nothing of the murder at Sandy Bay and had never been involved in stealing from yachts.

Then came the double whammy. One of the detectives revealed that he had seen Dodger's Facebook account where he posted news stories related to Bob's murder. Dodger denied this. The detective pressed him. 'Have you ever posted anything in relation to Sue Neill-Fraser's matter?'

'Oh, I doubt it.' Dodger maintained his clearly ridiculous position, saying that he didn't even know the password to his Facebook account.

Then the other detective jumped in, revealing that he had checked the records of Mara House for the evening of Australia Day, which showed Meaghan was 'to spend the night at [Dodger's]'.

Dodger was caught off guard. 'All right, yes.' He admitted that Meaghan may have stayed at his place. 'I used to be a male slut,' he boasted.

It's a bit like pulling teeth, interviewing characters like this, yet satisfying once you start having some success. So what was going on with these detectives? Having cracked Dodger's outer shell, discovered his Facebook fascination for following news of the Bob Chappell murder case and exposed his lies, why did they just walk away half an hour into the game? They closed the interview down at that point. Why? I wanted to know what he might have divulged if they had worked him hard, kept at him for a few hours of interrogation?

Coincidentally, one of the detectives who interviewed Dodger also investigated the attempted theft of the dinghy from Waimea Jetty in Sandy Bay a week or so before Bob's disappearance. The offender left behind a screwdriver and shifting spanner allegedly covered in 'blood'. As I noted earlier, for some reason the police report of that petty crime was designated 'Highly Protected'. I am sure that if Sue's barrister, Tom Percy QC, had known about the theft (and the 2017 police interview with Dodger) at the time of Sue Neill-Fraser's appeal, he would have put Dodger in the witness box. He would have made a meal out of him, finishing off what the cops had failed to complete.

'I can't go to jail'

FINALLY, MEAGHAN AGREED TO SIT DOWN IN THE HOTEL room that Tim and I had set up with cameras and sound. A controlled interview, filmed and formal. Journalists and authors do this all the time and we set up a room. Even though Eve wasn't there to see it, as she was holidaying with her family, she was elated. Over eight years she had spent a small fortune trying to prove Sue's innocence. Was this to be the moment on which everything would turn? Meaghan had dropped in to the hotel the night before with Sharyn. She'd seemed toey, and she and Sharyn had downed a quick drink before I'd taken her into the room to check out the cameras and microphones. Tim had wandered in behind us and I'd introduced them. She'd looked around and nodded at what she saw. Then, like lightning, she'd left, promising to be back the next day.

It wasn't a real surprise the following day to discover that there was a change of plans. However, the change would only be for the better. Snapper was coming along with Meaghan to hold her hand. I was rapt. I knew Meaghan felt safe with him. He guided her. What I wasn't certain of was whether Snapper, the head of the motorcycle club, would accept me, the ex-cop, now author and documentary film-maker, snooping around in Hobart. We had only spoken on the phone up until now and I knew I had to have my game-day play spot-on to get the tick from the main man.

I could hear Snapper approaching before I could see him. His ute could be heard roaring along the street. Its exhaust was so loud that heads turned, then quickly turned back the other way once they realised it was driven by a rough and tough biker. Snapper stepped from the ute along with Meaghan. They were chatting. I sized him up and I was a tad surprised. He wasn't that tall, but he was fit looking. He didn't appear to be a nutter. He seemed normal, whatever that means these days.

Snapper and I sat on bar stools in the downstairs lounge and had a beer. Meaghan sat with Kylie, the counsellor Eve had arranged to support her, just a bar stool away, in earshot. The drink was to soften the mood and it gave Snapper the opportunity to assess me. He explained that his late father was once a cop. And his daughter was in the police department in Victoria. I was taken aback, but it's often the way. Black sheep in police families. I found Snapper to be an all right sort of guy. Tough? Yeah. Savvy? Of course, he had to be to run the motorcycle club. And he'd need rat cunning to still be sitting on the bar stool next to me. As we talked I felt that he had great affection for Meaghan. These two were a couple, despite the age difference.

I broached the subject of Sue Neill-Fraser being in prison. He was happy to talk about it and it became obvious that he thought she had been wrongly convicted. At one point he said, 'It's not right.' I asked if Meaghan had discussed it with him and he said something I will never forget. 'She's told me she was on the yacht, but you've got to get her to tell you.' So true. By the end of our drink, it was time to get the show on the road. Walking to our room, I couldn't help but think that Snapper was on our side. He wanted Meaghan to talk about it. He had become an asset.

Snapper was camera-shy and chose to sit outside, in the corridor. He took a chair by the lift door and I took one alongside him. Meaghan walked into the room with Kylie and they sat and talked for forty-five minutes. Meaghan was to talk as much as she wanted with Kylie first, to relax and let go of any anxiety. They hit it off, instantly. Kylie's speciality is dealing with people having trouble discussing particular issues. In fact, she teaches this subject to psychology students in Melbourne. Her ear can pick up what the person is trying to say, where they want to take the conversation and what they want to avoid talking about. Once or twice I put my ear to the door, but all I could hear was the two women talking softly. The hypnotherapist, Alfred, remained on standby, in his room.

When it came time for Alfred to sit down with Meaghan, it all went to shit. His role was to see if she wanted to try hypnotherapy to help her remember what had happened on the night of Australia Day, 2009. He had barely walked into the room before Meaghan's voice echoed throughout the hotel. She was yelling. I bit my tongue and crossed my fingers. Snapper raised his eyebrows.

Things gradually quietened down, and Snapper and I talked a little about the chances of Meaghan getting an indemnity from prosecution. I explained that the lawyers involved in Sue Neill-Fraser's defence would handle that issue with great care.

He seemed to understand the legal issues and looked unfazed. Then we heard Meaghan yelling again.

I knocked on the door with Snapper standing alongside me. The hypnotherapist walked out, shaking his head as he headed back to his room. He looked as though he had seen action in Gallipoli. Snapper stepped inside and I followed. Meaghan had become aggressive. Wild. She was yelling abuse at Snapper and me, but still being nice as pie with Kylie. Meeting Alfred had tripped her barriers. She believed his hypnosis would put her under a spell; she would lose consciousness. How she came to that conclusion was a mystery. The day before she'd seemed keen to try hypnosis, but today she was dead against it. Perhaps she was afraid of what she might recall.

Kylie tried to get Meaghan to sit down and relax – the cameras were on all the time – but she refused, and she was still yelling. As she yelled she paced around the room like a caged tigress, working herself into a frenzy. Snapper tried to calm her down too, telling her she would feel better if she talked about what was troubling her, about what happened on *Four Winds*. 'Put it behind you,' he told her. He was extraordinarily patient, but she didn't want his guidance, and insisted on leaving, demanding that Snapper go with her. The room door was always unlocked, and she was free to leave at any time, but she was terribly conflicted. Snapper reminded her that she had made the appointment to talk about *Four Winds*. Meaghan claimed that she was 'fine to do it this morning, I was on a fucking roll'. Snapper reassured Meaghan: 'These people seem all right to me, darl.'

I had no doubt that Snapper was our winning card here. He was trying his hardest to help Meaghan get rid of the monkey on her back, persevering in the face of her disruptions and crazy claims. At one point, Meaghan said that Sharyn had threatened her. (Sharyn wasn't even in the room; she was downstairs.) Snapper replied, 'Bullshit, you're just using that as an excuse.'

Meaghan's mood was erratic: she would laugh and then become angry, raging about the hypnotherapist, whom she called a 'cunt'. Then she would demand to leave, and yet she stayed. Kylie also encouraged her to speak about the night on the yacht. 'If you want to do it with me here, we are going to have to get it finished ... Snapper is right here, he's behind you, and it's done.' I dipped my oar in, with little effect. 'This could be the biggest opportunity you've got. You probably don't see it.'

Meaghan then dropped a bombshell about the duress she had been under since January 2009. 'Eleven [Meaghan's words] fucking years it's haunted me, mate.' Snapper was quick to reply. 'Yes, we know that, and these are the people who are not fucking with you.' I was mighty pleased with Snapper's effort. He urged her on, obviously wanting her to divulge to us what she'd previously told him about that night: 'For two and a half fucking years I've known.' He tried to get her to relax. 'Lay down on the fuckin' bed. Put your fuckin' feet up.'

I played on the image of Sue in jail, trying to tug on Meaghan's heartstrings. Again, she claimed she'd been haunted for eleven years by the thought of it. 'Well, now's your chance,' I told her. 'We know it wasn't your fault.' She turned to Snapper. 'Can you please take me away from this shit?'

I tried again. 'Meaghan, it wasn't your fault.'

'Talk to him,' Snapper said.

I told her I believed that someone had done the wrong thing by her. She agreed this was true, but that I didn't know what she was going through. It was during this part of the conversation that Meaghan sat down for a few seconds and quietly said to herself, loudly enough for us to hear, 'I can't go to jail.' I was taken aback by these five powerful words. It all started to make sense to me. She feared imprisonment. I figured this was why she was avoiding an open discussion on the subject. The poor young woman was fearful of her own liberty, plain and simple. All I could think to reply was, 'You're scared.' She fell silent and seemed to be in deep thought.

Despite Snapper urging her to tell us what she knew, all our cajoling came to nothing. She shut down. And kept saying that she wanted to leave, although no one was restraining her. Every time it looked like the storm of emotion might break, she would arc herself up again and it would start all over.

Finally, as if it was her last word on the subject, the last crumb she would drop to us waiting dodos, she came up with another powerful comment: 'Well guess what, mate; it wasn't fucking me, so there's one for you.'

Snapper replied, 'We know who it was … Meaghan, we know who it was and why you were there with [sic].' That comment resonated with me. It's exactly how I saw it with Meaghan. She was a homeless kid in the wrong place at the wrong time with the wrong people, when something horrible happened. She saw something that had haunted her all this time. An act, or series of acts, that shocked her into suppressing her memories. I've seen victims of crime and innocent onlookers react this way in the past, especially girls and women.

Shortly afterwards, Meaghan stormed out of the room, slamming the door behind her. Kylie followed her out. 'Who's she scared of?' I named a crime family in Hobart.

Snapper agreed Meaghan had more fear for this family than talking to us about the issue. Snapper replied, 'She's never asked me to help. I put some names down, but she never changed her demeanour or looked at it or anything.'

As Snapper and I prepared to leave the room, he said, referring to Meaghan's shouting, 'Mate, I tell you, if I fucking fight with her then that's how she leaves most of the time, you know. People think that I've raped or killed her half the time.' We heard Meaghan yelling in the corridor. 'You can see how loud her voice is.'

On another day, I might have laughed at her tantrums. But this day was way too important.

The tornado that was Meaghan Vass lasted less than an hour. I headed for the bar and ordered a beer and sat, morose, with Kylie and Alfred. While we were working through our drinks, Kylie offered up an astute comment. 'Meaghan was certainly on the yacht.' I just nodded. I was already convinced of that by the size of the sample of her DNA. But what Kylie was saying was more profound. At no time in the hotel room did Meaghan say, 'I was never there.' Nor did she say, 'None of this has got anything to do with me.' She did say that she was trying to help. And that she thought of Sue Neill-Fraser daily. At times Meaghan seemed to be on the brink of telling all. Offering up answers. Then she stopped and went into her 'I can't remember' routine. However, the most chilling thing she did say was that what had happened that night had 'haunted' her for (in her words) eleven years.

Kylie left to catch a plane back to Melbourne. I asked her to make notes of the conversation she'd had with Meaghan alone before Alfred came into the room and the warfare started. She promised to send them through. I was buoyed by Kylie's cool-headed comments and decided we were only on second base. The game was still in play. A few days later, she sent me her notes. They were gold.

Revealed in Kylie's notes was that Meaghan had confided to her that she planned to say 'I can't remember' during the session. Meaghan had also said more than once that 'Sue is innocent'. And how, if she could remember what had happened, Sue would be released immediately from prison.

'Okay, so if you could remember, what would you say?' Kylie asked her.

'If I could remember, I would get her out of prison tomorrow. She hasn't got much time to live, she's old. She should die at home,' Meaghan said.

'You seem to feel for Sue. Is it important to you that you remember?'

'Yes,' Meaghan admitted. 'She's innocent.'

'Do you have any idea why you can't remember?' Kylie asked.

'Because of what happened. Maybe I've suppressed it,' Meaghan offered. 'You know that they say that happens.'

'What would life be like for you if all this situation with Sue was over?'

'For years I've had this over my head,' Meaghan said. 'I've been carrying this since 2009.'

Kylie noted Meaghan's certainty that 'Sue is innocent', but wondered how she could be so sure if she could not remember what happened. After absorbing this riddle, I asked Kylie to get to a lawyer as quickly as she could to swear an affidavit.

Yes, the game was still on.

The statutory declaration

A MONTH LATER I WAS BACK IN HOBART WITH A BAG FULL OF research to undertake and potential witnesses to meet. It seemed aggrieved people were coming out of the woodwork to talk to me. Trouble was, not a lot of it was relevant. Much of it was hearsay, inadmissible. In the few weeks since I had been away, getting a start on my manuscript, I had received a text from Sharyn saying she intended talking to Meaghan again, about *Four Winds*. *Going to have one last effort soon. Talk soon when I am able.* Snapper was also still on the team, willing to help Meaghan unburden herself of the horror she saw on the yacht that night. Then Sharyn called me; she was having some success. I told Sharyn I would fly back to Hobart to have one last try. I then went to see Eve Ash, cap in hand, and asked for more money. Eve, always the optimist, took out a second mortgage and found the funds.

I arrived back in Hobart on 21 April 2017. Sharyn had agreed to meet me for dinner and a chat. She'd rarely been out to a restaurant, such was her life, so she opted for a Chinese cafe in North Hobart. We discussed drafting a simple statement on paper for Meaghan that she might be happy to sign, rather than trying to have her sit still and talk through what she knew, in front of cameras and microphones. Sharyn saw merit in the plan. I vividly recalled my meeting with Meaghan in Sharyn's house a month earlier when Meaghan said she would be happy to swear an affidavit. It was time for that affidavit.

The reason I chose this path was the reaction Meaghan had to a formal interview with cameras. She reacted badly, despite having Snapper there to offer help. Why not opt for a softer way, by a plain paper statement. After all, Meaghan was the one who said she was happy to go that way.

I rang Snapper and he, too, thought that drafting a statement for Meaghan to sign was a good idea. He added that Meaghan would never tell anyone who she was on the yacht with; her statement would have to be about her only. I got it. It was stepping stones, with Meaghan. She could say what she was comfortable with now, and she could always build on it later.

I went back to my Airbnb accommodation on the rise above Sandy Bay and punched out a very short, easy-to-follow narrative of what Meaghan had previously told me. A summary of the salient points. I drew on what I believed she had said to Snapper, as well as what she had said to me by phone, in the hotel room with Kylie, and at Sharyn's house. It acknowledged that police had told her, in 2010, that her DNA was on the yacht. The statement was not much more than one hundred words, and had taken eight years to come about.

My name is Meaghan Vass. My date of birth is 14 October 1993. I am 23 years old. In 2010, I was told my DNA was found on the Four Winds *yacht off Sandy Bay, Hobart. I was on the* Four Winds *yacht on the night of Australia Day, 2009. I was there with people that I won't name. I don't want to give any details except that I was on the yacht. The lady Sue Neill-Fraser was not on the yacht. I have never met her, I don't know her; I just know she is in prison. I don't want to say why I was on the yacht and I don't want to say any more.*

The lawyers in our team saw nothing untoward in this draft statement: it was a summation of commonly known facts, supplied by Meaghan. The next day I drove to the motorcycle club headquarters and banged on the massive metal front door. The outside sensor lights went on and CCTV cameras were pointing at me from all directions. It felt like I was onstage. I probably was, my every move beamed inside and being viewed by a gang of well-fed angry men. Snapper came to the door and I waited while he fetched Meaghan. They lived in a small mobile home in the rear yard of the club grounds. Meaghan appeared calm, and I tried to be as pleasant as possible, reiterating the points covered in the statement. I could see that this Meaghan, the one in front of me, was a softer person than the version of her that I'd seen tossing a hypnotherapist out of a hotel room. I told her to forget about the cameras of the previous month and the hoo-hah of the hypnotherapist. If she still wanted to unburden herself, I would leave the statement with her and she could read it over. If she agreed with the content, she could sign it in front of a lawyer. I let her know that if she wanted to add or remove any wording she could. Or she could toss the statement in the bin if she so chose.

Meaghan looked it over and nodded, then handed it to Snapper. They would get back to me, she said. I gave Snapper my mobile phone number. When I left, the big metal door slammed shut with a thud.

I planned to be in Hobart until 25 April, Anzac Day, when I was required to be in Melbourne for a family remembrance of my grandfather, who'd served in World War I. So I could only wait around a few more days in Hobart. A couple of days after giving Meaghan the draft statement I had a call from Snapper. Meaghan had misplaced the statement. He asked me to drop around another copy, which I did. The next day I went back to the clubhouse. Meaghan and Snapper asked me to introduce them to a lawyer who could oversee the signing of the statement. Meaghan wanted the lawyer to come to Sharyn's house, and she wanted Snapper with her. Again, Meaghan was the softer version of herself. I guessed that she and Snapper had talked over this course of action a lot in the past days. There was also something she wanted added to the statement: that she had thought about Sue Neill-Fraser 'every day for the past eight years'. She also wanted to say, 'Nobody understands my grief.' She seemed pleased and I left.

The next day I delivered the statement to lawyer Jeff Thompson, who was invaluable to the pro bono team working in Hobart. I briefed Jeff on the wording of Meaghan's statement and the reason for the lack of specific detail. Still, it established that Meaghan and others were on the yacht the night of Australia Day, 2009, and that Sue Neill-Fraser was not. Once I briefed Jeff, I left Tasmania. I went back to Melbourne, sharing some time with my beloved mother and reminiscing about her father, our family's Anzac hero. On the night of 27 April, while I was in Melbourne, Jeff walked into Sharyn's house, carrying a bible. In the negotiations with Snapper and Meaghan around the signing and swearing of Meaghan's statement, the issue of an indemnity from prosecution had arisen. Jeff was of the view that Meaghan, who indicated she might have more evidence to offer, should be protected from prosecution and he wanted to add a clause to that effect to the statement.

As always, Meaghan would not be rushed. She, Snapper and Jeff sat around for an hour drinking tea. Jeff explained the potential ramifications of the statement. He also explained that in due course he would need to make a request for indemnity to the Director of Public Prosecutions. For that reason, the statement would be a statutory declaration, rather than an affidavit. Jeff recalls that Snapper offered Meaghan advice and comfort and that she seemed relaxed. At the business end of the night, Jeff read out every word of the statement, slowly and carefully. He also got Meaghan to recite every word as well, to make sure she understood the contents. Then the statement was signed and sworn by Meaghan.

She and Snapper left the house and headed back to bikie HQ. Jeff sat for a time with Sharyn, thanking her, before heading home. On the way, he rang to update me. His news gave me a lift. It had been a long road and, at last, we might just have turned the corner in this massive dog fight. I sent off a text to Snapper. *You did a good thing today. Thanks for all your efforts. Meaghan did a good thing too, please say thank you. Jeff will look after her. Don't worry! Colin*

Given all the stories we hear about dodgy, violent bikies, it was refreshing to know that there was at least one thoroughly decent biker in Hobart. One who was trying his hardest to help. Although in doing so he was putting his girlfriend at risk. The police who had prosecuted Sue Neill-Fraser would be disappointed by the content of Meaghan's statutory declaration. It indicated that Sue had no part in the death of her partner, making them look like chumps. The DPP might also take a dim view of contradictory evidence falling onto his desk, facts that might embarrass some powerful people. Still, I am a firm believer that the truth must come out, and hoped that any risk or attention the statement drew towards Meaghan would be manageable. Besides, there was a grandmother doing hard time in a concrete cell. I also thought then, and still do, that getting this eight-year-old monkey off Meaghan's back would ultimately help her move on.

About a week later, Jeff Thompson was back at his usual legal work, trying to save a single parent from being evicted from her home for overdue rent. In his haste to get to the tribunal, he bumped into Meaghan Vass. He made a point of stopping and chatting. Curiosity got the better of him and he asked Meaghan why she hadn't told the truth at Sue's trial in 2010. He watched Meaghan deal with his question. Before any words came out she started to fidget, and she held her head in her hands for a while. She seemed to be lost in memory and became distressed. Jeff tried to calm her. Finally, she looked up at Jeff, tears welling in her eyes. 'Because I was fucking scared. I had no one, no one.' Jeff felt great sympathy for the wretched young woman in front of him. He could only imagine how difficult life had been for her. 'Did you have someone to accompany you to court? Or when the police met with you?' he asked.

She began to cry. 'I was all alone. I had nobody.' A compassionate man and lawyer to the underdog, Jeff understood how frightening an ordeal a Supreme Court murder trial would have been for a sixteen-year-old homeless girl without any support. Jeff continued to see Meaghan occasionally around the traps. They always had a few friendly words and he always left her company with an enormous sense of sorrow – for Meaghan and for Sue. Both were locked in their own prisons. One was a concrete cell. The other was a repressed memory of a horror endured late one night.

SANDY BAY
CRIME SCENE

N

Four Winds yacht

Pablo's yacht

0 50 100 150 200

Home of witnesses
that were ignored

Red jacket

Napoleon St

Sue's dinghy found here

Stephen Gleeson's yellow Ford

Sandy Bay
Rowing Club

Witness
Field of Vision

Marleville Esplanade

Sue left dinghy here

Bay
Chandlery

The Royal
Yacht Club

Margaret St

Sue's red jacket

Hairdresser's
house

Sue Neill-Fraser having fun on the *Four Winds* yacht, January 2009.

Bob Chappell on *Four Winds* on 25 January 2009 – the day before he was murdered.

The *Four Winds* yacht. On Australia Day night it was very dark; only 0.1% luminescence.

Lunchtime on 26 January 2009.
Sue at the Royal Yacht Club of Tasmania, hours before Bob was killed.

Sue's dinghy found floating immediately in front of Stephen Gleeson's yellow Ford.

ABOVE: Position of red jacket on the fence of 26 Margaret Street.
BELOW: It was also seen on the Rivulet bridge, on the same morning.

The position of the yellow Ford on the spit of land looking over at *Four Winds* and Pablo's yacht.

Note the high sheds, blocking views from the yacht clubs. Wrest Point Casino is in the background, a kilometre away.

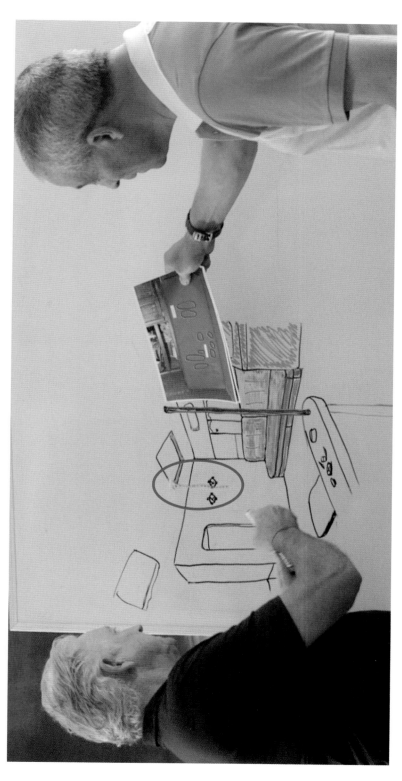

Colin McLaren and Charlie Bezzina discuss the way they believe Bob's body was removed from the yacht through the saloon starboard hatch above the blue couch. The rope dangling from the hatch into the saloon is circled. All this was ignored by the police. The couch had long vertical blood drips, directly below the starboard hatch.

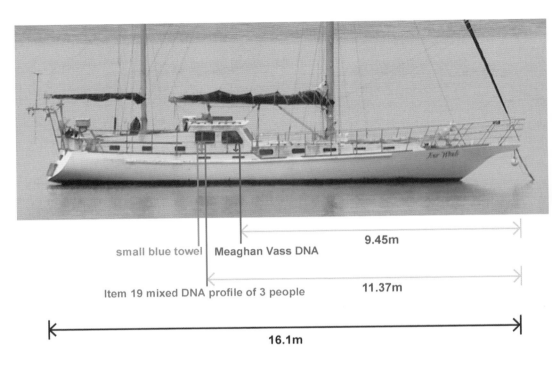

small blue towel   Meaghan Vass DNA   9.45m

Item 19 mixed DNA profile of 3 people   11.37m

16.1m

Colin McLaren, Robert Richter QC and Eve Ash days before their meeting in the premier's office.

I've been smack in the middle of two full-on bushfires in my life. So often it seems they are caused by just a spark. A tiny, insignificant bit of ash can become a fully fledged fire. Jeff hadn't suffered through any bushfires in his fifty years, but he was about to experience a metaphorical one. Rumours of Meaghan Vass's sworn declaration were seeping through the cracks in the walls of the offices of the DPP and police headquarters. Jeff was getting sideways glances from suits and courtroom gowns as he moved about his daily tasks. He caught local lawyers and barristers pointing him out. One day, standing in the halls of justice, a couple of detectives walked past him and glared at him. He was uneasy. The stares and the unwanted attention got worse. Like an Aussie bushfire, things around Jeff Thompson were heating up.

Jeff made an appointment with Daryl Coates, Tasmania's new chief prosecutor. Tim Ellis was no longer with the DPP. Coates, his successor, had an assistant prosecutor, Jack Shapiro, who had been assistant to Ellis back in the days when Sue was tried. Jeff walking into that particular lion's den actually troubled me more than the thought of fronting up at the motorcycle club headquarters.

When Jeff plonked Meaghan's statutory declaration on the DPP's table and took a seat, he was hoping to discuss the issue of her indemnification from prosecution. The meeting soon descended into hostility. Jeff, as usual, remained calm and respectful in his approach; however, the new DPP's mood appeared to worsen as Jeff tried to workshop the statutory declaration and discuss the immediate needs of Meaghan.

The DPP read the short yet powerful statement, focusing on the part where Meaghan stated that she was on *Four Winds* 'with people that I won't name'. Coates insisted that he be told who these persons were. He became animated, his voice high-pitched and angry. Jeff explained that Meaghan was not prepared to name them, and any further information would need to be prefaced by an indemnity from prosecution. A very normal process in cases where fear plays a factor in a witness's testimony.

I have been involved in many murder cases in which indemnification from prosecution has been used to get to the truth of a matter. Coates knew the system; he had probably signed off many indemnities before. Sometimes it's the only available path to the truth, but in this instance the DPP was not at all interested. He demanded over and over to know who the others on the boat were. Jeff was in no position to answer. All he could say was that Meaghan might offer up the names should she be indemnified. That was the purpose of the meeting. When Coates continued to press him, Jeff took a guess and mentioned the names of a couple of persons of interest who had appeared in the many affidavits he had helped gather. It was of little use. The application was soundly rejected. Jeff left Coates with a copy of the statutory declaration.

Jeff was profoundly troubled by the meeting. He felt physically unwell and took a walk to mull over what had just happened. He pondered the state of law and order in Tasmania. He sat on a street bench and rolled over his involvement in the Sue Neill-Fraser case in his mind: witnessing Stephen Gleeson's photo identification of Meaghan; learning about her being on the foreshore that night, intending to steal from yachts; meeting Meaghan and Snapper only days earlier; and the impact Meaghan's declaration was having on him. And potentially on Hobart and on Tasmania. Despite taking a series of long and deep breaths to calm himself, his gut was clenching. He felt like vomiting. He sat for half an hour, dwelling on all he had learned and witnessed, before heading back to his office.

Part III

Smashing through success

During the darkest, most dreadful days of this ordeal, locked away, I continued to believe that justice would prevail. Words cannot describe the horror of being accused, then wrongfully convicted of a crime which involves the suspected murder of someone close. I have been unable to write or work for a few days due to the great sense of sadness and loss. It really is devastating to reflect that we still don't know what happened to Bob or where he is.

I regularly point out to inmates that 'if life gives you lemons, make lemonade'. I am very grateful to know that there are people out there concerned with human rights and justice issues. I certainly would not have survived this life-changing ordeal without family and supporters. How wonderful to meet Robert Richter QC. I felt quite honoured! Would you please pass on how very grateful I was to him for meeting with the powers that be. I fear there is huge resistance to change in this state...

Excerpt from a letter from Sue Neill-Fraser to a friend, sent from prison, 2017

Welcome to politics

By May 2017 I was starting to feel Sue Neill-Fraser fatigue. As much as I was a committed member of the team, I was becoming jaded. My bad heart was a constant worry and my exhaustion wormed its way into my mood. I hadn't found time to rest properly. Each day I was overly conscious of my chest cavity, as twitches and pains came and went. I never felt right.

Daily there was something to do, someone to research. My main problem was that I had no authority or legal standing in Tasmania. I was just an author, chasing the facts for my book. As well as a participant in a documentary by Eve and Tim. May 2017 would mark twelve months since I first became involved in Sue's case. The avalanche of facts, suspects, persons of interest and potential evidence my research had thrown up amounted to a workload that could easily keep four or five detectives busy for a year. But I didn't have the benefit of police resources such as databases, criminal records and access to background information. I was acutely aware of being alone. If truth be told, I felt that Tasmania Police would prefer

I fell under a big red bus, never to be heard of again. But, I couldn't just walk away from a woman in prison, even though we hadn't ever met.

There was little doubt Tasmania Police were monitoring me, Eve and possibly Tim Smart. Jeff Thompson's swearing of Meaghan Vass's statutory declaration was by then common knowledge. I was beginning to feel things would get dirty; however, none of us had expected the DPP to come back with such a negative response. And because the documents we'd uncovered seemed to indicate that the police had got the original investigation horribly wrong, perhaps I shouldn't have been surprised when I felt that prying eyes were looking at me as carefully as I was looking at them.

I became circumspect in the way I spoke on my mobile phone and what I wrote in my emails. My cryptic and sometimes abrupt communications amused my friends and loved ones. All I could hope was that whoever was watching me, listening in, would keep their interest professional. I was not out to harm anyone; I just wanted to help right a wrong. Just like Eve, Jeff and Robert Richter. I didn't want to become the target of any rogue cop. It's a dangerous police department that cannot accept that, at times, it may come under scrutiny. Law enforcement shouldn't be so precious. Every police force in the world gets things wrong from time to time. I wondered if Tasmanian law enforcement officials had ever heard of Andrew Mallard of Perth. Or Lindy Chamberlain. Two stark and deeply troubling examples of wrong convictions.

* * *

One idea I worked up with Eve Ash was that it might be useful to talk to Lara Giddings. Giddings was a savvy politician who had been in government a few years earlier and was now biding her time in the Tasmanian opposition as the shadow attorney-general. I thought she might relish the opportunity of receiving a confidential briefing about what I had discovered in my research into Bob Chappell's disappearance. Maybe I was a tad optimistic, but I thought she might be able to make political mileage out of the findings. So did Robert Richter. He thought a 'white paper' might be the answer.

I set about preparing one such paper to present to Giddings. Eve, who had spoken to her many times over the years, undertook to arrange a briefing meeting with her. My only stipulation was that Giddings should allow an hour for the meeting, and that she should be alone and prepared to read my document. Eve came back with a date, time and place, and a short time later, she and I headed back to Hobart.

Eve was footing all the expenses, as well as continuing filming for her documentary about Sue's case. She had absorbed all the costs since she first pointed a camera at *Four Winds* way back in 2009. She had lost count of the number of visits she and others in the team had made to Hobart, each of which involved hotel accommodation, meals, taxis, hire cars, fuel, and on it went. It would have run to thousands of dollars each trip. She estimated that she had spent over three-quarters of a million dollars in her quest to unravel the facts of Bob Chappell's disappearance. I know she had every receipt along her journey, paperwork that filled shoeboxes. I had come to view Eve as an extraordinary and brave Australian. A woman who literally put her money where her convictions were. So the very least I could do was continue with the case. My part was to fall in behind the lady with the orange eyewear.

Eve and I arrived at Parliament House in Hobart and were shown to the House of Assembly meeting room. Lara Giddings sat at the end of possibly the biggest table in all of Tasmania. A mass of red timber – jarrah or mahogany, I guessed. I also guessed it had been around since colonial days. I wondered how many death sentences had been discussed around this mighty fine piece of furniture.

I placed my paper in front of the shadow attorney-general. It was about sixty pages in length, half text and the rest photographs. I told her it was my 'white paper' (a name that stuck), independent research for my book into the death of Bob Chappell, then asked her to read it. Eve and I sat in silence as she took in every word. To her credit, she read it all. As she got into the meat of the paper, she became more and more animated. Clearly, it included information she hadn't previously been aware of; revelations that caused her to shake her head in bewilderment.

After forty minutes she looked up and took a deep breath and slowly let it out. She uttered just one word, under her breath. 'Fuck.' Then slowly pushed the document away from her, as far as she could, into the centre of the table. Then, just as slowly, she drew her hands back, freeing herself from the report. She next clasped her hands neatly together in front of her, like a student about to hear from the teacher. She looked at Eve and me.

For a few seconds, silence hung in the air. Then Giddings spoke. She made it clear that should my white paper be correct, Sue Neill-Fraser may have suffered a massive wrong. She would be shocked and saddened if that were so. The three of us then spoke for twenty minutes, trying to see a way through the forest of legal and police issues that had shrouded the case. Eve and I pleaded with Giddings to raise the matter in parliament. We discussed trying to get the current attorney-general to either read the white paper or meet with me so I could brief him on the information which suggested a wrongful conviction had occurred.

Ultimately, Giddings said she was unable to champion our cause or raise the issue with the government. Furthermore, she would not take a copy of the white paper. She was blunt: her fingers would not touch the document again. She took the position that 'the matter is before the courts'; therefore, she could not interfere. What she was saying was that Sue's appeal was booked in for hearing some time in the future. It was now a court matter.

With no strategy to take forward, our meeting came to a close. We were politely escorted out of the building, into another bleak Hobart pre-winter day.

As we left empty-handed, Eve informed me that Giddings had been the deputy premier and attorney-general back when Sue Neill-Fraser was investigated, prosecuted and jailed. The mess had happened on her watch. After the initial shock of hearing this, I realised Giddings was not to blame. The shortcomings began on the street, with one or two of the detectives who investigated the murder. Giddings was too high up the chain to be held to task. Still, I had hoped for much more from her. I was fed up with Hobart and its politics. It's fair to say I had lost regard for the wonderful state of Tasmania and all the decent people who live there. People who deserve better, in my view.

I came to a sad realisation. So many of the people we were coming into contact with had some form of involvement in the original investigation, prosecution or management of the case against Sue Neill-Fraser. Perhaps they were too close to see the problems – but surely they should be open to the possibility of mistakes? They are always possible. Along with Robert Richter, I wondered if our efforts could bring about a truly transparent, independent review that re-examined the case and revealed the flaws of Sue's prosecution. I hoped so.

Back at Hobart airport, Eve, Tim and I waited for our flight. Our trip had been disappointing, and I had fallen into a dark mood. Tim, forever the cinematographer, wanted to capture my low spirits, and Eve wanted to discuss the disappointment of our visit on camera. I wanted solitude. I'd had it with Eve's documentary project. I wanted to go into my man cave and sulk. And I did.

Tim was sick of my moods, tired of my brooding. He threw a few sarcastic quips my way, and when I responded badly he let me have it with both barrels. I was a 'moody, sanctimonious prick', who was ignoring all the hard work that he and Eve had put into the documentary. His words hit me right between the eyes as I sipped my Sullivans Cove whisky. As a fellow documentary filmmaker, I should have realised the pressure those two were under, not just that day, but constantly. Tim didn't deliver his words quietly. Half the airport lounge heard them. I sensed about twenty pairs of eyes on me, the owners of which had become abruptly aware that they would be travelling on an aircraft with a sod. A rude prick. A sea of faces glared at me. Eve busied herself rearranging the empty glasses in front of her. I surveyed my landscape. I was past the point of no return and I was angry. My response to Tim's comments, which were absolutely spot on, by the way, was to get onto my front foot and attack. That's the cop in me.

I told Tim he could get fucked. A businessman two tables away glared at me while sipping his beer. He became my next target. 'What the fuck are you looking at, you buffoon? Why don't you mind your own fucking business and drink your silly beer?' I relaunched at Tim, hurling a similar degrading insult. Tim pushed back his chair; Eve did likewise, distancing themselves from me.

The businessman stared at his laptop and nervously gulped his beer. I scowled at the other travellers, who looked here, there and anywhere except at me. Then common sense reasserted itself. I became horribly aware of my poor behaviour. It was time for an unnecessary toilet break. I got up and strode towards the gents.

I splashed my face with cold water and looked at the idiot in the mirror. Lost in my own downer, I had forgotten all the hardship Eve had suffered, not to mention the extraordinary debt she was encumbered with from funding the whole shooting match. Likewise, I had taken Tim for granted and stopped being conscious of the physically hard work he was faced with, lugging his trolley of cameras and lighting to and from and all around Hobart. Then there was the constant pressure on him, as director of photography, to come up with the magic. I reminded myself after another splash of water that I was in the company of two very special people and I should be more of a team player.

By the time I returned from the toilet, the atmosphere had cleared a little, and Tim and Eve had returned to the table. I declined another whisky and the three of us sat in silence for the next thirty minutes. We kissed and made up on the flight home, but I still felt both enormously guilty and enormously burdened. I was a bit like a monkey required to dance and chatter each time the organ-grinder – Eve – wanted me to talk to her camera, to offer up my words of wisdom on how the research was progressing, and to explain all the twists and turns in our tale. I needed, somehow, to reprogram myself and find a better attitude. Which, in time, I did. My friendship with Tim was restored and we would go on to sip whisky together again.

* * *

Back in Melbourne, Robert Richter, Eve and I sat around thinking the case through. Trying to find a door to open, one that wasn't going to be slammed in our faces. Lara Giddings then offered up a surprise. Eve had been calling her regularly and applying subtle pressure by asking if she had any ideas that might help us. Giddings confided to Eve that the contents of the white paper had deeply troubled her and suggested that she might be able to set up a meeting with the acting attorney-general, where we could present him with our white paper. We were elated. If the attorney-general was amenable, then maybe, just maybe, a fresh investigation could be launched. One that we hoped might be undertaken by independent investigators from another state.

To Giddings's credit, she lined up a meeting with the premier, Will Hodgman. The acting attorney-general, and the Tasmanian solicitor-general, Michael O'Farrell, would also be in attendance. We were to have thirty minutes on 11 May 2017 with these three, the most powerful people in Tasmania, as far as law was concerned. They had been informed that Robert Richter QC would present a white paper and would lead the briefing. Eve and I would also be there. Three against three: not bad odds, I thought.

When the day arrived, we were ushered into the premier's office. Three hands reached out to shake ours and we sat down. My first impression was that we were dealing with three very stony-faced men. I hoped they would loosen up and allow Robert to make our points.

Robert spent the first ten minutes making it clear that we had unearthed a trove of information that undermined the findings of the original investigation. I handed each of the officials a copy of the white paper.

Robert assured them we were not on a path to harm reputations, but that many avenues had gone untapped in the original investigation. He reminded them that he had written to the attorney-general back in 2013 calling for a royal commission and that his views had not altered; there needed to be an independent investigation.

So far, the only reaction we had received was blank faces. Things were not going as well as we had anticipated. Robert then mentioned Meaghan Vass and the DNA found on the yacht. We had made significant discoveries concerning her involvement, he told the three men, and she had sworn a statutory declaration admitting she had been on the yacht on 26 January 2009, and that Sue Neill-Fraser was not. Their faces remained blank.

I jumped in and asked if the group would read over the first twelve to fourteen pages of the white paper, which served as an ideal briefing of the most damaging evidence. The premier opened his document to page one; the other two men kept theirs closed. Then the oddest thing happened. The three of them pushed the documents away from themselves, into the centre of the table, just as Lara Giddings had done.

Robert continued the fight, outlining his ideas about an independent inquiry. He mentioned a few suitably qualified people who might be available. I too mentioned names. Blank faces. We realised our attempt to enlighten the government of Tasmania on the most controversial criminal case in Australia was looking pointless. In desperation I told them that, in my view, the original investigation was 'the worst major crime investigation I have ever seen'. That didn't go down well.

Robert valiantly tried to engage the men on what he obviously saw as a miscarriage of justice. None of them took up the issue. He asked that Meaghan Vass be considered for indemnity from prosecution. This request was ignored. The matter of the white paper came up again. Robert suggested they should each take a copy away to read. The premier and the attorney-general declined. The solicitor-general held on to his, although reluctantly.

Robert's request that they take the report away was against my wishes. I had made it clear to Eve that I wanted no copy of my report left in Tasmania. The document revealed all the evidence crucial to Sue's case in the event of a retrial. Such evidence could be ammunition for the prosecution. I have been on enough major investigations over the decades to know that you don't share your evidence with the enemy. I also know that witnesses are the responsibility of the detective who signs them up. With this in mind, I had given the more sensitive witnesses an alias to make it difficult to identify them. I wasn't naive. Naturally, I would not go against Robert and his judgment, nor would I counter his offer. His wisdom is greater than mine. I did, however, stress that the white paper was confidential. The solicitor-general nodded and kept his copy. He then stated that he would get back to us, in time. However, there was definitely no love in the room. There were lots of stares, pregnant pauses and – overall – a feeling that nothing was being accepted or offered in return. As if by remote control, we all stood at the same moment and went through the awkward nonsense of handshakes and half-baked smiles before leaving.

Going down in the lift with a silent Robert and Eve, I had a massive sense of dread. One copy of the white paper was not under my control. Within it was information critical to getting Sue Neill-Fraser a retrial. We had tipped our hand.

I have only experienced that level of dread twice in my life before. It's a very difficult feeling to describe. I first felt it when I was investigating the murders of uniformed police more than twenty years earlier. I was up to my eyeballs in the case and under threat from the bad-ass thugs who, I was sure, correctly as it turned out, had killed the police. The feeling came upon me like a massive wave, accompanied by an overwhelming desire to get as far away from the source of my feelings as possible. Another way I try to articulate this feeling is to describe myself as walking hastily away from a petrol tanker about to explode.

The second time I felt it I was a year into an infiltration of the Mafia. I was buying huge rocks of pure cocaine, gaining evidence, hand over fist. I was even offered a truck load of cannabis to buy, and had conspired with the upper echelons of the Mafia to import a plane load of drugs. I was in, as we say in the covert world of policing, over my head, but the police hierarchy were rubbing their collective hands together, knowing that we were close to shutting down a troublesome cell of Mafiosi. Then came that horrid feeling. That wave. That petrol tanker feeling. That desire to run, flee it all.

Once outside the premier's building I did everything I could to overcome this feeling. Despite having suffered it before, experience was no help to me. The best I could do was take in the crisp air of Hobart and try to collect my thoughts. I worried, privately and silently. I stood aside from my colleagues for a moment, pretending to blow my nose, but really I was trying to take stock. I felt dreadful about that meeting.

I met up with Jeff Thompson and welcomed his calm presence. We decided to make a quick visit to Meaghan and Snapper at the motorcycle clubhouse. I had told them about our meeting with the premier and how Robert was going to raise the issue of Meaghan's indemnity from prosecution. Meaghan was waiting anxiously to hear the result. We found Meaghan and Snapper sitting inside their little mobile home in the rear yard. The four of us chatted, more like mates than anything else. The first thing we noticed was how calm Meaghan was. The change in her was miraculous. I even got a few smiles out of her. It was a cold day and I was wearing a scarf. Meaghan was joking with me, playfully teasing me about my scarf. I let her have her fun, thinking how wonderful it was to see her relaxed and showing a humorous side. Jeff explained that the premier's meeting was a work in progress, and that Robert had put the issue of Meaghan's indemnity on the table. All we could do was wait. Both Snapper and Meaghan seemed pleased enough, believing that the wheels of justice were turning in their favour.

I explained that I was going to be absent for a couple of months; I was going away to work elsewhere. Meaghan looked quickly at Snapper, then at me, then at Jeff, as if she was searching for an explanation. Jeff jumped in, saying that he would be there for her, and that he would work closely with her as the indemnity issue developed. She seemed happy with that. We explained that the indemnity matter would be helped greatly if Meaghan could remember more about the night on *Four Winds*. She smiled and nodded, as if she was thinking it over. Jeff then told her that, because he was working on Sue

Neill-Fraser's legal team, she really needed an independent solicitor to help her. There had to be distance between Meaghan and Sue. She agreed, and Jeff promised to introduce her to a suitable lawyer. Our chat over, Meaghan walked us to the front gate. She wished me well and teased me one last time about my scarf. She laughed for the first time ever in my presence. Just a giggle as she turned away and walked back inside. I have not seen her since.

* * *

I felt a sense of pride and achievement when I thought about my meetings with Meaghan. My hard work was paying off and the young woman who had travelled such a hard road showed real signs of turning a corner. Within a couple of hours, I was back in Melbourne, packing my suitcase. I was off to Italy for two months. What Meaghan didn't know, nor anyone else for that matter, was that I desperately needed rest. Despite my heart procedure three months earlier, I was still getting chest pains way too often. My family doctor and my cardiologist were worried. I needed to take a long break from the stress of my research and lie on a banana lounge under the Northern Hemisphere sun. But I couldn't resist taking my laptop with me and making a long overdue start on this manuscript. As I worked, I reflected about my meetings with Meaghan. I took comfort in hoping that Meaghan might finally unburden herself from the darkest of her secrets. I kept my imaginary fingers crossed for the tough girl from Hobart.

But I wasn't completely at ease. I constantly worried about that lone white paper we'd left in Hobart. What sort of impact might it have, good or bad? And the feeling of dread stayed with me.

I would later learn that after a week my white paper had been posted back to Eve. With a scathing letter from the solicitor-general, who told us in no uncertain terms that he saw no reason to open an independent inquiry into the past investigation. He had every faith in Tasmania Police.

Turning up the heat

By late July 2017 I was back in the saddle, although moving more slowly than normal. The deckchairs on our *Titanic* had shifted in my absence. Barbara Etter had resigned. And true to her ways she wasn't talking to anyone. She just needed to move on, and she did. The highly regarded Melbourne solicitor Paul Galbally stepped into the breach, which pleased me greatly. He bounced the ball on his involvement with a one-day conference, a talkfest that proved wonderfully helpful. We then all set about our tasks.

Despite our renewed optimism, August delivered an utter shock to our team. That petrol tanker had exploded. Out of the blue, the Hobart-based lawyer Jeff Thompson was raided by police. His home office was turned upside down and his case files seized. He was marched down to police HQ and interviewed. In time he was charged with perverting the course of justice for meeting and talking with Stephen Gleeson about the photo folder identifications. There was a vast team of detectives working on all of us – Jeff, Eve, Tim, myself, Gabby, Sharyn and who knows who else. Even the young IT woman in Eve's office had a Tasmania Police calling card placed in her letter box, requesting an interview. I went from peace of mind to panic stations in a week.

The police were claiming that Jeff had overstepped his legal mark with the photo folders he had shown to Gleeson. The police alleged Jeff had been involved in a conspiracy. Jeff denied this emphatically, but it all fell on deaf ears. He was a charged man. And his name was blackened.

Just as worrying was what was happening to Gabby. She too was charged with perverting the course of justice for – allegedly – standing over Meaghan and trying to get her to speak to me. All I could think was: where was the standover? I'd sat in a hotel room for three long days and nights and never got to meet Meaghan. The police seemed to focus on a phrase that Gabby had uttered, that she would 'put Meaghan in the boot of her car'. A threat, the police said. I listened to Gabby on Eve's tapes and heard her say to her child, who was crying, that she would put him in the boot. It was just the way she spoke. Tough girl stuff. In context, nothing. In fact, a nonsense.

Sharyn was also approached by police, hauled into police HQ on at least two occasions and interviewed. A five-page statement was taken from her. Why? It appeared it was just for assisting us with Meaghan's statutory declaration. For providing her home as a place to sit and talk about Meaghan's statement, and to go through it with her before she agreed with its truthfulness and swore it. Police were looking for anything to discredit what we had achieved.

Stephen Gleeson was also questioned and charged. He must have pondered the visit he'd received a year earlier when detectives went to the prison and asked him why he was talking to me. They'd threatened to charge him should he continue. A fact that he'd sworn to in an earlier affidavit.

The long arm of the law had reached out and grabbed a fistful of witnesses and a lawyer and squeezed the daylights out of them.

We were all stunned for days. Eve, Tim and I wondered when it would be our turn. We had not heard of similar actions by police anywhere in Australia. It was shockingly heavy-handed and there was much discussion in the legal team as to whether the charges against Jeff Thompson and our witnesses amounted to contempt of court. Opinions were sought. The advice was that it would require a massively expensive legal exercise to challenge the actions of the police. Money that we, as pro bono players, didn't have. All we could do was wait it out and watch the landscape, and support those bruised by the pummelling of their reputations.

A fundamental pillar of our judicial system is the right of appeal. It demonstrates that we are an advanced, civilised society. Sue Neill-Fraser was approaching the time when she could exercise that right, and her pro bono legal team was working hard. Every detective knows it's part of the game; you step aside and let the convicted person get on with it. The appeal system suits a person like Sue who has never been in trouble before – she'd never even received a traffic fine – and then all of a sudden is convicted of murder.

Sue may not have expected much from the appeal process. She may not have expected anything from the individual cops who hunted her. But surely they could have acted with a bit of civility and let her hearing unfold without incident. After all, it was her last roll of the dice. But sadly, with the raiding of Jeff Thompson and the seizing of all of Sue's appeal material, civility and humanity were not chips on her poker table. For police it had become a game of grab what you can, issue search warrants and snatch it all, just two months before the appeal date.

I was at my wits' end and considering escaping to somewhere outside Australia. The writing was on the wall. But there was still so much to do. A mountain of work sat on my shoulders. Eve had recently been part of a television show on the Seven network, a one-hour special on *Sunday Night*, detailing the many contradictions in Sue's story. It rated well, and threw up leads; viewers rang in, offering information. Interestingly, none of the leads pointed to Sue's guilt; they were all to do with her innocence. Eve gathered them in, and they needed to be followed up.

* * *

It's not uncommon for untrained people undertaking research to get swept away with enthusiasm. They try to go it alone to achieve success. Eve fell into that trap. A lead came her way and, instead of handing it over to me, she decided to follow it up herself. A man from Sydney, named Peter, rang her, as a result of the TV show, with a fascinating story. One that, on face value, could help free Sue.

Peter told Eve he was a 56-year-old engineer. He refused to give her his surname. He claimed to have tried on numerous occasions to pass on information about Bob's disappearance, once as recently as three years earlier, but no one seemed to listen to him. He'd spoken to Barbara Etter, Sue's lawyer at the time, but she hadn't called him back. He'd also called Crime Stoppers, reported what he knew in full, but didn't hear anything further from the police. He had kept notes about what he knew in his diary from 2009. He thought his information could be the key to getting Sue out of prison. His information went like this:

A day or so after Bob Chappell went missing, 'Rowdy', a friend and work colleague of Peter's, called around to his place early in the morning to have a cup of tea with Peter and his wife. They were talking about the disappearance of the man off his yacht moored in Sandy Bay when Rowdy said, 'I know what happened to him and who killed him.' He then named someone's daughter as the killer, along with a couple of males. Rowdy said the girl's mother and stepfather knew the whole story of what had happened.

Peter was horrified and told Rowdy to tell the police what he knew. Rowdy said he couldn't because he was a friend of the family and worked with the girl's stepfather, as well as the stepfather's cousin.

The girl was into drugs and living on the streets, prostituting herself, Rowdy said. She was living on Franklin Square with an older 'weathered' guy. But she also had a boyfriend who was about 22 or 23 years old.

The girl rang Rowdy on Australia Day night from a public phone box in Liverpool Street. She asked Rowdy to pick her up from the Brunswick Hotel, along with a grey-haired bearded man in his forties or fifties whom she was with, and take them to her mother's place. The girl confessed to what happened as they drove there. They'd gone out to the boat with a younger man, she said, in a dinghy she had access to through her mother's boat business.

Rowdy said the girl and the man she was with wanted to steal something particular from a yacht, something that someone had 'ordered'. They would sell the stolen goods to this person to get drugs. Both the 'weathered' man and the younger guy had worked as deckhands and they were all involved in stealing from yachts and boats. Apparently, the three of them came across the owner of the big yacht, Bob. He wasn't helpful, and the girl hit him with a pot; he fell downstairs and was bleeding. The younger man finished him off. They wrapped him in an orange raincoat and dragged him up and out of the boat and into a dinghy. The older man got rid of the body at the bottom of South Arm Peninsula on the outskirts of Hobart, close to the open sea. Rowdy also said that the girl became frantic about a red jacket and he had to take her back to Marieville Esplanade to search for it. They drove up and down, trying to find it.

Peter's story is remarkable for several reasons. It was highly credible because it was filled with the facts we knew, such as the street names, times and date and description of the weathered man, which were remarkably in line with what I knew about the night Bob was killed.

In short, Peter's recollection of the 'Rowdy' story is uncannily possible. His words indicated to me that he couldn't have invented his statement. There was too much detail that I considered accurate. The information that meant most to me was how the homeless girl had a stepfather and she was frantically searching for a red jacket. It squared with what we knew about the jacket that was one of the Crown's key pieces of evidence. It explained how the jacket got on the fence at 26 Marieville Esplanade. And why it wasn't covered in Bob's blood. The girl wore it as she fled.

Rather than briefing me and handing over the report, Eve lined up a meeting with Peter and headed off to Sydney with

Tim. Just before the planned meeting, she told Peter that she intended to film him speaking about what he knew for her planned television program about Sue's case. He went to ground. Eve would ring him numerous times in a vain attempt to repair the mess. All to no avail. Peter didn't want to be famous. He'd never wanted his information to be anything other than confidential. He didn't care for the idea of a cameo role in a TV show. Eve and Tim were left with an expensive night in Sydney and no witness. We would never hear from Peter again.

I was livid when I found out. Filmmakers trying to be detectives! That incident dinted my adoration of Eve. At least for a short while. Up until that point, I thought she should have been nominated for Australian of the Year for her dedication to her search for the truth about Bob's disappearance. I still respected her enormously and admired her. However, her actions in this instance had been naive.

I tried to repair the damage, ringing Peter at least twenty times over many days, on a series of different phones, without success. In the meantime, we confirmed aspects of Peter's story, namely that he had called Barbara in October 2015 and told her a near-identical story, but she had never got back to him. The file sat among the copious number of papers and reports that she had collected. It was never actioned. I therefore assumed he had told the same story to Hobart Crime Stoppers; however, that had been years ago and no one had seemed to be listening. Not surprisingly, as Sue was already in jail.

* * *

We poured all our resources into finding Rowdy and confirmed much about what Peter had said. He was married, and he seemed unable to settle into work; he'd had a few too many jobs over his lifetime. Then we hit a Eureka moment. Rowdy's Facebook page showed he was close friends with Meaghan's mother, and Meaghan's stepfather, a local fisherman. They went back a long way. Rowdy lived in a rundown house in the suburb of Moonah, and he had two kids, both teenage daughters. I decided to travel, under the radar, back to Hobart.

My decision was a hard one as things were getting tropical for me. Jeff Thompson's recent arrest rang alarms bells, signalling that I should not go to Hobart if I knew what was good for me. But Rowdy was the missing link to the truth. It was vital to speak to him and have him confirm the story he'd told Peter. Robert Richter, Paul Galbally and others on the team agreed that Rowdy was our best hope of getting to the truth. I planned my flight.

I would arrive in Hobart on a Sunday afternoon, as most detectives have that day off, spending it at home with the family. Rowdy would also be likely to be at home. We decided to enlist a local lawyer to help me, someone who could prepare an affidavit should Rowdy cooperate.

Robert Richter and I went through the names of lawyers in Hobart we could trust. It was becoming an extremely short list. In the end, we settled on someone and I told him my plans. All he had to do was meet me at the airport and accompany me to Rowdy's house. From there we would be guided by Rowdy's truthfulness or willingness to help. I expected to be back in Melbourne for dinner, hopefully with an affidavit that would result in a retrial. Robert Richter wished me well and handed me a note on his letterhead, detailing my task, in case police pulled me aside or tried any other sort of crap.

On the Sunday morning I left my apartment with my bag full of notes and papers related to Peter and Rowdy. I was about to get into my car to drive to the airport when my mobile phone rang. It was the Hobart lawyer. He was backing out, fearful of what might happen. His concern was that should Rowdy want to talk – and therefore be handed over to the lawyer to take an affidavit – the situation might compromise him.

I recall standing beside my car, with the door open, as the bad news was delivered. The lawyer attempted to explain his reservations, but I wasn't in the mood. No is no in my book, and there's not much use in trying to soften a negative. Our phone call ended and I sucked in a few deep breaths.

I rang Robert and we talked it over. He was concerned that I would be vulnerable if I was alone in Hobart. We quickly ran through our options and decided I wasn't flying to Hobart that day.

Enter Charlie Bezzina

ONE THING I LEARNED AS A TEAM LEADER ON THE TASK forces I worked on in Victoria Police was how to think laterally. And strategically. I sat up all night and picked over a dozen scenarios, one after the other. Each strategy was designed to get me through the front door of Rowdy's house and to get him talking, then get home again. Robert Richter was insistent that I do nothing illegal, such as using a false name to book a return airfare to Hobart. I agreed: the fruit of a poisonous tree could easily go against us. In the morning I'd decided what to do and made a phone call to a man I regard as one of the top detectives in Australia, Charlie Bezzina, otherwise known as the king of homicide crime scenes. We hadn't spoken for eighteen years.

Charlie and I are the same age. He served in the force longer than me, a staggering thirty-seven years, most of them as a detective in the Homicide Squad. He was retired from policing and itching to get his teeth into something interesting. He had taken to writing a weekly column for a national newspaper and had published a book of memoirs. Over his years in the force he had investigated about three hundred suspicious or unnatural deaths, two hundred of them murders. Charlie's involvement in the Sue Neill-Fraser case, at any level, would give all of us a great boost. I had a bit of a detective crush on Charlie, I don't mind admitting. He was thorough, measured and highly skilled.

As well as his fabulous detecting skills, which transferred into a high 'solve rate', he was also a nice guy. Three months earlier, Robert Richter had sent Charlie a copy of my white paper. Robert and I had wanted his thoughts on the case. This was around the time we'd been more or less tossed out of the Tasmanian premier's office. Charlie had kept his copy and, proving he still had a good detective's curiosity, had surfed the net, researching the case against Sue. He'd spent three months looking up court transcripts, affidavits, media reports and anything that he could get his mitts on. By the time I rang him, the day after I'd cancelled my flight to Hobart to find Rowdy, Charlie was dangerous with knowledge. I only had to ask if he wanted in. 'In a heartbeat; this case is a disaster,' was his answer.

The next day he and I sat around my apartment reading every affidavit, statement and notation on the case. We laboured on until the wee hours. Then we focused on Rowdy. I didn't need to waste too much time on what was required; Charlie saw instantly the importance of knocking on Rowdy's door. The only problem was that Charlie was committed to another job for four or five more days, and couldn't head down to Hobart till that was finished. We had no other options. Charlie was our man, Robert Richter agreed. He and Charlie had gone head-to-head in the Supreme Court in many a murder trial and they had a healthy respect for one another. All we could do was wait until the following week. We figured that no one had spoken to Rowdy in the past eight years; what difference would a few more days make?

* * *

The following week Charlie hit the chilly streets of Hobart and made for Rowdy's place. Should he be successful in getting Rowdy to swear an affidavit, we had Jeff Thompson on standby, keen to help out, despite being on bail and fighting to clear his name.

Charlie walked up to Rowdy's ramshackle house and tried the front door. A pair of howling dogs did their best to jump the six-foot side fence. Rowdy and his family were not at home. Charlie retired to the sanctuary of his hire car and listened to the scratchy radio. Within minutes he noticed a woman walking along the street, carrying bags of groceries. She turned into the driveway of Rowdy's house and opened the front door. With Rowdy's wife home, Charlie pounced.

The woman looked about forty years of age. Keeping it simple, Charlie explained what his inquiry was about. The woman didn't need much explanation; she was all over it. To Charlie's dismay, she told him that the police had knocked on their door a week earlier and sat down with her and her husband, Rowdy. When they left, the police took with them a signed statement, declaring that Rowdy had stayed home the entire night of 26 January 2009. His wife recalled that she and Rowdy had sat together all night, watching TV and drinking red wine. At some point, they both went to bed and slept. Rowdy never left the house. 'You've got it all wrong,' she told Charlie.

The veteran detective was gobsmacked. He had been involved in thousands of door-to-door inquiries and had taken an equal number of statements in an extraordinarily long and distinguished career. But what this woman was saying made his jaw drop. How was it that she could recall the details of such an uneventful night eight years earlier: staying in, watching TV and drinking red wine? Her recall was extraordinary.

Charlie went over her account with her once more. She was adamant, and she had nothing more to say. Nor did she seem at all curious about why it was so important to talk to Rowdy. Charlie knew that he wasn't able to take the matter any further. The wife and Rowdy were now police witnesses. Signed and sealed, and the veteran homicide detective could do nothing whatsoever about it. In fact, if he continued to talk to the woman, he could be accused of harassing a police witness. All Charlie could do was walk away, empty-handed.

Minutes later he was parked down a dead-end street and speaking to me on his mobile phone. The call was riddled with expletives. Suffice to say, we were bitterly disappointed. The more we talked the more we came to believe that someone must have been monitoring my phone calls or reading my emails. We had been checkmated. If only I had gone down to Hobart the week before and knocked on Rowdy's door. If only we had downloaded an encrypted mobile phone service so that our communications were untraceable and unable to be intercepted. If only...

I was left to break the sad news to the team. The loss of potentially a key witness. Just like we lost Stephen Gleeson to police charges as well as Gabby and Sharyn to police pressure. Things were looking sad in our camp. Charlie blunted his disappointment with a visit to *Four Winds*, spending a serious amount of time getting to know the craft. True to his skills and talent, he walked over every surface and looked closely above and below decks and at the engine. He even took his own video footage of the vessel. He wanted to make his own assessment of the place where Bob Chappell had most probably been murdered.

Like me, Charlie had great difficulty in understanding the Tasmanian police's claim that Sue Neill-Fraser winched the body of Bob Chappell out of the saloon up to the wheelhouse and onto the decking. He was convinced the task would be impossible for a woman of Sue's build and strength. And if by some remarkable chance she had been able to winch up the body, she would have shown signs of bruising, cuts, scratches, muscle strain and the like. Charlie also agreed with my theory that Bob's body was removed from the saloon through the skylight hatch, by two or more persons.

By the end of his inspection, Charlie believed that Bob first sustained a major blow, possibly to the head, while he was near the steps leading up from the saloon to the wheelhouse. This was evident from the blood spatter on both walls next to the steps. Charlie also concurred with my assessment that the primary reason for cutting the water pipe at the toilet and turning on the water valve was to allow a rush of water to wash away forensic evidence of the struggle with Bob Chappell. With the help of Chris Smith, the salvage agent and new owner of *Four Winds*, Charlie also studied the fuse box. It was clear to him that whoever disarmed the bilge pumps did so with a degree of knowledge about the workings of yachts.

Later that night Charlie rang me again as he was about to board his plane home. 'I agree with all your findings,' he told me. 'Well done.' Even though it didn't advance our case,

I was chuffed to have one of the very finest pay me such a compliment.

* * *

Once Rowdy's wife had taken the wind out of our sails, I realised we were getting smashed. We had to take every precaution. From that day onwards, no one spoke on a normal phone service again. We took to the encrypted mobile phone communication regime favoured by drug dealers, terrorists and former prime minister Malcolm Turnbull – the WhatsApp phone app.

I thought a lot about the rules that bound our game. I'd been a cop. I knew what happened. Nightly, I tossed and turned despite a burning desire for sleep. Often I was depressed, knowing the strengths of the Tasmanian police team. They had legislation to wave over us, to threaten us with, and, in the case of Jeff Thompson and the witnesses, to use against us. Laws that could stop us all in our tracks. They also had manpower. How many exactly they were devoting to their task we didn't know, but many more than us. And they had what I could only conclude was, at best, a lazy media and, at worst, a biased media on their side. Altogether, a formidable force. A gang far more powerful than a mix of exhausted pro bono ex-detectives, lawyers, supporters and filmmakers. My God, I was tired.

Then, out of the blue, came a snippet of information that would act like a few cubes of sugar to an exhausted man, giving me the strength to carry on. I had asked Eve to get her clever IT colleague to do some social media research. Her expertise is in all the things I know nothing about: the internet, Twitter,

Facebook, Instagram. She was able to run, surf, swim, or whatever they do, around the IT world with ease. Give her a task and she will tap into some seemingly innocuous information that ends up being something tremendously important.

I asked her to check the Facebook accounts of Rowdy and his wife to see if she could find out when they married. Two days later she reported back. She had uncovered the bomb we were looking for. Rowdy and his wife only got engaged in April 2012 and didn't marry until December 2012. More startlingly, an informant told us they only started dating in late 2009. Ten months after Bob Chappell was murdered. From the evidence it seemed Rowdy and his wife didn't even know each other at the time of Bob Chappell's disappearance. Or, at least weren't dating at that time. Rowdy, in fact, had still been married to his first wife, the mother of his two teenage daughters, in January 2009. Another Eureka moment, one that we would keep up our sleeve. Maybe for a royal commission.

Interpol, on the run

THE CHARGING OF JEFF THOMPSON WAS A MASSIVE BLOW FOR our team. I can't overstate the effect it had on all of us. It wasn't just that Jeff is the type of man you immediately want to be friends with, it was also the way the charge rammed home how murky and dangerous the game we were playing was. In truth, it wasn't a game at all.

Jeff had never felt fully accepted by Hobart's legal fraternity. He was an outsider. Initially he was snubbed because he wasn't a graduate of a Tasmanian university. Jeff had gained his law qualifications at the Australian National University in Canberra. He held a masters degree in law. In time, he'd deciphered how the legal politics worked in Hobart. There was a club, a clique, that you needed to be in. And Jeff wasn't in it. The lucrative work fell into the laps of those in the know. Judges were mates with senior counsel. Solicitors were buddies with magistrates and the high-rolling legal officer jobs in government went to those in the club. As Jeff stood apart and observed it all, scratching for work, he saw what others had warned him about, what newspapers had written about. There was nepotism at every level.

Running through the nepotism was a vein of pomposity
and elitism. It was colonial in style, very olde-English, private
schoolboy stuff. Jeff wondered how long he could persevere,
chasing work, trying to embed himself into this clubby league
of (mostly) men. His most astute observation was possibly his
most disturbing. Some of Hobart's lawyers, in Jeff's opinion,
were ignorant of various aspects of the law and its complexities.
He felt there was a lack of diversity in the legal fraternity. This
worried him, as a lawyer and a civil libertarian.

In his struggle to build contacts that might lead to paid
work, he undertook countless hours of legal aid and pro bono
work, for the benefit of the needy and disadvantaged. He saw
hundreds of cases in which clients on the lower rungs of society
were being shafted. He did what he could, offering help and
a smile. When Barbara Etter, Sue's lawyer, reached out and
asked if he could help with a wrongful incarceration case, Jeff
signed up. He came to believe the legal system – a system that
was already troubling him – had let Sue down badly.

Jeff gained a real sense of pride from the work he was doing
in Barbara's team. Unlike the Hobart legal fraternity, the
barristers and solicitors from the mainland he was working
with welcomed him with open arms, and with respect. He and
his wife thought of moving on from Tasmania. They began
renovating the family home, readying it for sale. It was then,
in August 2017, as he was working in his office, that the state
of Tasmania came down on top of him and he was raided by
the police.

All the material Jeff had amassed while working on Sue's
case – the affidavits, reports, persons-of-interest photo folders
and other legal documents – was confiscated, as was his
computer. The police alleged all this material was needed

to prove a conspiracy to pervert the course of justice. This 'conspiracy' centred around his accompanying me to Risdon Prison to show Stephen Gleeson a folder of photos of young women. Non-lawyers are prohibited from taking anything into a prison, so I'd needed a lawyer with me. One who could oversee the use of photo folders in an identification process, and give authenticity to the outcome. Without prompting, Gleeson had pointed out Meaghan Vass as the 'homeless girl' he had seen on 26 January 2009. I hadn't met Jeff before – it had been our first meeting – but somehow, in the police view, Meaghan being identified by Stephen Gleeson amounted to a conspiracy cooked up by Jeff, me and Stephen. The proposition was absurd. If you apply logic, which I often do, why would two men who had never met before conspire with a prison inmate, under CCTV cameras, to do anything wrong? It was nonsense and this rubbish needs to be brought to light in a royal commission.

The raid on Jeff and the charges against him were definitely going to blacken Jeff's name and spoil him as a potential witness at the Sue Neill-Fraser appeal. I could only conclude that Jeff and I were getting too close to the truth. During the raid on Jeff's office, the detective in charge openly told him that I was the architect of it all and that I would be dealt with soon. It stood to reason that the police might well decide to press charges against me too. The detective was Maverick, the detective who was key to the case against Sue Neill-Fraser back in 2009. The same detective who might suffer criticism, should our findings about his investigation be publicly ventilated. Funny place, Tasmania.

The charges against Jeff Thompson shocked the mainland media. The Walkley-award-winning investigative journalist

Nick McKenzie wrote a series of powerful feature articles for
the Fairfax media in the weeks following the raid. Nick raised
many worrying questions about the Tasmanian legal system. I
was alarmed, not just for Jeff, but for myself, especially when
Jeff told me how a detective at the raid had stated that I would
be charged next. The police stated as much in newspaper
articles after the raid. And the charges they referred to were
conspiracy and perverting the course of justice. I couldn't
believe this was happening. It was at this point that I took to
my heels and headed for the outback, then on to Sri Lanka.

Despite my escape overseas, I was still busy with
preparations for Sue's appeal, feeding reports to Paul Galbally
and Robert Richter. One thing I discovered in the police
material was that there had been an unsuccessful attempt to
identify 'inconclusive' samples of DNA (probably blood stains)
taken from the lower and middle treads of the steps leading
out of *Four Winds*' wheelhouse. Detective Maverick had asked
at Mara House if Meaghan had a 'cut foot' around the time of
Bob's disappearance. A cut foot would explain the blood drops
on the steps. Blood that had not been identified and still sits
in the forensic laboratory in Hobart. But why would she have
been barefooted? I drafted a report to the legal team suggesting
that Meaghan may be the owner of that blood. Little did I
know then that my hunch would soon get a big boost.

There was, of course, the swamp of other DNA exhibits
that had been ignored: the 195 mm colourless hair belonging
to Person D found on the skylight hatch (through which I
maintain Bob's body had been extracted from the yacht);
and swabs 81, 82 and 83, taken from the levers on the hatch,
inside the saloon. I drafted a document highlighting the LCN
methodology of DNA testing and suggested Paul Galbally

seek to have all the forensics looked at again. Paul sent a report requesting as much to the office of the Tasmanian Director of Public Prosecutions. He evidently hit a raw nerve. His demand was refused. Paul's only recourse would be to fund an expensive contest in the Supreme Court to overturn the DPP's decision. An expensive court action for a pro bono team with no funds in the kitty.

* * *

In a mad rush to leave Australia, I handed Charlie Bezzina two files that needed urgent attention. The first concerned a man whom I will refer to as the Hairdresser. He lived close to the foreshore of Sandy Bay, in a house alongside a tiny walkway that doesn't appear on any street directory or Google map. The walkway allows access onto Margaret Street and then down to the foreshore. Margaret Street is where the red jacket, which the police alleged was Sue's, was found on the fence at number 26, the red-brick house at the end of the walkway.

The Hairdresser contacted Eve via an intermediary in September 2017. He had seen something on the night of 26 January 2009 that troubled him, and that had been on his mind ever since. He had tried telling a retired policeman what he knew, but was told to shut his mouth. I rang the Hairdresser, who seemed like a very decent, switched-on family man.

The Hairdresser told me that back in 2009 he would often walk his dog at night, after his kids had gone to bed. His normal route took him down the walkway that ran alongside 26 Margaret Street, then onto the foreshore. Sometimes, he would walk with his next-door neighbour, Simon, who also had a pooch. Simon's house was ramshackle, a rundown rental property, a haven for the lost souls in the area. Drunks, thugs and homeless people alike would treat it as a crash pad.

On the night of Australia Day, the Hairdresser was having trouble getting his son to sleep so he and his dog missed out on their walk, but he was standing outside when he saw Simon returning from the foreshore. He was with three other people. One was an older man, in his late fifties, a burly tough guy who was sharing the house with Simon. He was a heavy drinker and the Hairdresser and his wife often suffered through his noisy drinking sessions late at night. The other two people were younger. One looked to be a street kid, a young girl, maybe fifteen or sixteen years old. The other was a tall, thin guy, maybe a bit older than the girl. They seemed to be a couple. A conversation started up and introductions were made, although the Hairdresser was unsure of their names so many years later. He recalled Simon saying that the girl and her boyfriend had 'just got off a dinghy' at Sandy Bay. This was late at night; it was dark.

Charlie was all over the report like an ant on a spat-out mint. He locked down a meeting with the Hairdresser and booked a flight to Hobart. We held our breath, hoping Charlie wouldn't be pulled over by police or followed to the Hairdresser's house. I was in a different time zone and I paced around in the dark. The hours ticked by, then Charlie rang me on WhatsApp with his news. The Hairdresser had confirmed his earlier remarks and added that the girl and her boyfriend looked dishevelled. (Later, at Sue's appeal, he would tell the Supreme Court that the girl wore 'no shoes'.) After their conversation, Simon and his friends walked into Simon's rundown house and the music was turned on. It was the 'no shoes' comment that dovetailed, in my mind, with Maverick seeking information about Meaghan Vass having a 'cut foot'.

It turns out that the older, burly guy (unrelated to the Sue Neill-Fraser case) was convicted a year later of the murder of a man at Eggs and Bacon Bay, south of Hobart. He was locked away for twenty years. It was beginning to make sense. Simon's house had been frequented by some of Hobart's worst.

Charlie showed the Hairdresser a folder with photos of eight girls of similar age and appearance. After much deliberation he pointed to one of the pictures and said, 'If my life depended on it I would pick photo number three as the homeless girl.' Charlie smiled his wry Maltese grin and got the Hairdresser to sign his selection. It was a photograph of Meaghan Vass.

We were over the moon. As was Charlie. I recall hanging up the phone feeling good for the first time in six months. I ordered an umbrella drink from room service and quietly, over another four drinks, got shitfaced. Then slept like the dead.

But the old dog detective wasn't going to get too carried away. Charlie was concerned that the police might come at the Hairdresser, find out about his evidence and interfere. We all agreed we needed to keep it under wraps. He buttoned up his paperwork on the case and handed it to Paul Galbally, who booked a flight to Hobart to have the Hairdresser swear his evidence.

The Hairdresser's statement would help debunk Meaghan's testimony at the original trial that she hadn't been on *Four Winds*, and, just as importantly, that she hadn't even been at Sandy Bay. Her puddle of DNA proves she had been on the yacht and the Hairdresser's affidavit proves she was in Sandy Bay, at night, on Australia Day, 2009. Further, and this is the icing on the cake, she had just got off a dinghy, barefoot and looking dishevelled.

We knew Sue's dinghy was found abandoned against the rocks, three metres away from Gleeson's yellow Ford sedan, untethered, just bobbing in the water. We knew Sue walked down to the foreshore that night and saw homeless people around a gas cooker, at the yellow sedan. We also knew that Gleeson picked Meaghan from a folder of photos as the girl who tapped on his car window and said she and her companion were going to 'steal from yachts'. We also knew there were drops of blood on the steps leading out of the wheelhouse, yet to be identified, and that Meaghan wasn't wearing shoes that night. We also knew, because of the presence of the burly tough guy who was convicted of murder, that on the night of Australia Day, 2009, Meaghan Vass and her boyfriend were running with bad dudes. Bad, violent dudes.

Charlie's second chore was also screaming for attention. During Sue's original trial much was made of a large fire extinguisher that the Crown alleged Sue used to weigh Bob's body down in the water. The jury gobbled up this story, despite there being no evidence that a large fire extinguisher had been on the yacht. We were at a loss as to how to challenge evidence that seemed to be an invention. We obtained four witness affidavits that stated there had been no extinguisher on board, as far as the witnesses could tell. Then one day, as Charlie was snooping around Hobart, he spoke to a woman who told him about a man named Panton, who had been raided by the same police who'd investigated Sue Neill-Fraser. They'd been looking for a fire extinguisher. This coincidence tickled Charlie's fancy. The ant was onto another spat-out mint.

It took a while to find the elusive Panton, and as luck would have it he lived in Williamstown, a bayside suburb of Melbourne, having left Hobart years earlier. Charlie decided a cold call was his best shot to see if he could win him over. Charlie's caring-cop routine worked a treat. He developed a genuine rapport with Panton, a retired painter, and Charlie ended up having a few phone calls with him. They agreed to catch up, face to face, in a waterside cafe.

Panton told Charlie he'd moved to Hobart in early 2009 and taken a bedroom in a house in Prince of Wales Bay. This was around the time of the death of Bob Chappell. The house was owned by his mate, who had a teenage son, who was stealing from boats, as well as milking fuel and selling it. The kid's parents were battling to stop the illegal ways of their wayward son.

One morning, Panton was home alone. He assumed the teenager had crashed for the night on a boat. Suddenly four or five car loads of police pulled up. They stormed into the house with a search warrant. Leading the way was Detective Inspector Peter Powell, the same man investigating Sue Neill-Fraser for the murder on *Four Winds*. They set about their search, looking for outboard motors, they said, and Panton thought it strange when they upended his small bed. An outboard motor would be too big to hide under it, he told a detective. He wondered what they were really looking for. One of the detectives (he was unsure if it was Peter Powell or another) said, 'We are also looking for a fire extinguisher.'

This made more sense to Panton, but the cops didn't find the fire extinguisher they were seeking. They got back into their fleet of cars and roared off. The timing of this raid and the search for an extinguisher, just after the murder of

Bob Chappell, is telling. It has to be asked: how many fire extinguishers normally featured in the work lives of detectives in Hobart? Why were they searching for one at the same time as their dance cards were full with the Sue Neill-Fraser investigation? They must have suspected that the teenager had stolen an extinguisher from *Four Winds*. We knew that the teenager was friends with Meaghan's old boyfriend Dodger so obviously there was a strong link to be gained in all this. I cannot fathom any other reason for four or five squad cars of detectives descending on the home of one youthful, low-level thief. This number of cars meant they were very, very serious.

Charlie, with the help of our lawyer in Melbourne, David Gonzalez, turned this remarkable piece of information into an affidavit. As David was getting Panton to swear to his testimony, it came out that Panton also knew of Sue and Bob as a couple. 'I never observed their relationship to be a violent one and viewed it as a normal long-standing relationship.' Needless to say, after Charlie rang me with this latest information I reached for the house phone again and ordered another round of umbrella drinks.

Within days we received more valuable information from an informer we codenamed Deep Throat, a person well known and well connected in the Hobart underworld. Like the source with the same codename involved in the US Watergate political scandal in the 1970s, our source's identity must be kept secret. Our Deep Throat knew the teenage thief, who was a similar age to Meaghan Vass, and said he had been associating with her back in 2009. He had been stealing from yachts for many years, Deep Throat told us, and he was known to wear gloves when he was thieving. Deep Throat, on one occasion, had seen stolen boat and yacht parts at the teenage thief's house. Jeff

Thompson could confirm some of this: he had once been in a busy courtroom when the teenager had pleaded guilty to a fistful of theft charges. He estimated the teenage thief must have accumulated pages of police charges over many years.

Deep Throat knew of two occasions when Meaghan had been living around the Sandy Bay area: once with a girlfriend called Ashley, and, interestingly, she had also lived with Pablo for a short time at the Shamrock Hotel, on the edges of the CBD, about two kilometres from Rowing Shed Point. Jeff Thompson went to the Shamrock Hotel and spoke with the owners. They confirmed that Pablo was indeed living there while he tried to sell his yacht, just after Bob Chappell went missing. Pablo remained at the Shamrock for almost twelve months, trying his darnedest to sell his only asset, his yacht.

Jeff also confirmed that Meaghan was a regular drinker at the hotel, in company with none other than Pablo. They sat at the same table. Yet Meaghan and Pablo would both give evidence at the appeal hearing in October 2017 that they had never met. At Sue's appeal, her barrister, Tom Percy QC, would ask Pablo about Meaghan. Pablo would clearly state that she was not known to him, full stop. Yet the publican at the Shamrock had poured them drinks for a period of twelve months, as they drank together, in the front bar.

Isn't that perjury? More importantly, why were they keeping their relationship secret? My memory drifted back to Meaghan telling me in January 2017 that she was on 'Pablo's yacht' on Australia Day, 2009, before going on to 'the old guy's yacht' where 'a fight broke out'. Of course, you'd want to keep that relationship secret. This falsehood had been maintained since 2012, when Pablo was first interviewed by police. It shouldn't be such a wrestle for the Hobart cops to pull the facts together on this mess. But as I was becoming all too aware, Hobart's small-town environment didn't seem interested in whether its institutions of law and order had got it badly wrong.

I also recalled back in March 2017, in Sharyn's home, when Meaghan and I spoke about her DNA being found on *Four Winds*. She told me, 'I remember knocking around with [the teenage thief] and [Dodger].' She then said, 'I have no problems doing whatever I can to help Sue. Horrible situation she is in.' Then she went quiet. This was Meaghan: half-truths, then regressing into her memory, her chamber of secrets.

After the Panton affidavit we all agreed that Deep Throat should remain a valued asset. We considered Panton's information to be highly credible. As a thief from boats, the teenager was now a person of extraordinary interest. In fact, anyone who is known to steal from boats or yachts should be considered important.

* * *

A few days after the Panton affidavit was sworn, I heard of an issue that might cause problems. This was as Paul Galbally was pulling his paperwork together for Sue's appeal hearing to resume in October 2017, and working on his witness list. It is courteous, indeed proper, that each side in a court case provides a list of witnesses it intends to call. Paul opted to do everything properly, so he included the Hairdresser's name and a summary of his evidence on the list. It is possible in some circumstances to withhold a name from a list until the last minute, especially if the witness is controversial. I was worried that someone might try to get to the Hairdresser, perhaps prevail upon him to change his evidence, should the office of the DPP let slip what he intended to say in court. But it was Paul's case and I respected him greatly, so I could only keep my fingers crossed.

A day later I rang the Hairdresser. He told me that the police had contacted him and questioned him about his intended testimony. It appeared to my observations that the office of the DPP and the police act as one. Yet, they are supposed to be independent of each other.

* * *

During this time, I would spend five weeks in Asia, moving from one hotel to another and rarely venturing outside my room. While it was tropical in these parts, it was equally 'hot' in Hobart and Melbourne. The pressure on Eve Ash and Jeff Thompson was unbearable. They felt isolated and were suffering. The three of us had become a team over the past months. A special bond had formed. We figured we were the Apple Isle's three bad apples. We spoke up to a dozen times a day and passed on documents. Each day was filled with searching for and sifting through records, files and court documents to find missing evidence. And I was working day and night on this manuscript.

The heat in Australia, however, got so steamy that Eve jumped on a plane and took off to Bali with Big Paul, her partner, for three weeks. She was exhausted. Jeff Thompson was also feeling the strain; his family was starting to fall apart. He had recently taken a part-time job as a legal officer at the Department of Justice and all of a sudden colleagues were looking at him sideways and his normal legal work, which he did from home, was drying up. He felt he had become persona non grata. Then, without warning, he was sacked from the department. He was told that, in the opinion of his superior, he might breach the department's confidentiality. Might? This was the last straw. It was time to jump ship and take a break. Jeff packed his family up and they bundled off to Malaysia to become a family again.

Eve, Jeff and I contacted each other every few hours, joking about how Tasmania's most wanted people were now all stashed away in Asia, eating string hopper curries, gado-gado and hawker cuisine. It was funny the first time we joked about it, but after a few days it became very miserable. I predicted they would soon tire of exotic Asian food and the heat. And they did. We sat about on our banana lounges, a couple of thousand kilometres apart, sweating, working and worrying. It was as if we had become an Interpol team; we were scattered everywhere.

Inside the Supreme Court of Tasmania

I CREPT BACK INTO AUSTRALIA ON 30 OCTOBER 2017, THE DAY Sue's appeal was held in the Supreme Court of Tasmania. I waited, and listened to the court gossip from Melbourne, fielding calls and hearing updates. Paul Galbally, who was acting as the instructing solicitor in Sue's defence, and Tom Percy QC had flown in to Hobart the day before. Eve had done monumental work in listing ten of the most salient points of our case. I had assisted her from Kuala Lumpur, digging up facts and snippets that would help Tom and Paul. They had summoned more than a dozen witnesses to help get their case across the line. Ten of the witnesses were ones that Charlie or I had discovered. We were anxious as to how they would stand up under pressure. Cross-examination is hard work for the uninitiated. Many a witness has been pulled to shreds by an aggressive barrister, and the Director of Public Prosecutions himself, Daryl Coates, was leading the charge, representing 'the people', and, therefore I believed, those who had undertaken the shoddy original investigation into the death of Bob Chappell. Jack Shapiro was his second.

Paul Galbally planned to present fresh and compelling evidence, which, had it been available at Sue's trial, might have saved her from a guilty verdict. It's a tough gig, mounting an appeal process; everything seems against you. Sue seemed to be taking it in her stride. She was outwardly calm, although I was told by those within her family circle that she was racked with fear.

Meaghan Vass was our first witness. Paul had found her sharing a little flat on the outskirts of Hobart and had served her with a subpoena. She had gone to ground about the same time Jeff Thompson was charged with perverting the course of justice, as had many of our informers. Since that day, police had swamped the Hobart underworld, banging on doors, forcing conversations with people who had been helpful to us. People stopped talking, stopped ringing with information. It just dried up, from a torrent to nothing.

Meaghan stood in the witness box and raised the bible, swearing to tell the truth, the whole truth and nothing but the truth. Then came the result of all the police pressure. She recanted her statutory declaration. Outright. The information contained in the statement was 'not fucking true', she said.

Tom Percy reeled, then rallied. In response to his questions, Meaghan agreed that she was out all night with her boyfriend Dodger on 26 January 2009. She also agreed that she'd signed the declaration, but she was muddled as to who was with her when it was presented to her. 'I was made to sign that piece of paper,' she claimed. She then demanded a five-minute break, becoming flustered and aggressive and finally running from the witness box, yelling, 'I can't do this anymore, Damien.'

The court was adjourned. Tom Percy wrote down her last comment, as did many others in the courtroom. Damien was the name of the detective sergeant who, alongside Maverick, was behind the raid and charging of Jeff Thompson and the investigation of Gabby for perverting the course of justice. During the adjournment, Meaghan spoke with Damien. Many in the court wondered why. I wondered what it was that she couldn't do anymore, and why she sought comfort with a cop, as opposed to family or friends. Then the hearing reconvened.

When Meaghan returned to the stand, Tom Percy raised the passage in her declaration that said she was 'there [on *Four Winds*] with other people'. She answered by stating that the comment was false; that Gabby had made it up. Each passage of the declaration Tom raised with her, Meaghan claimed was false: 'I was made to sign it out of fear.' When asked whether Sue Neill-Fraser was on the yacht that night, all Meaghan would say was, 'I can't remember.' I had heard that a few hundred times before.

Meaghan then told a wild story about Gabby: 'the one that made up the statement that we're reading'. She said Gabby had threatened her, telling Meaghan that she would be placed in the boot of a car if she didn't sign the statement. Inconveniently for Meaghan, Gabby had been locked away in Risdon Prison since 18 February 2017, and remains there. No one can get to her and she can't get to anyone else. Certainly, she was unable to have any contact with Meaghan. She had been incarcerated for almost ten weeks before Meaghan signed her declaration. So, Meaghan's silly claim had to be invented. But by who?

As Tom Percy pressed Meaghan for more information she simply locked up, saying forty-one times that she 'can't remember'. She was doing what she always did; she shut down. At one point, she admitted to thinking about Sue every day for the past eight years. At another, she yelled, 'I would go and unlock the cell door for her if I could. But I can't. Please, can I go? Please can I just go?' Meaghan could offer no explanation about how her DNA got on *Four Winds* and she never denied being on the yacht. Tom Percy sat down, his questioning of Meaghan complete. The courtroom went silent until the whispers started. Tom Percy and Paul Galbally's appeal case was starting to look awfully sad. Observers in the courtroom told me later that the only smiles in the room were on police faces.

The prosecutor stood to enjoy his turn in the limelight. His work was all but done, even though he hadn't asked the key witness anything. Nevertheless, he still had a few carefully selected questions he wanted to toss Meaghan's way. And my way, I guess.

Meaghan admitted that she was out on the night of Australia Day, 2009 with her boyfriend Dodger, and accepted that a photo identification by Stephen Gleeson as being of Dodger was indeed of Dodger.

Under the prosecutor's questioning Meaghan reiterated that Gabby 'wrote out the statement that's in front of me and made me sign it'. She didn't recall discussing the contents of the statement or applying for indemnity from prosecution with Jeff Thompson; rather she said she was simply shown the declaration and asked to sign it. Bizarrely, she also suggested that Eve was in the hotel room along with Kylie, Alfred, Snapper and I, when we were trying to record her memories of the night Bob disappeared. Meaghan had never met Eve, who was in Bali at the time of the hotel meeting, having a family holiday.

Then came the bombshell. The prosecutor suggested that I offered Meaghan money for her statement. She agreed: 'He did say there would be money.' Hearing this lie, I was shattered.

My name, my work, were being poisoned. Who had placed that lie, and the others, in Meaghan's head? What was really happening here? Meaghan couldn't have thought all this rubbish up on her own. Someone was pulling her strings.

There was one comment from Meaghan that I took away as a positive. She was asked, 'Did [Gabby] introduce you to another person by the name of Colin Maclaren [sic].' To which Meaghan replied, 'Yes.' The fact is, despite travelling to Hobart to meet Gabby, for the purposes of meeting Meaghan, the planned introduction never eventuated. Meaghan failed to appear. The only time Gabby introduced me to Meaghan was on the mobile phone, a week before my trip to Hobart, when she told me she'd been on *Four Winds* with others and there had been a fight. That was the only conversation I had with Meaghan when Gabby was present. (Later, when I had a chance to read the transcript, I wanted to scold Meaghan for her outright lies; on the other hand, I wanted to thank her for reminding me of the one and only time Gabby introduced me to her. This, in some way, confirms my conversation with Meaghan back in January 2017. The conversation where she told me that she was on the yacht and there was a fight.)

Tom Percy challenged Meaghan about her claim that I had offered her cash for her statement. 'You have never been promised any money, have you?'

'No,' Meaghan answered. Of course she hadn't, I don't pay witnesses for comment. Soon after, Meaghan stepped down from the witness box and walked out of court, back to the low-life streets from whence she came. And my name had started to take on an indelible shade of black.

* * *

An interesting aside is that I later noticed, when reading the court transcripts, that the prosecutor referred to me as a 'private detective' in his questions to witnesses. At first I thought nothing of it, then Charlie Bezzina pointed out that there are massive fines, up to $20,000, as well as serious prison time for unlicensed private detectives operating in Tasmania. Clever. I'm an author, writer and documentary filmmaker. I am not a private detective. I wouldn't want to be known as one as I have a pretty poor opinion of them. I became involved in the Sue Neill-Fraser case as a consultant to Eve Ash, and as an investigative journalist planning to write a book and as a documentary filmmaker. Charlie told me to be extremely careful. He could smell a rat, or two. And they were wearing suits. As insurance, I had my lawyer draft a letter to the DPP, outlining my writing career, and attaching the documents that I had provided to Risdon Prison back in 2016, when, as an author, I sought to visit Stephen Gleeson. The letter also pointed out that my tax returns have listed me as a writer for many years.

* * *

Stephen Gleeson was pulled from Risdon Prison to appear at Sue's appeal in early November. He stood by his previously stated belief that Pablo was involved in Bob Chappell's disappearance. He alleged Pablo had spoken to him shortly after Bob and Sue first moored *Four Winds* in Sandy Bay, just a month before Bob's disappearance. Pablo had told him that Bob was a 'condescending old cunt and I'd like to rip his teeth out of his head with a pair of pliers'.

Gleeson confirmed his identification of Meaghan as the homeless girl who knocked on his car window on the night of Australia Day. He also offered an additional piece of information that I was previously unaware of: Meaghan was carrying a bag that he thought had food inside it. This dovetails with the burglary in Blackmans Bay that same night, when seafood and alcohol were stolen. The police report of this incident was the one in which someone had tried to obliterate the name 'Megan'. (It's worth recalling in this context the vomit found in the laundry of *Four Winds*, samples of which were taken by a forensic scientist for toxicology examination. The samples went missing. Might the vomit in the samples have contained seafood?)

From the court transcript, it is plain that Gleeson voiced his frustration at the way his evidence had been repeatedly ignored: in 2009, when he walked into Hobart Police Station a couple of weeks after Bob's disappearance and told a policewoman that he suspected his best mate, Pablo, was involved in his murder; and in his 2012 police interview with Detective Inspector Powell, when he repeated this belief. He was blunt. 'The purpose of the interview [in 2012] is to twist it [his evidence] around … it clearly shows that it was corrupt and designed to stop me from telling the court what I'm telling them now … I'd call the interview a threat … an attempt to scare me off from this case.'

He also referred to the police interviewing him again in August, only months before Sue's appeal. (I, and the rest of Sue's team, only became aware of this when Stephen mentioned it at the trial.) 'You've asked me about every interview except the one that I report – Tasmania police nine years ago.'

By the end of his time in the witness stand, Stephen Gleeson was almost defeated, managing only one-word answers and sounding muddled. He had been asked 1651 questions about the events of Australia Day, 2009 over the course of two police interviews and one Supreme Court appearance. In all the task force investigations I have been a part of, never have I known a witness to be subjected to such protracted interrogations that have yielded nothing except to affirm his original testimony. I genuinely believe the treatment of Stephen is without precedent in Australia. His final word, after this intense scrutiny was, 'They [Meaghan Vass and her male companion] were definitely there [late at night, at his car window] on Australia Day.'

Balance this against the treatment given to Meaghan Vass, who was never subjected to a formal interview by police. She was never asked one solitary question in an official police interrogation. Why on earth not? The irrefutable evidence of her puddle of DNA demands that she should have been. As for Dodger, a gold-plated person of interest, he was only interviewed for half an hour. Police refused to consider that, just maybe, Dodger and Meaghan, and Pablo too, might have warranted more of an effort. Meaghan and Pablo – whose names I had circled in red all those months earlier in Eve Ash's makeshift muster room – were never seriously investigated to what I consider an acceptable standard. Nor was Dodger, even though the police knew he'd lied about his relationship with Meaghan and seemed unusually interested in the media reports on the court cases that followed regarding Sue Neill-Fraser.

* * *

When Pablo took to the witness stand at Sue's appeal, Tom Percy established that he was living aboard his yacht and that it was moored in Sandy Bay at the time Bob Chappell disappeared. Pablo also told the court that sometimes homeless people came aboard his yacht and they would drink together. He admitted his prior convictions for violence, which included stabbing a bouncer at a nightclub. He confirmed his friendship with Stephen Gleeson, who had lived with him on his yacht for a time, and said that Gleeson was living in a 'yellow XF 1983 Ford Falcon registration CK 067' parked at the Rowing Club car park when Bob disappeared. Gleeson used to cook meals with a 'Gasmate stove', a portable one-burner camp cooker, Pablo said. His knowledge of Gleeson and his belongings indicated he knew him well. It also indicated the reverse: that Gleeson knew Pablo well.

Tom Percy attempted to clarify the exact location of Pablo's yacht in relation to *Four Winds* when Bob disappeared. Pablo agreed that he was aboard his yacht in Sandy Bay on the night of Australia Day and that he saw *Four Winds* sailing towards Bruny Island the day before. He recalled details of the yacht, such as its size and the fact that it had two masts. Percy also established that Pablo saw Stephen Gleeson the 'next day' after Australia Day. This is consistent with what he'd said to police in his two previous interviews: in 2012 and in August 2017 (more about this second interview later). Pablo stated that Stephen used to come on board his yacht, for a drink: 'He used to yell out from … the seawall [Rowing Shed Point] and then I would come over and get him and take him back to the boat and have a cask of wine with him.'

This evidence established that Pablo's yacht was moored relatively close to the shoreline; close enough to see Gleeson and to hear him yelling that he wanted to come aboard for a drink. It was also consistent with what he had already told police: that he was moored 'just off the starboard side' of *Four Winds*. As noted earlier, the rowing sheds are four to five metres in height and run most of the length of Rowing Shed Point. From this spot, vision of the bay is limited to the north-east, the direction in which the two yachts were moored. Percy then asked how close the two yachts were to each other. In response, Pablo delivered a bolt out of the blue: 'Well, from there to there would be a kilometre.' He explained further. 'We looked at the legend yesterday and one of the DPP representatives said that it would possibly be a kilometre.' This was totally at odds with what Pablo had consistently said previously.

Percy reminded Pablo of the interview he'd given to police in 2012, when he said that he was moored much closer to *Four Winds*. Pablo simply repeated the glaring contradiction: 'We've checked the legend and it's approximately a kilometre according to the legend.' At this moment, just as Tom Percy was about to question Pablo about this blatant inconsistency, the prosecutor, Daryl Coates, raised an objection. Percy was shut down, unable to probe the extraordinary revelation that Pablo had sat down with a DPP representative and worked out a revised location of his yacht's mooring. The reason he was shut down is Percy had called Pablo to the witness stand and lawyers can't cross examine their own witness. A technicality that ended Percy's run at Pablo.

When the prosecutor, Coates, came to question Pablo, he endeavoured to establish when Stephen Gleeson told him about Bob Chappell's disappearance. Both men had stated previously that they spoke about Bob's murder and the flooding of *Four Winds* the morning after Australia Day; that is, 27 January. Coates initially ascertained, as Percy had done earlier, that Pablo was on his yacht the night of Australia Day. Coates then said, 'The next time you saw Mr Gleeson did he tell you, "You should have been here yesterday?"' With the inclusion of the word 'yesterday', Coates had inserted twenty-four hours into the timeline, suggesting to Pablo that Gleeson had spoken to him on 28 January, rather than 27 January.

Coates reminded Pablo that Gleeson had told him that 'There were police about and the *Four Winds* had sunk and Mr Chappell was missing.' Pablo agreed with this, repeating Coates's version of what Gleeson told him: 'You should have been here *yesterday*. It was a real circus here. They had the police rescue squad and the fire brigade here.'

Coates reinforced the altered timeline: 'So you didn't see Mr Gleeson on Australia Day. You didn't see him the next day?' Pablo agreed with this. Coates locked it off with one final comment: 'It was the day after [28 January] that he saw you and he said, "You should have been here yesterday." 'Is that right?' And, yes, Pablo agreed.

The Supreme Court of Hobart had been told a new version of the events relating to the morning Bob Chappell was discovered missing. It wasn't Pablo who had altered the story; it was Daryl Coates, the DPP, who had introduced the new timeline: that Pablo didn't see or talk to Stephen Gleeson until 28 January. In fact, the wording even changed. 'Earlier', recorded in the transcript of Pablo's 2012 police interview – 'I've come in with a hangover and, um, he said, um, he said, "Ah shit, you ought to have been here *earlier*," ' – became 'yesterday'. It helps this timeline that Gleeson had mentioned fire trucks and cops being around, which meant it could only have been the same morning Bob Chappell went missing.

Even in Pablo's police interview in August 2017, just a few months before Sue's appeal, Pablo recalled it was the day *after* Australia Day that he had spoken to Gleeson about the sinking yacht.

The changed timeline is locked into the court transcript, not once, not twice but three times, with the insertion of the word 'yesterday'. This seems extraordinary to me. And contrary to everything else (on this salient point) that had been gathered before, from court extracts, transcripts, statements, records of interview, and witness testimony.

Later in his evidence, Pablo attempted to recall something that happened the day after Australia Day, the day the yacht was seen taking water. He mentioned something to do with a 'neighbour'. He said, 'The day the boat was sinking, apparently one of the neighbours had …' Coates jumped up and objected. He stopped him from going any further and repeated the altered timeline: 'You didn't see him the next day. You saw him the day after, the twenty-eighth.' Pablo's reply was a soft 'Mmm'.

Eddie Hidding, who worked at the Bay Chandlery, was also called to give evidence by the defence at the appeal. When I interviewed him as part of my research back in 2016, he told me he had seen *Four Winds* and Pablo's yacht in a close cluster. However, when the DPP suggested that Pablo's yacht was a kilometre away, Eddie simply agreed. Despite the fact that it was an impossibility. For Eddie to have been able to see both yachts when they were a kilometre apart, he would have had to stand on the roof of the chandlery, looking through a set of binoculars, beyond the vast collection of yachts moored at the Royal Yacht Club. It was not what he had sworn in his affidavit after I talked with him.

The Crown's contention that Pablo's yacht was moored a kilometre south of *Four Winds*, out on deep water, would put his yacht opposite Wrest Point Casino. It made a mockery of Eddie's view of the two yachts. It also ran completely counter to what another witness for the defence, Stephen Shields, who also worked at the Bay Chandlery, had stated. Which was in line with what Eddie stated originally. Additionally, Grant Maddock had told me about the position of the two yachts, when I interviewed him in 2016; again, his recollection was that both yachts were close together. Beside these witnesses all saying the same thing, how on earth could Pablo communicate with his 'best friend' Stephen Gleeson by calling to him to come out to his boat to drink wine if he was moored a kilometre from the shore. How could he have even seen Stephen from this revised location? Not to mention the barrier of the rowing sheds in his line of vision.

The greatest issue in the way the evidence seemed to change was that as all these witnesses were defence witnesses, Tom Percy was limited in what he could cross-examine them about, due to the rule where he isn't able to do so. All I could do was shake my head in frustration.

Shifting the goalposts

It's worth revisiting Pablo's original 2012 police interview and other witness testimonies to understand how far the goalposts had been shifted by November 2017.

In Pablo's 2012 police interview he stated that his yacht was 'about three hundred, two hundred, two fifty to three hundred metres away or something [from *Four Winds*]'. He went on: 'So he [Bob Chappell] would have been slightly off to the starboard side. It would have been slightly off to the starboard side.' It's obvious that Pablo was moored very close to Bob's yacht. Let's not forget too that in 2012 Stephen Gleeson also recalled that Pablo's yacht was moored close to *Four Winds*.

Five years later, in August 2017, unknown to Sue's defence team, police interviewed Pablo again. From the transcript, it appears that police were encouraging Pablo to change his recollection of how close the yachts were moored to each other. They pulled out a nautical map and presented it to Pablo. A discussion followed, and they seemed to reach a consensus as to where Pablo was moored, and Pablo marked the map to indicate the position of his yacht. The dialogue at this point strikes me as odd. One of the officers said, 'If you're happy with that location, can I get you to sign just beside that?' Pablo agreed and signed the map. He was asked again, 'And so to the best of your recollection that's where your boat was moored?' Pablo again agreed. The police response seemed overly enthusiastic. 'Cool. Thanks [Pablo], and I'll sign the bottom of the map too.'

Pablo's yacht, all of a sudden, was positioned a long way from *Four Winds*. As pleased as the detective may have been, he perhaps wasn't aware that I had spoken to witnesses back in 2016, whose statements corroborated Pablo's previous evidence that his yacht was moored close to *Four Winds*. Stephen Shields and Eddie Hidding from the Bay Chandlery both recalled Pablo and his yacht in some detail. Shields had even been aboard Pablo's yacht. Prior to the disappearance of Bob Chappell, whilst moored near to the *Four Winds,* Pablo contemplated selling his yacht and had asked Shields to inspect it and give some advice. Shields went aboard and inspected the craft. On another occasion, again prior to January 2009, Shields recalled Pablo's intention to moor his yacht on a small rickety jetty below the 'Shipwrights Arms street'. The little jetty is near to where *Four Winds* was moored. He advised Pablo against doing this as the jetty was fragile and not used for moorings. Ultimately, Pablo moored near to the *Four Winds*. At Sue's appeal, Shields told the court that Pablo's yacht 'might have been in that sort of vicinity' (of the *Four Winds*).

Eddie Hidding knew Pablo well. He made a sworn affidavit on 21 September 2016 stating his knowledge of Pablo and where his yacht was moored. Pablo was a customer of his, and Eddie recalled that he was a heavy drinker. As pointed out earlier, the position of the chandlery – a building with windows on only one side (and facing towards the wall of rowing club sheds) offered Eddie only a 'restricted view' of the yachts. I checked that limited view when I interviewed him and believe his field of vision was just upwards of 15 degrees, to the north-east. As he explained to me, he could only see a small number of yachts. Eddie recalled Pablo's yacht as being near *Four Winds* for about twelve months. He referred to seeing them 'in a cluster'. Eddie went on to make a mark on a bird's-eye-view image of the bay to show where the two yachts were, close together. He then signed the image, as did a justice of the peace. Eddie's view accorded with that of Stephen Shields, as well as that of another local yachtie, Grant Maddock, who was on the bay the night of 26 January 2009 and recalled the two yachts close together. Of course, Eddie's 2016 affidavit accorded with Stephen Gleeson's evidence too. There were numerous yachting people who put the two yachts together, including, back in 2012, Pablo himself.

Despite this wall of witness recollections, the DPP slowly and (some might say) masterfully shifted the goalposts to create doubt as to where Pablo's yacht was really moored. Two hundred and fifty metres away or … a kilometre away. Again, I just shook my head.

Interestingly, something else of interest was revealed in Pablo's 2017 police interview. He told police at one point that, 'Apparently somebody had cut the bilge line [on *Four Winds*] or something and um, and it was slowly submerging.' While it was common knowledge that a water inlet valve had been opened on the yacht and a water pipe had been cut, it was not widely known that the bilge pumps had been disengaged. It had never been reported in the media. How did Pablo know this?

* * *

Stephen Gleeson was also formally re-interviewed by police in August 2017, weeks before the appeal. This interview, conducted in prison, was also not disclosed to the defence. This time, unlike back in 2012, the detectives paid close attention to what Gleeson had to say, insofar as they were trying to trip him up on the information he had given to Sue's team in his affidavit.

Over a three-and-a-half-hour interrogation, police attempted to discredit Gleeson's identification of Meaghan Vass, yet he never faltered. He reaffirmed that he was in his yellow Ford sedan late on the night of Australia Day, 2009, when Meaghan tapped on the window and spoke to him, and that she was with a young man, slightly older than her. How was it that Gleeson could recall Meaghan and a young man tapping on the window of his car that night, eight years previous? they asked him. And why had he never mentioned this fact until he and I spoke? Gleeson explained that his memory had improved since he'd stopped drinking. He hadn't drunk alcohol in three years. He stood by his evidence.

The police also asked Stephen about me: when had he first met me and how had I approached the interviews I did with him? In his reply, he said he'd been told by prison security that our meetings were under surveillance and being monitored. Not surprising. Nor was I particularly concerned. I'd done nothing wrong or illegal. It did show, though, that someone, somewhere, was concerned about me. What was I talking about, what had I said, the police asked Gleeson. He fielded a volley of questions about these issues. Not surprisingly, given the inordinate number of questions the police asked, Gleeson made a couple of errors in answering them.

Much was made of a comment that I supposedly made to Gleeson during one of my visits: that Meaghan and a man named Adam were on *Four Winds*. Police seized upon it, asking questions. But Gleeson was wrong; I never said that. I have never put that proposition to anyone. If I believed a man named Adam was on the yacht, I would have noted it in my white paper. It doesn't appear anywhere.

Another simple error Gleeson made was stating I was with Jeff Thompson at a second interview with him. (The only time Jeff and I were at the prison together was when Gleeson identified Meaghan from a folder of photos.) The interview with Jeff that Gleeson was confused about actually happened when I was in Italy, 18,000 kilometres away. Such mix-ups happen; after all, Stephen had fielded 1651 questions. I can understand how he might have been confused a couple of times. Anyone would.

Nevertheless, throughout the interview, Gleeson remained unflappable, pointing towards the involvement of Pablo and Meaghan at Sandy Bay. At no time did police probe deeply into his evidence or try to uncover corroborating facts. They simply tried to trip him up, searching for contradictions in what he said. Gleeson's doggedness in maintaining the truthfulness of his answers and assertions was impressive.

* * *

As well as shifting the goalposts alarmingly, the appeal tossed up some intriguing snippets of information, previously not known to Sue's defence team. Stephen Catchpool, whom I'd interviewed in 2016, lived in a large house overlooking Sandy Bay and the rowing sheds. Before Bob Chappell went missing,

Catchpool recalled looking through his telescope at a yellow Ford sedan and a homeless man living in the car. This, of course, was Stephen Gleeson. He also saw a man who came and went from the area in a dinghy and talked to the man in the Ford. At Sue's appeal, when questioned by Paul Galbally, he identified the man in the dinghy as Pablo. This vital evidence, long known to police, had not been revealed at Sue's original trial.

And the evidence of Catchpool's wife, Jane Austin, whose photos of *Four Winds*, taken the morning of Bob's disappearance, were seized by police, had been suppressed too. Austin is an astute and intelligent woman, who ran for state parliament. She'd looked out at *Four Winds* around 8 pm on 26 January 2009 and made a remarkable observation. The police log states:

> *1945–2030hrs Jane Austin observes an inflatable dinghy*
> *– she believes is the zodiac – leaving the area of the*
> *Four Winds. States that she believed a male was driving*
> *it towards the casino. Male described as: – 40–50yrs*
> *weather-beaten sailor look – wavy thick reddish-brown*
> *hair, white collared short sleeve (or rolled sleeves) shirt. The*
> *person was sitting in the rear left of the dinghy steering the*
> *outboard with his right hand...'*

The description of the person in the boat matches Pablo, and Sue Neill-Fraser owned a Zodiac dinghy. Yet Detective Maverick added the following comment to the police running sheet:

> *Person fits description of Sue Neill-Fraser – witness was*
> *some distance from dinghy and presumed it was a male due*
> *to the way the dinghy was sitting low in the water at the*
> *rear...*

I had to read this many times over before I realised it was not an attempt at humour. I was gobsmacked at the reaction to Austin's evidence. I applied that great Aussie benchmark, the pub test, to Jane's observation. Would anyone in a public bar think a weather-beaten male, with the look of a sailor, upwards of fifty years and with thick, wavy, reddish-brown hair and wearing a white collared shirt would look like Sue Neill-Fraser? What was going on with Tasmania Police and this vital piece of evidence?

Worryingly, Jane Austin was not called at Sue's trial. The defence was not made aware of the evidence of the weather-beaten man. I found this out during my research and fell into that gobsmacked state once again. Nor do the photos Jane took appear in the police files I have studied, and they were not tendered by the prosecution at the trial, except for one that showed *Four Winds* taking water on 27 January. None of the pre-Australia Day photos, which may have been valuable, at least in confirming the position of Pablo's yacht, were tendered. I wonder why not?

Another potential piece of evidence that I found out about was also ignored by the police. A claim from a woman living on the foreshore that she heard a 'male, distressed voice' in the middle of the night on 26 January 2009. It might have assisted police work out when Bob Chappell was killed. Yet it was simply filed away. Naturally, it was not passed on to the defence or mentioned at Sue's trial.

Yet another puzzle was why Barbara Etter, Sue's lawyer, was denied access to images police lifted from the security footage of Wrest Point Casino taken that night, as well as dozens of photos taken by local residents. Details of the images were redacted from the police reports Barbara obtained. Why on earth? What secrets loom among these images?

Indeed, throughout the long lead-up to Sue's appeal, in the years following the original trial, the goalposts moved all over the legal playing field, as Barbara would come to understand, time and again. A startling example was the police contention that Sue was observed with an injury to her thumb on the morning of Bob's disappearance. According to the police story, a couple of hours after Bob Chappell was declared missing, a constable 'discovered' a laceration to Sue's left thumb moments after he met her on her arrival at the foreshore. At Sue's trial, the constable alleged she was shielding the injury with a Band-Aid. When she removed the Band-Aid, supposedly at his request, a cut was exposed, that 'appeared to have been made by a knife'.

Bear in mind this was mere hours after *Four Winds* was found sinking. At this point the only police consideration was where Bob Chappell might be. Murder wasn't even considered as a possibility that day; it wasn't until Phillip Triffett made contact with police the following day that foul play was in the air. Fascinatingly, no one else recalled the constable asking Sue to remove the Band-Aid. He made no mention of his extraordinary observation in his notebook, nor did he photograph the laceration or speak to Sue or her children about it. His written police statement made that same day, tendered at Sue's trial, has no reference to a laceration. He claimed in court that he told a sergeant at the foreshore about Sue's cut thumb, yet the sergeant never made mention, anywhere, of this vital observation.

In fact the damning 'evidence' was only recorded months later when Sue was under suspicion for murder and the good constable wrote a passage about the supposed cut in his revised statement. He claimed that he'd rung the detective sergeant in charge at 9.30 pm on 27 January 2009 to inform him of the laceration to Sue's thumb. At trial, the detective sergeant declared that as a result of that phone call, he had 'grave fears for the life of Robert Chappell'.

The detective sergeant spoke to Sue the next day but failed to mention or inspect the laceration. He also failed to photograph the wound, have a doctor examine the cut or seek a forensic opinion on the wound, which would have a starring role at Sue's trial, fifteen months later. The laceration didn't even get a mention on the investigation log. Not only that, through a Right to Information request, Barbara found there was no record of a 9.30 pm phone call on the police phone that night.

The morning the laceration was supposedly discovered, the same detective sergeant was with Sue for hours. He supervised Sue's inspection of the vessel, where she opened and closed cupboards, and tried turning on the bilge pumps. Obviously, he saw no cut to her thumb, as surely he would have dutifully noted it in his notebook. At 11 am on the morning police were salvaging the yacht, the same detective sergeant took a saliva swab from Sue for DNA elimination. Yet he failed to swab her allegedly injured left thumb for DNA.

Furthermore, when the detective sergeant eventually interviewed Sue in March 2009 as part of the murder investigation, he didn't mention the laceration 'made by a knife'. And none of the countless witnesses who were standing with the grief-stricken Sue on the foreshore, on the morning she was told that Bob was missing, possibly murdered, recalled any cut to her thumb. This despite many of them comforting her and embracing her as she and they watched the team salvaging her yacht. Bob's own son and daughter were there, as well as Sue's two adult daughters and Bob Martyn. None of them recall any cut to Sue's thumb or any discussion about a cut from any police officer.

The constable who discovered this 'evidence' stated at Sue's trial that when he asked her about it, she replied it was a 'recent' injury. Damning? Certainly, if it were true. Yet the constable never mentioned her comment in his notebook, his earlier statements (which weren't signed until the morning of the preliminary hearing) or in his oral evidence at the preliminary hearing. He just saved it up for a rainy day, I guess. Sue repeatedly offered to have her thumb tested by medical experts, to determine if a cut ever existed, but the police never took the offer up. Such was the nature of the legal playing field Sue and her team had to negotiate.

How the mighty fall

THE APPEAL PROCESS THAT HAD ENGULFED THE LIFE OF SUE Neill-Fraser, the media and many witnesses presented by her loyal and pro bono team of lawyers would ultimately grind to a halt in November 2017. Adjourned yet again, until the new year. A work in progress some might say. Or a longwinded never-ending story, others might consider. The reason it was put off until 2018 was simple court stuff: the unavailability of a witness who was working in America. So, Sue would flop back into her wheelchair and get shunted back to prison to wait for a new calendar date to come her way. I recall feeling an overwhelming sense of sadness for the woman I had never met. Swallowed up in legal administrative mumbo jumbo, surely, she was, by now, the most patient person in the country. Inside, or outside of prison.

However, as everyone waited for the court bell to ring again and turned their attentions to other issues, a few of the brave who stood in the Supreme Court and told their story faced a less than welcoming outcome, including Sue herself.

There was a disappointing postscript to the pummelling Stephen Gleeson endured in the Supreme Court. Like the heavyweight boxer who took one uppercut too many, yet doggedly refused to surrender, Gleeson ultimately fell on the canvas, knocked out. Following his grilling at Sue's appeal, he was hauled into the Hobart Magistrates Court weeks later, without a lawyer to represent him. Flanked by detectives, he finally threw in the towel and pleaded guilty to one count of perverting the course of justice.

Those in the courtroom were unclear as to why Gleeson pleaded guilty. Perhaps it had something to do with the massive session of questioning he'd been subjected to in the Supreme Court. At one point, he'd unwisely said he was prepared to lie to help Sue Neill-Fraser, as he believed her to be innocent and that police had lied throughout their dealings in the case. A silly comment made under stress. A throwaway line. But in its utterance, Stephen Gleeson destroyed himself and his value as, potentially, a powerful witness for the defence of Sue Neill-Fraser.

Magistrate Glenn Hay, who heard the charges against Gleeson, seemed to sense that all was not well with him. Three times he urged Gleeson to speak to a lawyer, and to refrain from making his plea until he received legal advice. Gleeson looked defeated, lost and kept repeating that he was 'trying to save a woman's life' and he was 'up against corruption at the top of the police force'. He was angry and fearful, claiming he had been threatened by motorcycle gang members while in prison. And now he was looking at added jail time.

It was a bitter blow to all involved in Sue's defence. Despite the circumstances of his life and his history of violence, Gleeson has some admirable traits, such as persistence and, in my opinion, honesty. Barbara, Sue's lawyer for so long, found him to be raw and honest. Belinda Lonsdale, the senior counsel from Perth assisting at Sue's appeal, was moved by Stephen Gleeson's civility and street-level decency. Jeff Thompson saw a vein of blunt honesty in Gleeson, not common among prison inmates. I feel deep sorrow for Stephen Gleeson, who has endured a hard life on Hobart's sometimes mean streets. In my humble opinion, he deserves better.

Another casualty of Sue's appeal was Snapper, Meaghan's protector and sometime boyfriend. At an extraordinary meeting of the motorcycle club, a resolution was made to sack Snapper, its founding member, not just from the presidency, but from the club. He was told to pack up and move on, after forty-two years. He was banished, made homeless, like his sweet pea, Meaghan, who by then was living with him at the clubhouse. Both were seen carrying their stuff along a long lonely road, in the arse end of the factory zone that houses the club. Deep Throat would tell us that Snapper was devastated. He vowed to have nothing more to do with Meaghan; his efforts to help her had all been for nothing.

As for Sue, she was sitting alone in her cell one day, making Christmas cards for her grandchildren. Her cell door was kicked open and she was raided by a team of security guards. Sue, a model prisoner, couldn't imagine what they were looking for. All the goons found was the little pair of scissors used by Sue for her craftwork, which she had been using for years with permission.

Her half-made cards were tossed into the rubbish bin and Sue was transferred to a high security cell, to share space with Gabby, who was on remand for perverting the Tasmanian version of justice. She was also denied visitors. Police probably hoped Sue and Gabby's talk would confirm they had conspired together. No doubt there was a recording device concealed in their cell. Sue was onto the manoeuvre in minutes and complained, to no avail. She then went on a hunger strike and three days later, thanks to the intervention of her lawyers, she was returned to her own cell. The whole sordid saga made front-page news across the country.

Enough is enough

THE TIME I'D SPENT IN MY ASIAN SAFE HAVEN SEEMED LONG ago. As worried as I was back then, about my own liberty and the wellbeing of Jeff Thompson and Eve Ash it was nothing compared to how things were progressing. Everyone on Sue's side of the legal ledger felt the case was almost doomed, what with the way things ended when the appeal was adjourned. There was a sense of despair amongst the team. It was December 2017 and I was in Melbourne, busying myself with this manuscript and gathering documents.

Eve handed me a file that would bowl me over. It was a detective's investigation file that had surfaced, and the defence team had no prior knowledge of it. We received it as a part of the documents that Barbara Etter had surrendered when she quit the case and it had taken this long to land on my lap. Essentially, the file was a compilation of the work documents of Detective Maverick, who had investigated Meaghan Vass once her DNA had been identified as one of the samples found on *Four Winds*. Maverick seems to have worked this angle of the case alone. I recall being fascinated by the set of documents that were obviously genuine. Maverick was the one detective in this complex yet fascinating case who was in the centre of every discovery, every stage, every twist and turn. To have his file was a gift. Any experienced detective can read another detective's file, work sheets. It's just a matter of putting the file in chronological order and following the progress. To help the task I was able to see that most of the papers had Maverick's police registered number stamped on the pages, which helped to verify the file. I got to work.

The file held police reports on burglaries at Blackmans Bay, south from Sandy Bay, in January 2009, including a break-and-enter at 126 Roslyn Ave (a house under construction near the foreshore), on the night of Australia Day, 2009. Beer, wine and seafood were stolen. The report detailed the arrests of teenagers, about Meaghan Vass's age, for theft. In the top right-hand corner of the police report was a handwritten notation that had been scratched out. Eve Ash and I wondered what information might be so sensitive that it needed to be eradicated. We played with this document for a while.

We scanned the document with the obliterated note into a computer, then enlarged it 200 per cent. Then 400 per cent. When viewed with the backlight of the computer, the following handwritten words were seen: *'All kids said Megan ... sitting out front of the burg [burglary].'* The handwriting seemed the same throughout the file. Therefore, the work of one person.

I couldn't help but wonder why did someone try to destroy this note? Maybe because the resurrected words indicated that a 'Megan' (perhaps a misspelling of Meaghan) was keeping nit – watching out – while someone robbed a shed close to the foreshore on the night of Bob Chappell's murder. The officer who investigated the Blackmans Bay burglary was the

policewoman detective friend who had once babysat Meaghan
as an infant. Further, Stephen Gleeson had recalled that when
Meaghan Vass and a young male companion told him they
were planning to steal from yachts, she was carrying a bag.
Did that bag hold stolen food and alcohol? Meaghan, as far as
I could decipher, had not been charged over this burglary.

There was a large number of other crime reports in
Maverick's file, all dating from around the same time, dealing
with break-ins on yachts or at marine facilities, many of them
involving the male teenage thief who factored in the raid for
the fire extinguisher mentioned by Panton, in early 2009.
Meaghan had told me, when we first met, that she was with
this teenager and Dodger the night of Australia Day, 2009.
And it was the thief's parents' house that was raided by police
searching for a fire extinguisher, according to Panton, in early
2009. Oddly, a police mugshot of Meaghan Vass taken around
this time was included in the file, despite her not having a
police record back then.

The file then jumped to February 2010 when Maverick
obtained a copy of Meaghan's arrest sheet for theft. (It was
after this arrest that a sample of her DNA was taken and
matched to the puddle of DNA found on *Four Winds*.) On 15
March 2010 Maverick requested more reports, on Meaghan's
background and her associates. There was a report noting that
Meaghan and her then boyfriend, Dodger, were spoken to for
threatening behaviour to others. This was dated 12 January
2009. (More evidence that Dodger was lying when he told
police in 2017 that he hardly knew Meaghan and had only
met her in 2016.) Here they both were, in trouble together
for aggressive behaviour, just two weeks before Bob Chappell
was killed. Their aggression was levelled at Meaghan's

grandmother, who reported that she was worried about her granddaughter.

Maverick had reports of many offences of violence and theft committed by Meaghan Vass. The offences related to late 2008, early 2009 and through to early 2010. In all, there were seventeen entries bundled together.

Soon after he learned that Meaghan owned the puddle of DNA Maverick made contact with Shari Collis, the manager at Mara House, the halfway house where Meaghan was staying. Mara House was also the place that Meaghan was missing from in 2009 over several days, including Australia Day night and the next day. The written replies from Shari Collis to Maverick's inquiries made it clear Meaghan was in company with Dodger, a self-confessed 'burglar and car thief', and that Shari had received information from Meaghan's mother that Meaghan had been involved in a 'break-and-enter' over those few days.

Each time Maverick requested additional reports on Meaghan Vass it was for 'information purposes only', a common strategy used by detectives to avoid sensitive information in an investigation drawing attention from stickybeaks and then being compromised. The reports of marine break-ins kept coming in. One report related to Dodger, who was pulled over by police in mid-January 2009, two weeks before Bob Chappell was killed. It revealed that Dodger may have been eavesdropping on police communications with a 'police scanner'. Organised thieves commonly use scanners to ascertain the location of police before they break into a property. A scanner is a useful tool for any criminal, and a pretty good indicator that the person who has one, or mentions having one, is active as a thief. And Meaghan had told me that her mates were stealing from yachts and boats back in 2009. She'd

even stated that 'nine times out of ten' the thief would have
been Dodger.

Maverick also wrote to the forensic scientist, Carl Grosser,
who matched Meaghan Vass's DNA to that found on *Four
Winds*. The scientist replied, 'As discussed on the phone I will
not be issuing another copy of the report with this updated
information unless requested.' Was there a desire to keep the
DNA match secret? Maverick sent many more emails to the
scientist, seeking more information about when Meaghan's
DNA was located on the yacht.

By the early afternoon of 15 March 2010, Maverick was
fully aware of several crucial facts: Meaghan's DNA was
definitely on *Four Winds*; she was involved with Dodger in
January 2009; and there were an extraordinary number of
marine break-and-enters around that time. Let's not forget the
police report of another break-in on the night of 26 January
2009, in Lutana, on the water's edge, where thieves entered a
vessel and turned off the power at the switchboard. A report
that was elevated to 'Highly Protected' status. I can't believe
anyone would deliberately keep it hidden from the defence –
but how can I conclude otherwise?

Maverick's next request was for information on calls to and
from Meaghan Vass's mobile phone number. This time, rather
than 'information purposes', he gave 'murder' as the reason
for his inquiry. The authorising officer for this request was
Inspector Peter Powell, the head of the task force that charged
Sue Neill-Fraser with the murder of Bob Chappell. Sue,
while this frantic search for information about Meaghan was
happening, was on remand and awaiting trial. Maverick made
more requests for information throughout 15 March 2010.
Each time, 'murder' was cited as the offence being investigated.

In the file there was also a photocopy of a notebook page dated 15 March, which may have been taken from Maverick's notebook – it's impossible to say. The entire entry has been obliterated. All the evidence was pointing towards numerous potential suspects in the death of Bob Chappell. Yet at that point, the police, led by Inspector Powell, had charged Sue Neill-Fraser with murder and, in my opinion, ignored all other suspects – seemingly flying in the face of reason.

The next day Maverick called up some forensic photos of *Four Winds* and Sandy Bay from the police database. At 12.51 pm he looked at the photo of the dinghy found untethered alongside the rocks a few metres from Stephen Gleeson's yellow Ford sedan. Why did he choose that image? Two minutes later he called up a photo of *Four Winds* taken from the starboard side, where Meaghan's DNA was located. Maverick then requested more records concerning Meaghan Vass; however, he misspelled her name, writing 'Megan'. The same misspelling that someone attempted to obliterate on the crime report of a break-in that occurred around the time Bob Chappell was killed.

Maverick heard back about Meaghan's phone records. There were '10 raised' results. What were those results? They don't appear on the file. Who did Meaghan ring, and who rang her around the time of Bob Chappell's death?

Maverick again wrote to the forensic officer about Meaghan's DNA, asking whether it may have been a 'stain, or droplet'. As we know, he was informed it was a 'large amount of DNA'. We know it was a puddle of DNA, the size of a dinner plate, way too big to be considered a 'droplet'.

By this stage of analysing Maverick's file, I could almost see him in my mind. The information flow was slowing down, and everything was pointing to Meaghan Vass and her friends as possibly being involved in the *Four Winds* saga. Maverick, like all detectives, made notes and a list of things to do. Each note he wrote was headed 'Meaghan Vass'. In one he noted: *Definitely on Board. So — when, where, why, who with, how (dinghy, boarded, etc), Intent, theft? /burglary/ Trespass = put to her.'... 'Do you have any info Re: murder of Robert Chappell.'*

The notes also reminded Maverick to 'caution' Meaghan; to warn her that she was not obliged to say anything unless she wished to do so, as whatever she said may be used in evidence. Yet Sue Neill-Fraser never had the privilege of a 'caution'. In my assessment of the file, there can be no doubt that, for Maverick at least, Meaghan Vass was a suspect in the murder of Bob Chappell. Trouble was, Meaghan refused to be interviewed; she failed to meet her arranged appointment with Maverick.

Meanwhile, Maverick received more information about Meaghan's phone calls over the specified period. Three people were listed as having contacted Meaghan; however, those details were not in the file. Why not? Other mobile phone numbers were then linked to Meaghan and the file kept building. Maverick wrote again to the forensic officer on 23 March and explained that Meaghan had stated she wasn't on the yacht, but that he 'was reluctant to believe her'. Yet Meaghan was never formally interviewed. Never put through the investigative scrutiny that the facts in Maverick's file should have demanded.

The next morning, within a few minutes, Maverick called up four more forensic photographs:

- 9.08 am: *Four Winds* before Bob's disappearance.
- 9.09 am: ropes strewn around the skylight hatch. If enlarged, loose coins and scuff marks on the white exterior surface of the yacht are visible. (This is where I believe Bob's body was lifted from the vessel.)
- 9.10 am: the place police say Sue Neill-Fraser winched the body of Bob Chappell from the wheelhouse. The ropes are all neatly folded up, bundled together. If the winch was used, the ropes would be strewn about.
- 9.12 am: a second image of the messy ropes, from another angle, with the loose coins and scuff marks showing around the skylight hatch.

I believe I know why Maverick looked at those four images. If it was me, I'd be worried about the original investigation and I would have checked alternative scenarios.

On 24 March, 38 minutes after viewing the four images, Maverick emailed Shari Collis at Mara House, asking if Meaghan Vass had a 'cut foot' upon her return to the halfway house. Why did he ask that? I think I know: the two drops of inconclusive DNA, possibly blood, on the steps leading out of the yacht. Maverick wanted to know if the blood was Meaghan's. Let's recall that when the Hairdresser saw Meaghan she was barefooted.

Throughout the day, more reports hit the inbox of the now – in my estimation – shocked detective. There was more information on phone calls made to and from Meaghan's phone, and an expanding list of her associates, many of them with criminal histories. Again, Maverick's requests for information were made for reasons of 'murder'. One of the last documents was an A4-sized note on Meaghan Vass: *Likely Scenario. Mara House – Priors – Motive – Dinghy – Jacket.* Perhaps Maverick realised that it wasn't Sue who had dumped her jacket on the front fence of 26 Margaret Street, as I have attested all along. There had to be another explanation. Maverick's notes went on: *Movements 25, 26, 27, 28, 29, 30 Jan '09; Mara House. Prior Activity.* Four Winds. *Dinghy; Worked on boats – Electricals, etc.; Trespass on Boats;* and *Medical reason for memory loss.*

These notations and reports painted a picture of Meaghan as a suspect in Bob's disappearance off *Four Winds*. Yet Tasmania Police did nothing further to investigate her, her friends or her known criminal associates.

Towards the end of the notations and reports in the file I would have, if I was the detective sifting through all this, looked at everything that could prop up the original police theory that Sue Neill-Fraser was the murderer, something that might get it across the line. The last pages in the file relate to a list of twenty-three police and forensic staff who walked onto *Four Winds* as first responders when it was salvaged, or examined the crime scene over the next two days. This list was then proffered at Sue's court cases as an explanation of how Meaghan's DNA got on to the yacht – on the sole of a boot worn by a cop or a scientist. Yep, wriggle room. 'Secondary transfer' would go on to be mentioned at every stage of the trial and subsequent hearings. It even got a mention in my interview with Inspector Powell, who seemed convinced of this unbelievable 'fact'. The dinner plate size of the DNA meant it was impossible for it to have got onto the yacht through secondary transfer. Interestingly, the police never referred to the size of the deposit during the trial. It was like the elephant in the room, no one went near it. In the reality of crime scenes DNA samples tend to be little spots or smears, like a spit or perspiration stain. Not a dinner plate size puddle. Had the defence been able to recall the forensic scientist, the full extent of the DNA puddle may have come to the surface.

So ended Maverick's file on Meaghan Vass. And Sue's defence counsel, never given prior access to it, missed out on a pot of gold.

Maverick's file made it crystal clear to me that the police failure to investigate Meaghan and her friends, and the continued insistence that Sue Neill-Fraser was the murderer was fundamentally flawed. I could not comprehend why Sue Neill-Fraser's legal team was denied information, reports and facts that would have allowed a jury to understand what really happened at Sandy Bay on 26 January 2009.

In 2017, the police were applying pressure to those who dared have a different opinion about the death of Bob Chappell. Their adversarial thuggery was at its height towards the later part of the year, when they alleged that our interview with Meaghan in the hotel room in Hobart had been filmed under duress. The claim, accompanied by a not so subtle threat, was first made in a letter to her lawyer. (The letter was shared with us by our contact Deep Throat, and we later received two other copies from different sources.) A police solicitor wrote: *I infer from your letter that the statement in the statutory declaration that your client was on the yacht* Four Winds *on the night of Australia Day is false. If your client made the statutory declaration of 27 April, 2017, attributed to her, she would, at face value, be guilty of making a false statutory declaration and the crime of perverting justice. Tasmania Police is in possession of evidence suggesting that your client made the statutory declaration of 27 April, 2017 under duress.*

There seems little doubt the police were hoping Meaghan could be pressured into reneging on her statutory declaration that she and others were on the yacht. And, as demonstrated at Sue's appeal in late October 2017, that's exactly what happened.

Trouble is, the defence obtained a signed statement from Snapper, in 2018, in which he recalled going to Sharyn's house with Meaghan and meeting Jeff Thompson. He said that Meaghan went through her evidence carefully with Jeff and signed the statement, making it clear that she and others were on the yacht. There was no hint of duress; it was just a fair and honest statement-taking process.

* * *

In early November 2017, the pressure continued to build. Tasmania Police were doing everything in their power to slam the door on us, and, on 31 October 2017 the New South Wales homicide squad, acting for Tasmania Police, raided the Sydney office of CJZ, the co-producers of Eve's documentary about Sue's case. CJZ staff were busy editing the hundreds of hours of Tim and Eve's film footage into six one-hour episodes, when Detective Maverick's demand was made. The search warrant cited, among many other things, 'all film footage involving Colin McLaren'. I was well and truly under the microscope.

The seizing footage included hours of me walking the shorelines of Sandy Bay and nearby Battery Point in search of witnesses, clues, answers. As I walked I'd talk to the camera to explain the laborious work I was doing, the sort of work all detectives should undertake if they wish to properly understand a crime. But of course I was working as an investigative journalist writing a book and assisting a documentary. One of the most damning sections of film related to my crime scene analysis and re-enactment. It flew in the face of the police version, and should have been an embarrassment for any detective who put his name to the investigation of the scene of Bob's disappearance and murder.

The footage was crammed with revelations, including my interview with Detective Inspector Peter Powell and another with a boat broker, Jeffrey, who had sold *Four Winds* to Bob and Sue. He was annoyed by the way his original affidavit about Sue and his dealings with her had been handled. A friend of his, a boat contractor, had passed on information to Jeffrey that he'd received directly from a Hobart detective. The 'information' was about Sue: the police knew she had killed Bob and that she had previously committed a similarly violent crime that she had got away with. (A load of bunkum, of course.) Sue's phone was bugged, police had told the contractor, and both he and Jeffrey should be aware of this if they were talking to Sue. Jeffrey now believed he had been manipulated by police, who had deliberately had this damning and incorrect information fed to him. His statement, as a result, had been peppered with negative comments about Sue. He now regretted it.

A letter from a solicitor for the Tasmania Police had requested the search warrant. It referred to the footage taken of Meaghan in the hotel in Hobart. The letter stated that the footage was 'recorded against the wishes of Ms Vass'. This was obviously false, as the footage itself proved. At one point, Meaghan is heard saying, 'Shh, shit, that's recording.' Plus at Sue's appeal Meaghan made a comment that demonstrated she was aware of the cameras. They were in the open, for all to see.

A search warrant must be sworn in the Supreme Court of the relevant state, with a supporting affidavit from police. Was the affidavit, the letter, false or misleading in this case? Had a falsehood – that Meaghan had been filmed against her wishes – been used to gain a search warrant? Was the issuing judge misled? And why, when Meaghan's on-camera interview lasted less than one hour, was the warrant for all footage Tim had shot? Was the whole warrant process a fishing expedition?

The seizure of the film footage was a double whammy. First, it helped the police understand in minute detail the strategy of Sue's defence team, and revealed all the witnesses who we had spoken to. Secondly, the cameras had been my notebook. In fact, in legal terms, my contemporaneous notebook. Yet, the cops had it all. So many people had revealed their concerns about the death of Bob Chappell that I hadn't yet had time to digest all the footage myself. When I cast my mind back over the dozens of people I had spoken to, trying to recall the evidence I had extracted, the more worried I became. Not only would I likely forget some of what they told me, but their confidentiality had been severely breached. I genuinely feared for the welfare of many of these brave witnesses, and can only hope none of them suffers reprisals.

I knew the revelations on the tapes would anger the Tasmanian cops. When the documentary went to air, their incompetence, their harassment of witnesses and their willingness to let an innocent woman remain in prison would be revealed on national television, and possibly around the globe. I couldn't stop thinking about the police, hovering over their playback machines, watching the film footage like a murder of crows. All their thoughts would be on the arseholes from Melbourne who were going to name and shame them. Yet all we were doing was offering a credible theory for the death of Bob Chappell. One supported by facts.

I found it difficult to sleep. For months I had been locked into a dangerous sleeping pattern, surviving on a mere four to five hours a night. Always wide awake by 4.30 am. That's the time that marks the beginning of the ninety-minute period when police conduct house raids and execute search warrants. When the occupant of the house, the target, is dead to the world and at their most vulnerable. I would wake with the same recurring image: crows flying across Bass Strait to Melbourne, hovering over my apartment building and swooping onto my floor. Followed by a bang on the door before it was kicked in. My anxiety elevated to panic attacks. I was exhausted and had begun to talk in slow motion. I stopped sleeping at home. My network of friends took pity on me. I would arrive with my armful of notes, carrying my laptop, to crash in spare bedrooms across Australia.

During this period, I thought a lot about Lindy Chamberlain and the debacle of her conviction for the murder of her baby daughter Azaria. The parallels are obvious. A shoddy investigation with forensic factors at the centre of it. Ordinary women caught in a trap. The fight for fairness. The legal system and the media against her. I came to the conclusion that we Australians have learned nothing from the utter mess that was Lindy Chamberlain's prosecution and fight for justice.

In 1980, I remember, I thought Lindy Chamberlain was as guilty as sin. Dressed in my police uniform, I quoted long and loudly, chapter and verse, words that indicated her guilt. I knew it all, back then. Really, I knew nothing. I couldn't see past the newsprint. Then, all of a sudden, the facts that proved Lindy's innocence started to make an impact. After Azaria's matinee jacket was found buried in red soil near Uluru, I, along with the rest of Australia, sat back and felt ashamed for believing Lindy was a killer. But we haven't held on to that shame. We, as a nation, have let the mess that was Lindy's unjust conviction fade into the red dust of the outback. Lindy proved her innocence eventually. Hopefully we will do the same for Sue Neill-Fraser.

One morning in late November 2017, after another night of poor sleep, I was told by Charlie Bezzina to buy *The Australian* newspaper and to turn to page five. There, thirteen paragraphs telegraphed a message to me from the crows in Tasmania:

A police raid on a leading TV production company, seizing footage, has dramatically escalated an inquiry into an alleged conspiracy to pervert the course of justice ... two people have been charged and Tasmania Police – now viewing the hundreds of hours of footage seized in the Sydney raid – have flagged potential for further charges ... another filmmaker and former policeman Colin McLaren has helped dig up allegedly new information.

I didn't need to be Einstein to work out that Tasmania Police were gearing up to charge me, as well as Jeff Thompson and Gabby, the two referred to in the newspaper and whose unfair treatment I outlined earlier. With what I might be charged, I didn't know for sure. But through the media, the cops were telling me I was on their hit list.

I have chased down some of the worst crooks in the country – armed robbers, murderers, paedophiles, bombers and even members of the Mafia. For all the threats levelled at me by that collection of thugs, crooks and gangsters, nothing had ever troubled me as much as what was happening to me now. Those who were supposed to protect us and fight for justice were abusing their power in order to scare and harass ordinary, concerned citizens. As worried as I was, I was also very pissed off. I'd had a gutful of intimidation. Enough was enough. Eve and I were now fighting for our liberty. I rang Charlie Bezzina.

Charlie and I met at a rundown coffee shop. I needed his clear thinking. We read over the newspaper article with its implied threat and tried to formulate a way through. We spent ages canvassing retaliatory strikes, tossing around possible solutions. Then Charlie nailed it. We would write to the Tasmanian Integrity Commission, spelling out the stack of errors in the original investigation. We would also outline the ridiculous position of the current investigation by Hobart police, which allowed the key detective on the 2009 investigation into Sue Neill-Fraser to reinvestigate now, in 2017 his own investigative mess. Where on earth is the transparency? And objectivity.

Eve and I got to work. We wrote a letter outlining the harassment and intimidation targeted at us, as well as at Jeff Thompson, Stephen Gleeson and Gabby, by a handful of Tasmanian cops. We wrote that, in our view, these police had violated Tasmania Police's core values of integrity, equity and accountability. The letter also included Charlie Bezzina's opinion of the inept investigation back in 2009. We attached my white paper on the shortcomings of the original investigation. We also added a second report that spelled out the actions of the detectives at the centre of this debacle. We felt it paramount to spell out the failings of the past inquiry. In effect, we pointed out most of what is in this book. As well, we mentioned the seizure of the film footage from CJZ, which was carried out, not to prove a conspiracy by myself, Jeff Thompson, Eve Ash or the many lawyers and witnesses assisting Sue Neill-Fraser, but as a giant fishing expedition – the intended catch being anything that could be used to intimidate myself and others trying to save Sue Neill-Fraser from further jail time.

With the identification of Meaghan Vass as the source of the puddle of DNA found on *Four Winds*, the house of cards that was the case against Sue Neill-Fraser should have collapsed. However, one lone detective was given the task of re-investigating the original 2009 inept investigation. An inquiry that this officer played a major role in. An investigation where he wrote up the evidence of the main witnesses against Sue Neill-Fraser, those being Phillip Triffett and Maria Hanson. The same detective who handled the discovery of DNA of the then street kid, petty thief Meaghan Vass. And so on. How can this officer have fresh eyes to assess his original investigation wasn't wrong? This is clearly inappropriate.

Eve and I ran our submission past Robert Richter and Remy van de Wiel, another QC, and incorporated their suggestions. Robert and Remy, wise men with 80-plus years of arguing some of the toughest legal cases in the land, vowed to stand by us, should anyone come after us. We deeply appreciated their support.

We felt our complaint was too hot to deliver through the normal channels; we needed someone to hand-deliver it to the Tasmanian Integrity Commission. We canvassed some options and settled on a retired cop, a man with much experience who was very supportive. He had often said that if there was anything he could do to assist me, he would be glad to help. I gave him a call.

The plan was for the ex-cop to catch a flight to Hobart, walk into the office of the Commission and hand the Commissioner our submission. He would then fly back to Melbourne. He was up for it. But the next day he phoned me. Our intended courier was suddenly reluctant. He was concerned for his reputation, should Hobart's finest intervene and pull him aside. (I couldn't blame him.) He pulled out. We were in limbo once again.

It was at this time that Charlie and I held a number of closed-door meetings with the investigative journalist team from the *Herald Sun*, the biggest-selling daily newspaper in the country. We were to learn that this same team had independently considered the Tasmanian cops were on the nose. They had shown interest in the story but needed something big in the way of new information to justify writing an exposé on the case. We met in my apartment and explained that we were about to hand-deliver a massive broadside to Tasmania Police via the Integrity Commission. Two of the team, Anthony Dowsley and Patrick Carlyon were all over it. It was more than enough for them to convince their editor to publish a series of articles exposing the tunnel vision, the missed leads, the lost opportunities and everything else that had gone on in the original investigation into Sue, and subsequently. Normally they would need at least a couple of weeks to write and research such a story, but due to tight scheduling they had just four days. And two of them were on their weekend. Undaunted, they forged ahead.

But we were still without a courier.

Charlie made a call to SureFact, a progressive investigative company staffed mainly by ex-cops. One of the co-owners, Mary Mansell, was an ex-detective, ex-prosecutor and ex-lecturer at the Detective Training School. She was just the person we needed to deliver our complaint. She listened to our story of woe and never batted an eyelid. Within two hours she was on a flight to Tasmania. Got to love a savvy ex-policewoman! Shortly after Mary had delivered our submission to the Integrity Commission, she was having coffee with Jeff Thompson. She spent the next five hours with him, listening to his story and hearing about life as a legal outsider in Hobart. She was horrified.

Together Mary and Jeff visited the house at Blackmans Bay, the one that had been burgled over the long weekend of Australia Day, 2009, when beer, wine and food were stolen. The crime scene where a 'Megan' was named on the crime report. They knocked on the door and confirmed the burglary with the occupants.

The Tasmanian legal system was taking its toll on Jeff and his family. In the fourteen months since he had been charged, and after the same number of appearances in the Supreme Court, he still hadn't been supplied any evidence of his alleged wrongdoing. He had become like a rodent on an ever-spinning wheel, getting nowhere. In desperation he lodged Right to Information requests for information relating to the charges against him, only to be denied. Tasmania Police refused to supply him with anything, claiming that it would take them more than 1100 hours to compile the paperwork. Much of the information would be redacted, Jeff was informed, and if they went ahead they would present Jeff with a bill for $107,000. The procedural unfairness levelled at Jeff rivals that which could be expected in third world countries with corrupt regimes. How did it ever get to this? Clearly, Tasmania Police were playing Jeff for a fool, stalling him until after all matters concerning Sue Neill-Fraser were completed. This ensured he would not be a valued witness for her. I was sickened by the way a good man had been forced to his knees.

Just as bad, as 2018 unfolded, Barbara Etter was brought before the Legal Professional Board of Tasmania and her practising certificate was withdrawn. Her crime? There was none. It all had to do with her defence of Sue Neill-Fraser and one other soul she believed had been wronged by the Tasmanian legal system. She fought the suspension, but the courts upheld it. There was an outcry from Civil Liberties Australia and many astute journalists, but Barbara decided she'd had enough. She took down her shingle and replaced it with an easel and set of paintbrushes. Her career was over.

For Eve and myself it was an agonising wait, as we second guessed the Tasmanian Integrity Commission. None of us knew much about the commission. Similar commissions around Australia are normally feared by police, and rightly so. Their role is to ensure police and the legal system don't step out of line. What would the Tasmanian commission do? Would they be shocked by what they read? How many investigators would they throw at the file? We pondered these and many other questions.

Two days after our complaint was filed, the first of the articles in the *Herald Sun's* exposé exploded in the media. It was a two-page spread detailing our complaint to the commission, supported by Charlie's and my thoughts about the inept investigation and the heavy-handed tactics Tasmania Police used in trying to thwart our efforts to expose the truth. We could hear the tom-toms from Hobart. The Free Sue supporters were bouncing social media comments all over

Australia. Insiders within the legal fraternity were sitting up and taking notice.

The next day we received a call from one such insider in the Tasmanian Department of Justice. He had bad news. The thinking within the department was that the commission was going to pass our complaint, with our files and all the supporting documents, over to Tasmania Police to investigate. What? The police we complained about to be investigated by their own? I was utterly lost for words. That would mean Maverick would get another bite of the cherry. This was absurd, beyond comprehension. We were also advised that the commission had no resources to undertake investigations; they were usually palmed off to the police. I hung up and stared into nothing.

The rest of the day I spent working the phones. To Robert Richter, to Charlie, Eve Ash, to my lawyer, Tony Hargreaves, and on it went. I was sickened. So was everyone else. Charlie hit the roof. Eve was in tears. Robert Richter and Tony Hargreaves confirmed with the Integrity Commissioner that it was possible that the complaint file would be given to the very people we were complaining about. Tony made it clear how inappropriate this was. What I wanted him to say was how fucked this was.

A short while later, I rang a barrister who lives in Hobart but works mostly in Melbourne. We workshopped the ludicrous situation of our complaint being gifted to Tasmania Police. Fears for the welfare of Eve, Charlie and myself were also playing on me. Being from Tasmania, the lawyer was familiar with the politics of the place. However, unlike Jeff Thompson, he was in the fold, in the clique. I pleaded with him to find a way to prevent the complaint file being handed over to the cops.

At this time, I was staying in the spare bedroom of a dear friend of mine, Liz Porter, a fellow true crime author. When my call to the barrister ended, I raced into my room and rummaged through my suitcase, tossing clothes and reports in all directions. Then I found it, my passport. I put it in my back pocket and sat down to a glass of shiraz with Liz and got thinking.

Part IV

What price change?

There is no doubt that once a conviction is obtained, the police, judiciary and government are most reluctant to reverse the finding of guilt. Does this mean a wrongfully convicted person is supposed to just accept their lot, in my case 23 years? I am running out of years. I believe the way forward is for the government to approve a Commission of Inquiry or Review ... empowered to properly assess all the evidence, including the original police investigation. How much longer will Bob and I have to wait for justice? We can only hope and pray it comes to an end soon. This is not only about the clearing of my name. It's for every Australian. If we don't fix the underlying problem, how long will it be before the peace of another family is shattered? For me the worst part of this whole nasty business is that the system has failed dismally to obtain justice for Bob ...

Excerpt from a letter from Sue Neill-Fraser to her family, sent from prison, 2018

Bombs over Tasmania

BY THE TIME LIZ AND I GOT THROUGH OUR BOTTLE OF Heathcote shiraz, we had a plan. The Hobart barrister had studied the legislation that established and guides the Integrity Commission and found something that might help us. Should a complaint received by the commission warrant it, the commissioner has the power to request that the premier appoint an independent commission of inquiry. I came alive again, and so did Eve and Charlie. We needed to get the commissioner to push the premier to exercise that power.

The trouble was, when Premier Will Hodgman had met with Robert Richter, Eve Ash and myself back in May 2017, he had shunned our calls for an independent inquiry or royal commission. He didn't even read the white paper I'd prepared.

Soon I learned of another setback. A recently published report by the Australia Institute, a think tank that conducts public policy research, found that the Tasmanian Integrity Commission had never fully investigated any matter, never had anyone charged and never held an independent commission of inquiry. For anything. Other state integrity commissions were making huge strides in stemming corruption across Australia, but the Tasmania Integrity Commission had a score card of 'zero'. The Australia Institute labelled it 'toothless'.

I read the report and felt a massive wave of nausea. Of all the deflating moments I had suffered over the past twenty months, it was reading the damning comments of the Australia Institute that floored me the most. It felt like we'd come to the end of the road as far as exposing the disturbing behaviour of Tasmania Police and justice officials was concerned, and there was nowhere else to turn. I read the report three times, hoping, praying that it was wrong. But its criticism was undeniable, backed up with telling statistics. That one report would cause more worry to Eve and myself than almost anything else we had suffered up to that point. We questioned what on earth was happening in Tasmania that caused the body meant to ensure integrity in the system to be 'toothless'. In addition to all my other feelings – frustration, incomprehension, outrage – I was now also scared.

We needed to put the Tasmanian authorities under pressure. Had a report as well-researched and volatile as our white paper hit the anti-corruption bodies of any other state in Australia, it would have resulted in a commission of inquiry or possibly a royal commission. But it seemed it would take a rolling set of explosions to detonate over Hobart to prevent the Integrity Commission from handing over our complaint to the very cops we wanted investigated. Explosions loud enough to wake up Premier Will Hodgman.

Two days after reading the Australia Institute report I had my plan ready. I rang Cathy, my agent, and asked her to create five PDFs of the most recent news stories about Sue Neill-Fraser. The media was on our side, at long last, and their stories were a revelation.

Already that same day, the *Herald Sun* had run an article about Bob Martyn, Sue's friend and one-time business partner. The article raised questions about what could have happened at Sue's trial if Martyn had been called as a witness. The answer was obvious.

That weekend we also scored an influential story in the *Mercury*, Tasmania's most prominent newspaper, which usually ran items slanted towards the police view. In this story, however, it quoted Robert Richter and myself. The headline read: 'New Twist in Murder Case'. It stated there was 'enough evidence to raise doubts [about Sue's conviction]' and detailed how Premier Hodgman had rejected Robert Richter's request for an independent inquiry back in May. It described how police had charged Jeff Thompson and others for perverting the course of justice, and mentioned that I feared being charged myself. The article quoted me: 'The using of legislation against people can't be underestimated in this case. And that scares me and a lot of other people.'

Only days earlier there had been another two-page exposé in *The Age* highlighting our complaint to the Integrity Commission and Charlie's and my opinion that the investigation into Bob's disappearance and murder had been inept and the case against Sue Neill-Fraser manipulated. It included her legal team's demand for re-analysis of all blood and hair exhibits in the case, using the latest LCN methodology.

Bright and early on Monday morning I walked into Cathy's office, laptop in hand. We sat down and drafted an email, briefly summarising the now infamous case of Sue Neill-Fraser and mentioning the complaint sent to the Integrity Commission, which, in all likelihood, was about to send the file to the very cops mentioned in the complaint. We then attached the five most recent media stories and sent the email to a string of journalists, media luminaries and politicians across Australia.

I looked up at the wall clock; it was 11.46 am. Cathy was sipping her third piccolo latte of the morning. She nodded. I winked. Then I pressed send, and watched my emails leave the screen. We then went to brunch, occasionally turning our ears to the south, in the hope of hearing the media explosions from across Bass Strait.

Two suburbs away Eve Ash also pressed send on her laptop. She had drafted a compelling report for the British High Commission in Canberra. Sue is a British citizen and Eve urged the high commissioner to pressure the Tasmanian government into holding an independent inquiry into her conviction. She received a reply within the hour from the high commissioner, who was keen to act. A file was created to watch over Sue Neill-Fraser's court case.

Lawyers working on Sue's case also sent a transcript of a conversation I had with a young woman twelve months earlier to the Integrity Commission of Tasmania. It's better that I not name her here. The young woman claimed she'd been asked to identify the red jacket as belonging to Sue. She refused. She told me she felt intimidated and the detectives who spoke to her only had one focus: any evidence against Sue Neill-Fraser. The transcript was another bomb we hoped might help persuade the premier to hold an independent commission of inquiry. The eagerly awaited outcome from the Integrity Commission came in early 2018 when we received a letter from the commissioner. A mix of good and bad news. First of all, of the thirty-three complaints that Eve and I lodged with the commission they found merit in thirty, citing that a proper investigation would be needed to flush out further and better particulars about the workings of Tasmania Police in the original Sue Neill-Fraser investigation and subsequent follow-ups. However, the bad news was no such investigation would take place whilst Sue was before any court of law. Therefore, our file was put aside until Sue had exhausted her appeal and legal options. And Eve, Charlie and the legal team knew that would be indefinite. Sue would never give up challenging her conviction. Nor would we. So, the Integrity Commission, at that time, was of no value.

I had just sat back to enjoy some respite from the frenzy this case had thrown up when I received a troubling phone call from one of Australia's most respected journalists. He had been informed by an impeccable source that it was only a matter of time before the Tasmanian cops charged me. He asked me if I was at home, and when I said yes, he advised me to get out immediately. And to stay away from my car. He had been told there was a listening device in each. His voice trembled as he wished me well and urged me to finish my manuscript. More of the same. Pressure. I believed I had surveillance on my mobile phone, emails and texts and now I was being told there were 'bugs' in my own home and car. I grabbed my passport and headed to the airport.

This uncertainty and upheaval in my life is my own doing. I have come to terms with that. We make choices, and Sue Neill-Fraser has been mine for two years. As I stepped away from my Uber and proceeded to board a flight to Argentina, I thought over the choices I had made. They came with loss and great sadness. I might not return to my beloved country, not in the short term at least. What was the alternative? Remand in Risdon Prison on conspiracy charges?

I left my gorgeous daughter back in Melbourne with my beautiful grandson. We would be separated over the festive season, as we had been for most of 2017.

I buckled my seat belt and stared out the airplane window and thought long and hard about reputations, legacies and southern justice.

Turning right

IN FEBRUARY 2018, I WAS ON THE MOVE AGAIN. I SPENT THE New Year period sharing a tenement with a family of geckos in Bangkok. It was stiflingly hot. The air smelled of rotting mangoes, exhaust fumes and food cart smoke. My only exercise was on the laptop. By Valentine's Day I had hit Europe, paranoia and warnings from my wonderful support team in Melbourne (whose keen ears picked up on rumours) keeping me on the run. I spent a month in France in a cold farmhouse, owned by a friend, tapping away on this manuscript as the snow fell all around. When the firewood ran out I moved on. I headed for Rome, and the wettest winter in more than a century. From Asian heat to European sub-zero cold. I was feeling the strain, having panic attacks. A sense of hopelessness grew within me as the cold months extended. But I was determined to complete this book.

One freezing day I spent two hours pacing the streets of Trastevere, the ancient Roman neighbourhood, looking every which way, worried who might be on to me. I feared a touch of madness was setting in. I had slept in seven different beds

in as many countries in such a short time, each stop was
just another cheap dump to set up my laptop and write my
story. But, as I worked through the night I ached to be home
with those I love. It was a couple of months into this block
of isolation and poor diet that I saw myself in the mirror.
An unshaven face, pale skin and heavy eyes; I looked years
older. I succumbed to tears. I wished Tasmania would vanish
from the map. I wanted the whole sordid affair to go up in
smoke. My mood was so dark I reached out, by phone, to a
friendly psychiatrist in Melbourne, who – as luck would have
it – had studied the injustice of the Sue Neill-Fraser case. He
knew it well. He also knew well that I was in serious trouble,
completely absorbed by the intended actions of a few rogue
cops and lawyers in Tasmania. He talked me through the
blackness, settled me down and demanded that I call him
every day, until I got over this mental hump, and came off
the Valium he prescribed. He figured I had witnessed, over
the past two years, the collapse of most of the foundations
that I had based my life on: strong but compassionate law
enforcement; a fair judicial system; respect; and the value I
once thought of as a great Aussie attribute – doing the right
thing. He feared I was carrying an exile and persecution
complex. Except in my case it was not a complex, it was real,
and it would need a lot of working through. We formed a
bond, and his help was a godsend.

  In time, spring arrived. A glimmer of sunshine appeared
outside my frigid window pane. It had been five horrible months
of sheer isolation since I had left the warmth of Bangkok. I was
on my way back, baby step by baby step. To help my mental
state, I kept tapping away, wearing out the keys of my laptop.
In July, at long last, my manuscript was finished, and I sent

it to my publisher. Then I walked outside to enjoy the Italian sunshine, and the hospitality of my favourite Villa Cheta.

I would spend an Italian summer with the sun on my back and a sense of slow repair. My daily Valium had reduced to once a week, dependent on what horror stories Eve fed me from Tasmania, or Sue's legal team. During what I call my recovery phase I worked with my editors to knock my words around and finalise this book. Then, out of the blue, it was September and Sue's appeal was back in court, after a wretchedly long delay. Poor woman. The Supreme Court judge was taking evidence from a few witnesses and was close to making his decision as to whether Sue might get a chance at, perhaps a re-trial. Trouble was he was perplexed, trying to work out Meaghan Vass's role in the saga, whether she really was on the yacht on the night of Australia Day, 2009, or not.

The DPP and police showed a few minutes of the footage they had seized the year earlier from CJZ. (Only a few minutes offered against the 500 hours they seized.) The footage was of me drafting the statement that I, the next day, put to Meaghan. For her to consider. A nutshell grab of her role on *Four Winds*. It was, in fact, a summary of what she had told me previously, and what she had said in the hotel room back in April 2017, and ended up being the infamous statutory declaration that the DPP and police took issue with.

The way the film footage was being presented to the court suggested that I had been caught off guard by a camera and the footage revealed me falsifying the statement. Nothing further from the truth would be possible. But, I wasn't there to defend myself and the media went mad, writing stories of me creating a 'fake statement'. The story circulated around one hundred and thirty newspapers and television and radio news broadcasts. My name was blackened. My reputation shot. So was the reputation of Eve Ash, who is also on the same footage assisting me in drafting the statement. Friends started texting me, asking questions and wondering how I had made such a blunder in judgment. No one knew that the film footage was made by myself and Eve; we filmed each and every stage of what we did. It wasn't a covert police camera, it was our own and we had nothing to hide. The media never bothered with this trivial aspect, their sensational work had been done and I slumped back into depression, reaching for the Valium.

Then luck tapped me on the shoulder. The judge returned to his court the next day to deliberate and a full courtroom sat in anticipation. Sue's rolling dice were about to come to a stop. Then, out of the blue, the judge stated that he had studied the film footage and said, in effect, that I had done nothing wrong in the footage. He explained that what I did – formulate a draft statement for Meaghan Vass – was 'doing what solicitors do every day when they are drafting an affidavit, based on instructions'. Tom Percy QC, for Sue, then stated, 'As long as you have seen the witness before, you're entitled to sit down and draft what you think they will say.' That is exactly what I was doing!

This time smiles were on the faces of Sue's legal team, not the cops. Then the judge took the issue one step further. Much had been made of Meaghan Vass on the yacht and the judge felt that he couldn't make his final decision until he heard from me. He suggested the defence seek an affidavit from me, outlining every twist and turn, every meeting I had with Meaghan and what the facts were. Apparently, my evidence had become pivotal to the case. The judge stated my evidence may be 'fresh' and may affect the outcome of Sue's appeal.

Tom Percy said he would make inquiries about an affidavit from me.

I almost fell off my chair, in my apartment in Palermo, when Eve rang me with this startling piece of news. In short, I was elated to now come under the category of a witness assisting the judge. And how my affidavit of facts might just turn the tide in favour of Sue Neill-Fraser. I paced the room for hours, wondering what to do: stay in hiding or risk going home?

Over the next two weeks I drafted my six-page affidavit with the kind assistance of Remy van de Wiel and, as always, Eve Ash. Then, with a newly acquired sense of security (who would ever fuck with a witness called by a judge?) I booked a flight home, to Melbourne, to swear my affidavit. And visit my cardiologist; my chest was full of pain.

True to form, I concluded that there must have been a customs alert on me as I entered my own country. Agents swarmed over me and went through me like a dose of salts, before photocopying my documents, and making a call to announce that I had arrived in the country. Luckily, my gorgeous daughter was on the same flight and carried my laptop, manuscript, USBs and files with her, past customs and out the airport arrivals doors. Half an hour later I joined her in the long-term car park and we hit the road. Just like I'd done for almost one whole year.

Once home I was met by Eve Ash. We hadn't seen each other for such a long time. With a look of horror on her face she dumped a ream of documents on my dining table, dozens of pages. She had received them from a confidential source. The documents were initiated by police and were now floating around the underworld in Hobart. They were a copy of all of my bank records from the Bendigo Bank and NAB bank since 2016. My Mastercard, Visa card, savings, mortgage and investment accounts. Along with account numbers. Plus, a full set of Eve's own banking details, hundreds of transactions. Accompanying this trove of reports were analytical spreadsheets by Tasmania Police who assessed my expenditure and made a comment. Like the $3,000 I spent for 'Forward Scout' work, then commenting with six question marks and surmising that I must have been up to something shifty. If they were any good at analysing they would have seen the corresponding credit card expenses adding up to $3,000 for hire cars, cheap hotels and meals of spaghetti in Europe! 'Forward scout' is the term I use, when making a documentary, I go ahead, scouting locations and setting up logistics and accommodation for the film crew.

Every suspicion we had had over the past two years, that the cops were crawling all over us, was confirmed in that brief meeting with Eve. The greatest worry was how there were dozens of police opinions (in my view flawed) against the inconsequential expenses of two private citizens – Eve and myself – who were filmmakers and, in my case, an author. Such as, an ATM withdrawal of a lousy $200 for running around money was perceived by Tasmania to be dodgy money, 'likely' to have been used to entice witnesses.

Overall, I reckoned that I had spent $100,000 in the past year, being on the run, across five continents, to avoid the police, and the police had my bank records to show it!

I had many years as a task force team leader. I can assess what it costs to mount and run a task force. I believe, with the effort by the Tasmanian police, against myself, Eve Ash and Jeff Thompson, as well as the witnesses who were charged, that the state of Tasmania would have spent millions to date. For what? And why? I know why. Reputations!

* * *

An expat Aussie asked me once why I get involved in investigating cover-ups. It's a good question. Much of my work over the past decade has been in this area. The reason I bother is because of something deep within me. First, need I remind you, I'm an ex-cop. I cut my detective teeth in the 1980s and 1990s, when corruption was everywhere. I went through my career on a diet of Bacon, Pilger, Masters, Hinch and Bottom, investigative journalists who gave a damn, and prompted a dozen royal commissions between them. They were agents of change; their collective mantra was 'fear should not be a shackle', as they worked bravely to uncover incompetence and corruption up to the highest levels.

As a community we should be entitled to scrutinise wrongdoing, question secrecy in our public institutions and demand clarification. There is a flood of irregularities in the Sue Neill-Fraser case. And it took a pair of brave women to take the fight up to those responsible and expose inadequacies in the police investigation and subsequent prosecution. Eve Ash and Barbara Etter fought the good fight against bullies and sods for a long time, just the two of them. Their resilience is staggering. So, when Eve asked for my help, eventually, how could I refuse?

Once I stepped in, I got sucked into the sewer pipe that was the Tasmania Police investigation of Bob Chappell's disappearance and likely murder. Before long I was up to my chest in the excrement that surrounded this horribly flawed case. I had two choices: let myself be carried along by the flow, out of the sewer, into a cleansing ocean or fight against the current and swim towards the source of all the shit. I turned

right and chose the second way: a difficult journey, often in
the dark and one that would scare me witless at times. I could
see little light, just Sue Neill-Fraser, way back in the distance,
sinking, but with her hand still held up. There were also
others, persons of interest who, I sensed, had the answers. I
was reminded of my time as a young detective as I searched
for a truth that could really stick. Like the stuff I found
myself swimming in. How, no matter what is exposed in an
investigation, the facts must always be presented. There is not,
and never has been, any room for fabrication of evidence.

As I worked on the Tasmania case, I saw others swimming
in the same direction that I was, and they carried lifebuoys:
Robert Richter, Jeff Thompson, Charlie Bezzina, Tim Smart
and Paul Galbally. I realised I had a chance to make a difference
and to do, possibly, the best work of my life. That's why I got
involved.

With regard to our shared belief in the flagrant injustice
of Tasmania Police's pursuit of Sue Neill-Fraser, we're in good
company. Take Bill Rowlings, CEO of Civil Liberties Australia,
who commented on Sue's case: 'Police filter the truth. Forensic
evidence is abused. The prosecutor invents a murder weapon,
and the judge agrees. A miscarriage of justice so blatant you
won't believe it possible in twenty-first century Australia.'

Eminent law academic, Dr Bob Moles, agrees: 'In this case
there is no compelling evidence to show that Bob Chappell
is dead, let alone murdered. If he was murdered there is no
compelling evidence to show how that was brought about.
Regrettably, this is a case built upon very little evidence, and
which serves to implicate the nearest and most helpless suspect,
and fails to investigate properly other more sinister or more
complex possibilities. This case begs to have a single informed

and impartial person to conduct an independent review of it to ensure the manifest failures in its investigation and prosecution are authoritatively determined.'

The man credited with unravelling the quagmire that was the wrongful conviction of Lindy Chamberlain, Chester Porter QC, also offered his words: 'If you look at all the alleged evidence against her [Sue], it's really just guesswork ... the police were quite convinced that Sue was guilty. And everything she said and everything she did had to be evidence of guilt. There is no doubt in my mind this case calls for an inquiry.'

With the help of Charlie Bezzina, I have tried to remain impartial when examining the facts around Bob Chappell's probable murder. Together, we were unable to find one snippet of a fact that suggested Sue Neill-Fraser killed her de facto husband. What we did uncover is the worst homicide investigation that either of us can recall. An entanglement of loose facts and discarded evidence sitting under a poisonous tree, teasing the unskilled with bad fruit. And while the days of Tasmania's penal settlement and its convicts have ended, it seems to me that the colonial system of justice in that state has not. You could swear Tasmania never went through any reforms. Sure, the convicts died off, but their system of justice appears to remain. I can offer no other explanation for the mess surrounding Sue Neill-Fraser's wrongful incarceration.

No other city in Australia pursues the twin ideals of incompetence and corruption with quite the same enthusiasm as Hobart. When it comes to asinine administration, the Tasmanian government is in a league of its own. Too often the media is splashed with headlines alleging nepotism, corruption, dodgy police work or appointments to the judiciary for pals of the government.

Sue Neill-Fraser's case highlights the unease I feel with regard to our Australian system of justice, adopted from the United Kingdom in the eighteenth century. It's lingered, without practical innovation, ever since. Adversarial by design, it pits the underdog against the almighty. The accused's usually meagre resources have little hope against resources able to be accessed by the offices of public prosecution, the police, intelligence agencies and prisons, all of which are underpinned by relatively generous budgets. This sort of justice ensures that the patsy who's been wrongfully convicted stands a snowflake's chance in hell of ever overturning a flawed judgment.

Truth remains an elusive ideal. I used to think truth was like the oak trees that are often planted around courthouses. Tall and solid. In actuality, truth is often whittled down to toothpicks and placed between the teeth of clever lawyers, out for a win. To be spat out at the end of the game that is a trial.

There are many questionable outcomes emanating from our courts. An alternate check-and-balance regime is needed to challenge the unjust convictions that our current system spawns. In my opinion, we need to create a federally staffed Criminal Case Review Board, that can wave an investigative and forensic wand over potentially unfair convictions. We should be embarrassed that this vital safety net doesn't yet exist in our country, a nation that prides itself on world's-best practices in law enforcement, such as speed cameras!

The travesty of justice inflicted upon Sue has been the doing of many men. Almost always men. I saw it often in my police career. I couldn't imagine women in the upper levels of the judiciary making such blunders; they have too much compassion. It would be fitting for all the women out there who are associated with the men who've played a part in the prosecution of this case to read this book and simply ask the man next to them one very tiny question. 'Really?'

Let's hope that Sue Neill-Fraser's case is the catalyst for our squabbling politicians in Canberra to unite on this issue and create a federal review body. It's our nation's most troubling incarceration case, a legal minefield only the federal attorney-general or prime minister can shake down.

* * *

On the eve of publishing this book I am still in limbo, still fearing what might come to hinder my liberty and, more importantly, what may result in the legal path for Sue Neill-Fraser. She seems to be one step closer to taking a long walk, away from the rural suburb of Risdon, towards the home of her family. But, who knows? That's still in the hands of the slow-turning wheels of southern justice. And my passport still sits inside my back pocket, just in case.

Meanwhile, I have become a smidgen like Sue, in that I'm always trapped. Although my imprisonment is in being continually on the run, hoping the Tasmanian authorities don't snare me at the next passport checkpoint. I'm always moving. Pushed into unwanted destinations, staying in grotty hotels, waiting in airport queues, eating lousy food and suffering a level of loneliness that I could never have imagined before this. Or wish on anyone else.

Who knows, maybe one day justice will be done. Perhaps I'll finally meet Sue and share a Tasmanian whisky with this remarkably resilient and patient woman, the recipient of a form of justice we thought was tucked away in the back pages of our history books. Here's hoping it's not inside Risdon Prison.

Epilogue

It's late on a Sunday afternoon in autumn 2013, somewhere in the murky jail years of Sue Neill-Fraser. There's a damp chill in the air and the low light gives the silhouette of Risdon Prison an ominous presence of concrete and razor wire. Outside, in the prison garden, Sue is thinking of planting the last of the spinach. Or perhaps silverbeet. She is in a quandary as to what would do better, this time of year, what with the weather fading. Her garden keeps her sane and allows her a fraction of joy amongst her countless days of broken prayers.

Hope. She needs it more than ever in the days following her failed appeal on sentence the previous year. The Director of Public Prosecutions, Tim Ellis, had stood before the Supreme Court, opposing any leniency for her. A bulldog for 'justice', he had a reputation for winning his cases. The eventual reduction in jail time was so small as to be a pittance, from 26 years to 23. Sue didn't view the result as any sort of victory.

On the Midland Highway, in her Toyota Corolla, a 27-year-old woman, Natalia, is heading towards home to Launceston, after a weekend in Hobart. She is gym-fit, a homeowner and her parents' pride and joy. She is gaining on the slowcoach ahead of her and she moves to overtake the vehicle in the designated passing lane.

In the opposite direction, travelling south came a big Mercedes Benz, with a heavy-set driver behind the wood-grained steering wheel. His Mercedes was drifting on to the wrong side of the road, as it had been now for up to a kilometre or so. The Toyota didn't stand a chance. On a sweeping bend, the Mercedes ploughed through it like a bowling ball careering into a skittle. Natalia's injuries were horrific, her car was concertinaed. She died well before the ambulance came to a screeching halt beside the wreck.

The driver of the rather less-damaged Mercedes, survived less scathed, with an injured leg. Director of Public Prosecutions Tim Ellis limped away and faced a gathering public clamour.

* * *

As the call for lights-out echoed through Risdon Prison, Sue heard a whisper from a fellow inmate; Ellis killed a young woman in a head-on collision. Gossip gets through even concrete prison walls. Sue lay back, deciding to forgo her book. To ponder the utter tragedy dumped upon the family of another victim. Sleep came slowly. Sue guessed that Ellis would give the system a run for its money. She was right.

The prosecutor would face a charge of 'causing the death of another person by negligent driving'. A man who knew his statutes, Ellis would run a not guilty defence, his own liberty and reputation was on the line. The State of Tasmania was generous, he was suspended for two years from his position of Director of Public Prosecutions on full pay, $430,000 per annum to defend the charge. His defence counsel was the eminent lawyer Michael O'Farrell SC, the now Tasmania solicitor-general, whom I last saw in the premier's office, with my white paper.

Mr Ellis would eventually go the way of Sue Neill-Fraser, found guilty. His whack was a suspended sentence. Internally, in his workplace, he was ousted from his mahogany office for the trifling administrative offence of 'misbehaviour'.

Timothy Ellis now practises law, his shingle swinging in the cool breezes of Launceston, also home to Natalia's family. Funny place, Tasmania. And Sue worked out that, in autumn, spinach does better than silverbeet.

Acknowledgements

IT WOULD HAVE BEEN IMPOSSIBLE TO TELL THIS SHOCKING story without the involvement of Eve Ash. I am constantly in awe of her energy as she seeks the truth. Additionally, in her own enigmatic way, Barbara Etter. I also must mention the calm guidance and legal and investigative support of two giants in their field: Robert Richter QC and Homicide Squad veteran Charlie Bezzina.

To all the friends who offered me warmth, a spare bed, a glass of wine, food on my table, and sometimes headache tablets, thank you. Some couriered documents to me; others kept the wolves from my door and graciously gave me the space I desperately needed to write this book.

Most importantly of all, thanks to my daughter, Chelsea, for her undying love, empathy and encrypted phone calls of encouragement. And to Siegrid, another victim in this mess. You weathered my absenteeism until it got too much. I don't blame you!

Also, to my friend and fellow author Liz and her sanity-saving brother-in-law, Dr Bill, thanks from the bottom of my heart. Also, the wonderfully gregarious Remy van de Wiel QC, for always standing by me. And lawyers Shaun Miller for his compassion and the title to this book and David Gonzalez for being there. Also, my cardiologist, Mark Horrigan, and Dr David Marsh; another battle, Marshie! The Burgens and Jeni for proofreading and John Pfeiffer for his stealth. Lastly, Oliver Larkin for keeping me sane and Anna, a constant inspiration in trying to help a desperate woman in need of her freedom.

A massive thanks must also go to Hachette Australia. You are my 'home' when it comes to writing tough stories. Vanessa Radnidge, the head of non-fiction, you are the bomb! And thanks also to my talented editors, Maryrose Cuskelly and Amanda O'Connell, headed by the extremely forgiving Karen Ward.

Lastly, and certainly most importantly, I am deeply indebted to the family of Sue Neill-Fraser, who have been through hell, yet generously gave me access to private photographs and excerpts from Sue's letters. Her words are a poignant insight.

Colin McLaren
cm@scuttlebuttmedia.net

hachette
AUSTRALIA

If you would like to find out more about Hachette Australia,
our authors, upcoming events and new releases you can
visit our website or our social media channels:

hachette.com.au
HachetteAustralia
HachetteAus